LIVING IN
SPANGLISH

ED MORALES

LIVING IN
SPANGLISH

The Search for Latino
Identity in America

 An *LA Weekly Book for*
St. Martin's Press ✻ New York

LA Weekly Books is a trademark of LA Weekly Media, Inc.

www.stmartins.com

The poem "I am Joaquín" on pages 81–82 reprinted with the permission of the
Gonzales family.

Design by Kathryn Parise

LIBRARY OF CONGRESS CATALOGING-IN-PUBLICATION DATA
Morales, Ed.
Living in Spanglish : the search for a new Latino identity in America / Ed Morales—
1st ed.
   p. cm.
   ISBN 0-312-26232-9
   1. Hispanic Americans—Ethnic identity.   2. Hispanic Americans—Social conditions.
3. Racially mixed people—United States—Social conditions.   4. Pluralism (Social
sciences)—United States.   5. United States—Ethnic relations.   6. United
States—Civilization—Hispanic influences.   7. Pan-Americanism.   8 Ethnicity—
United States.   I. Title.

E184.S75 M667 2002
305.868'073—dc21   2001048867

First Edition: March 2002

10 9 8 7 6 5 4 3 2 1

CONTENTS

ACKNOWLEDGMENTS

This book is a product of my journalistic and creative work over the last fifteen years, and reflects all the people and places I came into contact with during those endeavors. There are too many moments and feelings and colors and instances of humanity for me to acknowledge, but here are a few:

I wish to thank my parents, Zoilo and Maria Morales, for possessing the courage to come to New York from Puerto Rico as very young adults and making sure I would feel at home here. My loved one, Adriana López, for helping me see the intense passion and ecstatic contradictions of our Spanglish blood, and for never giving up on me. My sister, Marisa, and her husband, Rolando Briceño, and Adriana's parents, Victoria Vargas and Pedronel López.

For the conception and execution of *Living in Spanglish*, I would like to thank my agent, Daniel Mandel, who helped me make sense of a tangled mass of ideas floating in my head several years ago. I thank also Elizabeth Beier, my editor, for keeping me honest and focused, her assistant, Michael Connor, and Dana Albarella, my original editor at St. Martin's, who first took a chance on the idea. I give it up to *compañero* Felix Rivera in the SMP publicity department. Thanks also to Susan Bergholz, whose faith in my ability was crucial to what eventually bore fruit in this book.

Thanks to all my colleagues in the world of journalism: Gershon Borrero, Joie Davidow, Mandalit Del Barco, Julian Dibbell, Karen Durbin, Enrique Fernandez, Luis Francia, Annette Fuentes,

Richard Goldstein, Sandra Guzman, Maria Hinojosa, Lisa Jones, Andrea Kannapell, Dennis Lim, Evelyn McDonnell, Abby McGanny-Nolan, Evette Porter, Elaine Rivera, Rosana Rosado, Karen Rothmyer, Danyel Smith, Greg Tate, Peter Watrous, and the late Ross Wetzsteon.

Thanks to all the "Nuyorican" people I lived the life of an underground poetry star with: Miguel Algarín, Paul Beatty, Dana Bryant, Steve Cannon, Willie Correa, Julio Dalmar, Maggie Estep, Reg E. Gaines, Lois Elaine Griffith, Bob Holman, Tracie Morris, Dael Orlandersmith, Willie Perdomo, Pedro Pietri, Edwin Torres, and Mike Tyler.

Thanks to the encouragement and support of friends: Yuzzy Acosta, the late Ana Araiz, Ivan Benavides, Hector Buitrago, Jeff Chaffa, Julio Correal, Esperanza Cortes, Angie Cruz, Andrea Echeverri, Erica Gonzalez, Sonia Gonzalez, Michelle Habell-Pallan, Jaime Cardenas, Lalo López Alcaraz, Angelo Falcon, Richard Gans, Saul Hernández, Darius James, Paul Kachur, Phillip and Lilah Levin, Marta Lucia, Marc Nirenberg, German Pérez, Richard Pérez, Michael Pribich, Marusa Reyes, Alexandra Rosa, Abel Salas, Rodrigo and Luz María Salazar, Ray Santisteban, the Women of WILL, Fernando Zapata, and so many others.

Finally, two teachers, David Gordon and David Zilberman, and a visionary, Eddie Figueroa, whose souls have passed into eternity.

AUTHOR'S NOTE

When I use the term "North America," I am referring to the America north of the Rio Grande, even though Mexico is considered to be part of North America (it is part of the North American Free Trade Agreement, for instance). North America is a state of mind that allows for the popular misperception that Mexico is not part of North America. Lastly, North America is opposed to South, or Central, or Caribbean Latin America in a way that reflects the North/South tension that needs to be resolved by, among other forces, Spanglish.

INTRODUCTION

What I'm Talking About When I Speak in Spanglish, or the Spanglish Manifesto

HISPANIC, LATINO, OR BOTH

As a journalist who has covered issues in the Latino/Hispanic community for fifteen years, I often wondered if it would be possible to locate the essence of what it is to be Latino/Hispanic. I've interviewed hundreds of people who all seem to have a different idea of what their ethnic identity is, and what seemed to emerge was a set of stereotypes that had to do with food, dancing, or sexuality. What's more, there is a great resistance to attempts to make our community monolithic. The idea of being Latino (or Hispanic) was further problematized by the multiplicity of our nationalities (Puerto Rican, Mexican, Cuban, Colombian, Dominican, etc.).

This fruitless search almost caused me to admit that this was a problem that could not be solved in my lifetime. Like marketers who are still baffled about how to sell things to us, I could not come up with a definition narrow enough to be intelligible. Then one day, looking in the mirror, looking at the photos of my family, friends,

1

lovers, listening to the music, watching us on television and in movies, feeling the dance moving inside me, I realized that the working definition for Latinos (or Hispanics) should be "everything." All races, all creeds, all possible combinations. Then I thought we should call ourselves "Spanglish" because it was a word that expressed what we are doing, rather than where we came from. And the only way to get a real understanding of what I meant by Spanglish would be to dispense with this Latino (or Hispanic) thing.

What's in a name? A rose, no matter what name it goes by, will always smell just as sweet. For years the dispute between Latino and Hispanic as the proper term for those of us with Spanish surnames and varying degrees of South of the Border baggage has lingered like a bad hangover. Hispanic—a term invented by the Nixon administration, probably inspired by his friends in the Cuban exile community—was designed to allow the lighter-skinned to claim a European heritage. Latino—derived from Latin America, originally coined by Napoleon-era France as a public relations ploy to explain why a French emperor was installed in Mexico City—was a mid-'70s incarnation of the term meant to allude to a separate identity from Spain.

While Hispanic became the preferred term of assimilationists (although it is often used by working-class Latinos who identify less with their home countries than with the Spanish language they still speak), Latino became the preferred term of the intelligentsia, identity politicians, and young urbanites. Hispanic best describes a Republican politician in Florida, a CEO of a soft-drink company in Georgia, a lawyer in Texas; Latino, a professor in California, a musician in New York, and recent immigrants all over the U.S. Although Latino importantly alludes to an allegiance to, or at least a sympathy with, Latin America and the pseudo–Third World status that implies, its most significant implication is that Latinos are not just Spaniards, but a mixture of Spaniards, Africans, and indigenous people.

But until now, this idea that Latinos are a mixed-race people has remained static. It merely states that, in fact, our genetic makeup is the product of a long-term racial miscegenation process. But it doesn't say anything about what that means. There is a need for a way to say something more about this idea than the word "Latino" expresses. So, for the moment, let's consider a new term for the discussion of what this aspect of Latino means—let us consider Spanglish.

Why Spanglish? There is no better metaphor for what a mixed-race culture means than a hybrid language, an informal code; the same sort of linguistic construction that defines different classes in a society can also come to define something outside it, a social construction with different rules. Spanglish is what we speak, but it is also who we Latinos are, and how we act, and how we perceive the world. It's also a way to avoid the sectarian nature of other labels that describe our condition, terms like Nuyorican, Chicano, Cuban American, Dominicanyork. It is an immediate declaration that translation is definition, that movement is status quo.

> To be Latino in the U.S. is rather to participate in a unique process of cultural syncretism that may become a transformative template for the whole society.
> —MIKE DAVIS, *Magical Urbanism*

Living in Spanglish is an informal invitation to those who seek to end the tyranny of black and white. It's always been easy to see race in these terms, the terms of the opposite poles of the spectrum. It has even become a metaphor for truth in our society. As far as the reader's trust in veracity goes, these words, "in black and white," constitute truth. But, overhyped millennium celebrations aside, we are in a new age in America today. It is an age in which the nuances of brown, yellow, and red are as important, if not more so, than black and white.

When W. E. B. Dubois said that the problem of the twentieth century was the problem of the color line, Americans never really understood what he meant, nor committed to understanding it. But it seems clearer that in the twenty-first century, we're going to focus on the color line itself—what many observers call the border. The only problem is, as Jacques Derrida says, the closer we get to the border, the harder it gets to see it. Reality blurs. Uncertainty becomes a principle.

If you focus on that blurred border, you begin to understand that Spanglish is so much more than reading between the lines. There is, of course, *the border*, the literal region of the Rio Grande, where Mexico blurs into the United States and vice versa. At the border, an obvious and often awkward mixing of cultures takes place that makes up the superficial idea of Spanglish. But the border also exists deep within the territory of North America, now more than ever, in its major cities; it is an imported border that is expressed through a dynamic, continuing recombination of cultures. That is the Spanglish way.

> *The most humanized human collectives always appear, in the last resort, to be the product not of segregation, but of synthesis.*
>
> TEILHARD DE CHARDIN,
> *The Natural Limits of Humanity*

To almost everyone, Spanglish is an ugly word. In its most literal sense, Spanglish refers to a bastardized language, an orphan, a hybrid, a mule—in short a pathetic, clumsy creature incapable of producing viable offspring. During their reign as conquerors of Latin America, the Spanish referred to the child of an African and a European as a mulatto, a mule-ly being; it was a branding that made it almost impossible for someone to elevate their social status, except through intermarriage with a lighter-skinned partner. For centuries, many Latin Americans have been on a dreary quest to lighten the skin, better the race, *mejorar la raza*, to achieve social status. Unconsciously, it may have been my mother's goal; it was the implied subtext of *West Side Story*. But the mule is the creature that does all the work—on its back rides the hopes of a new economy. I say the twenty-first century is time for Latinos (and anyone who wants to come along for the ride) to find their Spanglish soul, to deny racial purity, and find relief in the cool waters of miscegenation. Liberate yourself from the white/black dichotomy!

Spanglish is the state of perpetual, chameleonlike flux. There is a regional tendency for certain Latinos to call themselves "brown," but while this is an interesting metaphor, it defeats the purpose of calling for the withering away of race. To become brown would be to become a third wheel, constantly fighting for turf with the more established "black" and "white." Moreover, although brown describes perhaps a majority of Latinos, it leaves out a huge number of us who are actually black and white. Spanglish is about not having to identify with either black or white, while at the same time having the capacity to "be" both. We can even be both Hispanic and Latino.

SPANGLISH, THE "LANGUAGE"

Unfortunate numbers of uptight Spanish speakers with a Latin American colonial mindset find it unsettling and distasteful that in the U.S.'s inner cities, Latinos are substituting English words liberally. English speakers flinch at anything that isn't in their native tongue. The Spanglish that permeates the everyday culture of Puerto Rico can become a maddening drivel of advertising speak. Spanglish's harshest critics feel that its practitioners are in danger of becoming illiterate, much the way Marshall McLuhan once predicted rock and roll would destroy literacy. Surf any Spanish-language Internet site and you'll find this phrase: Click *el* mouse *aquí*.

The task of understanding and evaluating Spanglish, the metalanguage, has been taken up by the academic establishment of Spanish-speaking countries, since Spanglish still represents Spanish under siege from an external invader. They argue over the diminution of Spanish because of the introduction of new Spanish words that are literal translations of English ones—*parquear*, the cognate of "park," takes the place of the more elegant *estacionar*, which could be literally translated as "stationing." "Marketing," spoken in a Spanish accent, is absorbed into the language, replacing the more elegant *mercado tecnia*, or "market technology." Undoubtedly, the Spanish words tell us more about the human condition, but isn't this just an arcane exercise in preserving European flourishes in an American hemisphere that is moving quickly into the future? The fetishizing of pure Spanish only serves a colonial mindset, preventing Latinos from participating in the more dynamic, adaptable world of English. Spanglish is Spanish adapting the crazy rhythms of English, and English inheriting the multicultural content of Latin America.

But Spanglish is altogether something else—it expresses something much broader and interesting than just a glitch in language. Spoken Spanglish is only a verbal manifestation of a powerful force that has been incubating in America since the beginning of the postwar era, and will almost surely be a powerful determinant of U.S. culture in the twenty-first century. The simple utterances "*Yo quiero* Taco Bell" and "*Hasta la vista*, baby," do not in themselves pose a major challenge to what we know as postindustrial America. They are merely the iconographic residue of a society in transition, like rock and roll, Andy Warhol, or phone sex.

Spanglish the movement, Spanglish the message, Spanglish the party happening next door right now is the active state of cultural mixing, the endless pursuit of resolving contradictions in politics and art, the upside-down overhaul of class structure, the carnival of multinational culture. Spanglish happens when you go to see a bossa nova or a jazz quintet and you don't notice that half the band is black and the other half is white, or brown, or Asian. Spanglish is when the role of race is played by such skilled actors that you don't notice they belong to a particular race.

When I speak of Spanglish I'm talking about a fertile terrain for negotiating a new identity. I'm feeling excited, as Gloria

Anzaldua did in her book *Borderlands/La Frontera*, about "participating in the creation of another culture/in a state of perpetual transition/with a tolerance for ambiguity." Gloria sees us as reincarnated Quetzalcoatl, becoming "the quickening serpent movement."

I am my language, and it is continually in the process of being born. I'm affirming my own existence while at the same time demystifying the mainstream, distancing myself from the monocultural other. Identifying the monocultural is a revolutionary flipping of the script because the prevailing discourse identifies *us* (and others) as the other, keeping intact the narrative of self-pity and victimization that casts us in the role of schizophrenic signifying monkey, which is nice work if you can find it, but is rapidly becoming obsolete. Identifying the monocultural other should be a brief process for defining purposes only; the mere act of identifying "others" is a Eurocentric act that is antithetical to practicing Spanglish.

SPANGLISH THE PHENOMENON

This is an open challenge to previously established conventions of categorization, it is a Hegelian rejoiner to a Kantian world, it's a playful variation of Marx's unlucky eleventh thesis on Feurbach: "Philosophers have interpreted the world in various ways. The point is, however, to change it." Okay, so it seems that material efforts to change the world have failed; in retrospect it seems so quaint to think we could have changed it by a crude stab at overturning power relations. But this is not "the end of history"—that remains to be written by the language inside us, and the metaphoric language of the future is Spanglish.

At the root of Spanglish is a very universal state of being. It is a displacement from one place, home, to another place, home, in which one feels at home in both places, yet at home in neither place. It is a kind of banging-one's-head-against-the-wall state, and the only choice you have left is to embrace the transitory (read transnational) state of in-between.

Spanglish is that thing you haven't quite figured out yet about where we're going. It's a kind of new romantic thing, where we are liberated from previously existing structures and allowed to breathe. Spanglish is the state of belonging to at least two identities at the same time, and not being confused or hurt by it. It's a new blow against the tyranny of outward appearances, a personal map of demographic possibilities. It's kind of like what Antonio Gramsci called the taking of an exhaustive inventory of the self. It's an overtly sexy decapitation of the subject.

> *To become "Hispanic" is to turn the idea of an ethnic identity inside out, because it is ultimately to shed any specific identity in the hope of participating in this life as an American.*
> —GERALD TORRES, "LEGACY OF CONQUEST AND DISCOVERY"

The old-school idea of being an American leads many of us to say things like, "Why can't we just be considered *American*, like everybody else?" Maybe it's because we're already American. The raison d'être of Spanglish is to revise the entire idea of being American. Most Americans don't know that an entire continent directly to the south of us considers itself part of America as well. To these people, who are essential to the phenomenon of Spanglish, these United States, (along with Canada, and maybe, Mexico) is called "North America." This is how Guillermo Gómez-Peña, that madcap, deeply feeling, *border*-line genius performance artist puts it: "Let's get it straight: America is a continent, not a country. Latin America encompasses more than half of America. Quechuas, Mixtecos, Yaquis, and Iroquois are American. Chicano, Nuyorican, Cajun, Afro-Caribbean, and Quebecois are American as well." So instead of asking why we can't be considered American like everyone else, let's ask, why can't everyone else be more like us?

To the vast Spanglish world to the south, multiracialism is a widespread, if often imperfectly realized, norm that is hardly the subject of inquiry. Because as U.S. Latinos, we are descended from a multicultural, that is, a large group of mixed-race people, we are positioned to be the primary proponents of multiracial America's future. The 2000 census shows a blip of an increase in the number of Americans who consider themselves "multiracial. America is in its infancy, at the one-cell organism stage, in terms of understanding what it means to be multiracial. But there is no prescribed form, no cultural norms involved in being Spanglish—the world of Spanglish is the world of the multiracial individual. We live in a crowded universe of multiracial I's. In order to understand what that future is, indulge me in trying to figure out what I am. I've spent my whole life trying to figure out what I am, what Latino is. It's the food, it's the sex, it's the music, it's the dance, it's the brownish skin, it's the whatever. So we have no fear when we speak a crazy bastardization of language called *yo no se que* (*je nois se quois*), Spanglish.

Spanglish, like everything else, could not exist outside the forces of history. The phenomenon of Spanglish was born as a result of the emigration of Latin American people to North America, which naturally flowed from the penetration of the south by the north. It is a wave of immigration that was made necessary by economic forces that the U.S. participated in very actively since its inception. As Juan Gonzalez describes in excruciating detail in his book *Harvest of Empire*, the conditions for this immigration are the direct result of the activity of U.S. and European ventures in Latin America, and the foreign policy pursued by the State Department in the defense of that activity. If you like polemic, there's Eduardo Galeano's *Open Veins of Latin America*, a relentless indictment of the forces that undermined Latin America's economies. If you like real-life stories, just talk to anyone working as a busboy at your favorite restaurant or stockboy at your local greengrocer, or the guy who delivers your take-out vegetarian ramen.

So we came here, tired, poor, hungry, and the reception we got was for the most part extremely hostile, and when it wasn't, that lack of hostility was predicated on our ability to present ourselves in the most passive, nonthreatening way. It can be argued that it was the same way for Irish, Italians, Jews, Poles, and so forth, all those European ethnic groups that make up the melting pot of TV culture. The classic mode of assimilation for most immigrant groups to the U.S. involves the insertion of a hyphen between their original culture and their acquired one. Becoming a hyphenated American entailed little more than adopting a version of American identity popularized in post–World War II culture, with a fleeting reference to a European culture, preferably one on the side of the Allies.

But the original culture of the Latin American, although giving Europe its due, is divergent from the Eurocentric north. Because of widespread miscegenation between Europeans, indigenous people, and Africans, as well as the existence of towns established by escaped slaves of both indigenous and African origin, and the fact that Spain was Europe's dark cousin, Latin culture has a decidedly different racial feel. The Roman Catholic Church, which, in its small way, harbored thinkers who objected to outright slaughter, did more to tolerate African and indigenous religions in the hope that they would link to Christianity somehow. Whether it was because of a few compassionate priests or the feudal incompetence of the Spanish crown, African tribes and their customs were left more intact in Latin America. Dominican writer Juan Bosch said, "Economic conditions in Santa Domingo may have produced the defacto, if not de jure, liberation of slaves to the extent that they might already have behaved as free men in 1659, although they were not free legally." And sometimes countries like Mexico actually exalted and celebrated indigenous culture to make it part of the twentieth-century idea of nationalism.

Vast regional differences create nuances and wide variations from country to country in Latin America, which inhibits the creation of a monolithic Latino identity. Latinos cannot consider themselves an intact "European" culture; we cannot resort to being a convenient, added-on hyphenated identity, a couple of hand gestures or reference to an ethnic cuisine. We are so close to our point of origin, so under the influence of our American hemisphere, that an amalgam, "Hispanic" or "Latino" must be used to describe our passage to the north. Latino or Hispanic is a state that one must choose, and actively cultivate, to achieve. It is the process of North Americanization. That's where Spanglish comes in.

Spanglish can be something you are and feel all along, in the barrio, on the streetcorner, in the bodega, on the dance floor. Most of us go through life this way. I, however, am a freak of nature. Classically sheltered Project Boy of the North Bronx—where even white people lived in public housing—I lived a deluded dream of class transition. First I imagined myself as hyphenated, something that for Puerto Ricans is a state of redundancy. (Puerto Rican—American is saying the same thing twice because of the 1917 Jones Act, passed by Congress, which made all of us American citizens even if we never left the island.) Then, in the attempt to consider myself "American," my identity evaporated completely, like liquid sizzling into nothingness on a hot grill. When I became aware of the mistake that I had made, the way I had been removed from the bosom of Latino-ness, I knew that somehow I had to spend the rest of my life making up for my error.

I didn't make the mistake, as Richard Rodriguez described he did in *Hunger of Memory*, of subscribing to a self-serving fantasy of my miraculous transformation from working-class Puerto Rican given the privilege of attending an elite Northeastern private university to public intellectual. I did not reserve my culture to myself, relegate it to a private sphere that would prevent me from taking my place in American society. I did not try to shave my skin away. I began a long struggle to understand the necessity of creating my new Spanglish identity, without leaving behind the architecture, the latticework provided by my indoctrination into the private club of liberal arts education.

Spanglish describes a feeling, an attitude that is quintessentially American, but it is both older and newer. It is a culture with one foot in the medieval and the other in the next century; we straddle a broad swath of human history. Spanglish is a catchy catapult for the imaginary proliferation of everything. The Spaniard, a slippery soul already a pastiche of Visigothic, Gallic, North African Islamic Jew, comes to the Antilles and beyond to enact slave plantation sitcom allegories. There are guest stars from Yoruba, Benin, Congo, Angola, and special appearances by the quickly exterminated Taino, the emasculated Aztecs, and the conquered Maya and Inca, whose Asian essence is preserved from the tribes who slouched toward Oregon across the Bering Strait. These wildly different elements have produced a multisubjective, all-taxes-included new jack identity that may soon serve to explain the crazy polyglot chaos that is growing by leaps and bounds in the North.

THE COSMIC RACE

Our Spanglishness is based on the multitude of racial memory that we carry inside. *Living in Spanglish* takes comfort in the pseudoscientific notions of José Vasconcelos in his famous 1925 essay, "La Raza cósmica." Vasconcelos's work has been denounced as racialism and racist, variously by late twentieth-century interpreters. The first criticism can be tempered by the fact that Vasconcelos was trying to debunk the fascist strain of Darwinists who felt that natural selection was a rational explanation of the dominance of Western European cultures over the rest of the world. "La Raza cósmica" argued that all races would disappear in one massive "fifth" race (the "final race") created by a flurry of race-mixing.

Vasconcelos was denounced as a racist because he implied that the Hispanic or Iberian aspect of Latin culture was the guiding light, and that indigenous cultures gained by mixing with Europeans while offering little in the transaction save for an exotic skin tone, some mysticism, and sensuality. There is no doubt that this argument is racist, but we'll give Vasconcelos a pass because he had trouble freeing himself from his Eurocentricity—he was purportedly of Spanish-Italian-Sephardic extraction, a first-generation Mexican. His idealism, if sometimes misplaced, helped Mexico create a uniquely compassionate rhetoric about its indigenous constituency, one that is still in effect even now as pro-corporate president Vicente Fox delicately negotiates with the Zapatistas. Installed as the chancellor of education almost immediately after the Mexican Revolution, Vasconcelos did much to institutionalize Mexico's indigenous culture as an essential part of that nation's postrevolution identity. Vasconcelos was almost singlehandedly responsible for the Mexican Muralist school of Diego Rivera, David Alfaro Siqueiros, and José Clemente Orozco.

> *It is necessary for us to remain nationalist until we are able*
> *to achieve a true internationalism, that is, as soon as the*
> *dangers of the many imperialisms that attempt to subju-*
> *gate, not to civilize, disappear.*
>
> — JOSÉ VASCONCELOS

Perhaps the most intriguing aspect of Vasconcelos's argument is his prediction that humanity was going to enter a new age of the spiritual and the aesthetic, and that the miscegenated fifth race, so well characterized by Latinos, would be the one to lead us from the impersonal material world. There is no shortage of hand-wringing in our elite journals of opinion that American culture, never much to speak of in the first place—many Africanists would argue that most of its energy is black-inspired—is in crisis, has gone flat as a pancake. And there is ample evidence that in fields like popular music and film, Latinos have become flashpoints for cultural revival. So Vasconcelos's bizarre fantasy may be closer to the truth than he could have imagined. How romantic, you might say, and you're correct, but in that sliver of utopian realism I see that overlap of modernism that we still need before we go on into the postmodern world of no nations. It's that almost naïve notion of being attached to an idea of nationhood that is beyond nations that sets us

13

up for the twenty-first century. It is the triumph of the spirit. One of Vasconcelos's most affecting statements, which became the motto of Mexico's National University says, with haunting prescience, *"Por mi raza hablará mi espiritu* (The Spirit shall speak through my race).

In *Living in Spanglish* I posit the coming of existence of this forward-looking race that obliterates all races, stripping away Vasconcelos's petty resentment of Anglo culture and patronizing Eurocentrism, and acknowledging a cultural-economic inevitability that is hemispheric convergence. To paraphrase a Latino saying (which is possibly ultimately from the Arabic tradition), *"Mi raza es tu raza."* So *Living in Spanglish* is not a racialist text. It is a call for the end of race. But in order to face down race, we must first immerse ourselves in it. In all of them. It's a contradictory thing, you will understand. There is still plenty of time for everyone to learn to speak Spanglish.

The spirit of Spanglish embarks on the migratory journey to the north, already loaded with the possibility of infinite subjectivity, multiple personality. When the Latino pulls up stakes in New York, Los Angeles, Chicago, Miami, or Houston, for example, he/she becomes Spanglish—a north/south creature that many of his/her forebears can hardly recognize and often come to reject. This is the Chicano, or the Nuyorican, or the Miami Cuban—still largely Latino, but recombined again, with North American influences, although never really becoming what most people imagine as American. These days Latinos are coming north from places like Puebla, Mexico, or San Salvador, places where urban culture is not unknown. Many people in Latin America have already been exposed to rap music in their own language before they even come to New York or Los Angeles; they become Spanglish even faster than their predecessors.

The cosmic race is not a race per se, it's just the idea of a large group of miscegenated people with a more or less shared culture that has been in development for five hundred years. (Even my roots as a writer go back to the first printing press of the Americas, brought from Spain to Mexico in 1535.) The cosmic race is the end of race, because race becomes a multiple factor, not a defining category. Since its first articulation, the essay by Vasconcelos, the idea of *raza* has been most developed in Mexico, with one major flaw—the African component of Mexico, which has a major Caribbean capital city in Veracruz, is muted. But when *raza* is used by Chicano student groups in California, or by Saul Hernández, lead singer of the Mexican rock group Jaguares, it is a powerful call to unity, an abstract nationhood divorced from European nationalism.

NORMALIZING THE IDEA OF RACE-MIXING

The Spanglish phenomenon is key to understanding or at least reevaluating the increasing debate over mixed-race Americans. There is a great fascination of late with the new biracial North America. While the average American has always been of mixed race to some extent, before the civil rights era, the country was largely segregated by race. But with growing attitudes of tolerance and the liberation movements of the '60s, intermarriage increased, and now we are confronting a new generation of biracial youth, with many clamoring for a separate census category. The experiences of this new multiracial generation are presented as revelations of our country's future.

The irony in all this is that just to the south, and increasingly within the U.S.'s own borders, there is a huge multinational tribe of bi- and triracial people. While Latinos are largely categorized as a single brown mass whose common denominator is the use of Spanish, we are actually an astonishingly intricate mix of racial and cultural heritage. In any Spanglish family, one can find a black person, a white person, an Asian person, a Semitic person, or an indigenous person. The crucial difference, in perhaps oversimplified terms, is that here in North America, one drop of black blood makes you black, while in Latin America, one drop of white blood makes you white.

15

The Spanish conquistadores and rulers of Latin America had a slightly different approach from their Anglo counterparts. Rather than pursue an assiduous form of segregation between the races, the Spaniards, who brought few of their own women to the New World, decided to mix with their conquered out of lust and necessity. Still, the Spaniards were always careful not to let race-mixing impede their racial superiority. It has been said that the son born to Mexico's conquerer Cortés and La Malinche was sent to Spain to marry into the noble Castillian line in exchange for a vow never to lead an Aztec uprising. As the Spanish presence in the New World dragged on, several hierarchies of racially mixed "castes" were established, with different names for the various combinations between European, indigenous, African, and even Asian used to describe the shades and facial characteristics of each combination. By the early twentieth century, Vasconcelos was proclaiming the great potential and eventual dominance of the *mestizaje*. We are a miscegenation-happy people.

But even though we are hyper-miscegenated, our biggest divisions occur between nations, usually no more than subtle differences in intonations in language, varying degrees of connection to Spain, coastal versus mountain cultures, and the relative amount of African and/or indigenous blood in certain cultures. The failure of Simón Bolívar's dream of Latin American unity has resulted in a constellation of catty rivalries between regional cultures that have more in common than they realize. But now, in Anglo North America, we are forced to make alliances despite our differences, and, speaking a new language, we are slowly putting the pieces back together to the Bolivarian dream of Latin American unity. This despite findings by some historians that Bolívarism, and many Latin American independence movements, rose in fear of escaped-slave revolts.

The new American biracial individual is often portrayed as someone plagued by an unpleasant reality: whether to choose "white," "black," and, to a lesser extent, "Asian" culture as a domi-

nant form of identification. Star golfer Tiger Woods calls himself—
"cablinasian," truncating caucasian, black, Indian, and Asian. With
higher rates of intermarriage occurring of late between whites and
Asians or light-skinned Hispanics, some now theorize that the color
line of the future will be beige and black. But Latino culture, particularly our Spanglish American variation, has never been about
choosing affiliation with a particular race—it is a space where multiple levels of identification are possible. It may be what Michel Fou-
cault calls a heterotopic space—"a kind of effectively enacted utopia
in which all the other real sites that can be found within the culture
are simultaneously represented, contested, and inverted." It is a
Spanglish space. If the postmodern era is characterized by unprecedented heterogeneity and randomness, then Latinos are well prepared to take advantage of it. We have spent the last several centuries
preparing for our role as the first wholly postmodern culture.

Although Simón Bolívar was greatly disappointed with Latin
America's failure to unite politically as North America did, his disaffection with Europe was primal, and by century's end, a consciousness of a distinctly non-European, non–North American
entity began to take hold. Spurred on by Cuban essayist José
Martí's signature essay of 1898, "Nuestra América" ("Our America"), Latin Americans began to recognize their "own Greece," the
pre-Hispanic cultures of Meso-America and Africa. Ironically, as
writers like Samir Amin and Martin Bernal have theorized, it is the
fallacy of a "white" Greece that is the central flaw of Eurocentrism.
If, as these writers claim, the Greece of antiquity had crucial inputs
from Egyptian and Phoenician cultures, and these tendencies traveled to Spain during the Moorish occupation, Latin America's heritage may be closer to Greece's than North America's. But taking
Martí at his word, most Latin American cultures have made great
strides to at least partially recognize indigenous American history
as integral to the idea of a Latino.

Some parts of Latin America—particularly Southern Cone
countries like Argentina, Chile, and Uruguay—overtly reject indige-

nous and African influences. But the heart of Latin America—Mexico, the Caribbean, and northern South America—developed cultures that, despite being headed by white elites, pursued a national identity that in some way acknowledged the darker-skinned, lower classes of the society. (It can be argued that indigenous and African cultures have been more relentlessly oppressed in economic terms in Latin America than in North America; witness the Zapatista rebellion and the struggle of indigenous tribes in Colombia against multinational oil companies. But that is probably more of a function of the much smaller aggregate wealth of the region. The constricted and underdeveloped Latin American economies provide no real safety net for the poor, and the amount of unassimilated indigenous people is much higher proportionately.)

Worship of whiteness is perhaps more insidious in Latin America—some of the most dramatic instances occur in the Caribbean. In the Dominican Republic, political leaders have denied African influence despite its obviously darker-skinned population, and in Puerto Rico a recent poll revealed that over 80 percent of Island Puerto Ricans believe themselves to be "white." Again, whiteness in Latin America often means "not black" rather than "pure white."

MULTINATIONAL MULTIPLICITY

But Latino culture has not been developing in a hermetically sealed area South of the Border, where air quality and water purity cannot be guaranteed. It has been evolving directly in conjunction with North American culture through massive migrations, which energize Latino populations that have already been living in the U.S. and Canada. It is for this reason that many Latinos refer to two sites of experience: *aquí* and *allá* (here and there). The rapid transfer of information via commodities and media images, and the back-and-forth lifestyle of transnational Latinos are central to the postmodern experience. *Aquí* and *allá* is a people-based echo of the activity of multinational capital.

Latino culture, which is constantly evolving both north and south of the border, involves an increasing, if nonsystemic, proliferation of identities that allow us to choose from an array of guises, accents, class mannerisms, and racial solidarities. Martí, whose roots were in Spain and the Canary Islands, but who ultimately became one of the champions for Cuban independence in 1898, insisted in his famous essay that "we feel the inflamed blood of Tamanaco and Paramaconi coursing through our veins." Referring to rebellious indigenous tribes from Venezuela, Martí is establishing a principle of Latino culture—allowing all of us to recognize the varied nature of our genetic information and cross-identify with a particular ancestry for political or aesthetic reasons. This is the same principle that, in a country like Cuba, allows for an apparently light-skinned man to become a leader of a religion like Santería, an African religion masked by Christian artifice roughly parallel to Haiti's voodoo.

So if Spanglish culture is characterized by the multiplicity of its racial and class identifications, then its implications for identity politics in the U.S. are enormous. Growing out of the liberation movements of the '60s and '70s, identity politics has been widely criticized by both the American right and left, and the varyingly neoconservative writers of color like Stanley Crouch, Dinesh D'Souza, and Richard Rodriguez. At the dawn of the George W. Bush administration, a new "multicultural right" ideology is coming into focus in which a conservative "minority" elite are the role models for a new assimilation process. The neoconservative stance has made it widely acceptable that identity politics is divisive and encourages self-victimization and lack of taking responsibility. On the other hand veteran '60s liberals like Todd Gitlin and Jim Sleeper argue similar points that follow from the right wing, but believe that the divisiveness caused by identity politics weakens the general left cause, taking away the focus from class politics.

But since class is so closely associated with race in both North and Latin America, the muddling of race becomes an antidote to class prejudice. More importantly, the infusion of Latino-ness, the con-

sciousness of Latin America, into North American discourse introduces another level of class analysis. The hemispheric class structure
introduces a vast underclass, the army of workers (along with workers in Asia and other parts of the Third World) that has made the so-
called Clintonian era of prosperity possible. The working-class
dream of Americans is based on the nightmare of the underclass of
Latin America. The new immigrants from Latin America never quite
lose touch with their homelands; in fact, they are often actively
engaged in transferring wealth to the families they have left behind.
They are transcending the post-colonial, semi-European class stasis
of Latin America and engaging in North American class mobility.
Through Latinos, America's domestic policy becomes foreign policy.
The same kinds of forces, that is, the direct cultural identification
with outside countries that led America into World Wars I and II,
will eventually lead it to confront the economic destruction it is visiting upon the south.

> *The making of an American begins at that point where he*
> *himself rejects all other ties, any other history, and himself*
> *adopts the vesture of his adopted land.*
> — JAMES BALDWIN

Living in Spanglish argues that we are already American. The
Chicanos say, "We didn't cross the border. The border crossed us."
There is a trauma involved in trying to make sense of life on the
border, on the hyphen. But the mistake many writers and observers
have made is the demonization of the hyphen, the self-negation of
being on the border. Neither white nor black, we are, poor Latinos,
wallowing in a pool of nothingness. We will never be anything until
we're somebody else's idea of what it means to be an American.
But we are not defined by negation, we are the celebrators of contradictions, the revelers in the thorniness of the human condition,
the slayers of category.

In this book, I'd like to argue that Latinos give the chance for

America to move beyond identity politics, although not quite in the way the neoconservative (or, neoliberal, if you must) consensus would like them to. The Latino cultural "style" has the potential to free everyone from the guilt of having to reconcile with a strict definition of identity. For every biracial or middle-class black kid who comes home from school crying because street kids think he/she speaks too white, the Latino model offers a chance for that speck of whiteness to be part of a spectrum of behaviors and identities that are all "American." For every white person who thinks he/she is devoid of rhythm, incapable of dunking a basketball, or dancing a mambo, there is a chance to "feel the blood" of our "own Greece." America will finally become a total hemispheric concept. *Mi raza es tu raza*.

EL PLOT THICKENS

Living in Spanglish will seek to analyze the emergence of Spanglish from its origins in Latin America, when the Bolivarian dream of independence failed because of individual countries' inability to transcend almost feudal, postcolonial rivalries. Already at a trade disadvantage with North America and Europe, Latin America has an inability to accumulate capital and world market leverage that has left it unable to establish its countries as world powers. The — migration to the U.S. by Latinos, then, became an involuntary spasm of people unable to control economic forces.

Spanglish becomes a protective reflex exercised by Latinos, in a way parallel to the one pioneered by postslavery African Americans, as a mode of survival in a hostile environment. Incubated in the Southwest borderlands by Mexicans from California to Texas who suddenly found themselves living under the U.S. flag as a — result of the war with Mexico, Spanglish manifests itself culturally in the twentieth century. Mambo becomes all the rage in Manhattan and parts beyond, but sometime after the JFK assassination and the emergence of the Beatles, our emerging Spanglish reality was blunted by the coolness and ironic detachment of the hipster era. The musical hybrids of the '50s and '60s like cha-cha and bossa nova had been championed by the heroes of the dying Brat Pack era, and were dismissed as inconsequential, nihilistic, and anti-intellectual by the scions of the counterculture. Spanglish is forced underground by a realigned post-Vietnam culture, engaging in the radical politics pioneered by the African-American civil rights movement.

In the '60s and '70s, Latino nationalism not only entailed a revival of interest in Latin American culture, but perhaps more importantly, incubated the first fully developed Spanglish cultures in New York, Chicago, and Miami, and much of Texas, Florida, and California. Latinos were feeling their oats as Americans, but many did not choose to cooperate with the melting-pot consensus, which mandated that American culture be considered superior to all foreign cultures. Spanglish was developing a new way of being American, one that will be increasingly important in the coming century. *Living in Spanglish* discusses the culmination of this process—how Latin America itself is gravitating toward North American culture in a process that hints at a convergence between North and South.

America is moving. Intracontinental jets whiz back and forth between New York and L.A., jobs move from Michigan to Mexico, as Mexicans migrate to Michigan, and suburban SUVs make tracks for Blockbuster evenings of video rapture north and south of the border. Almost imperceptibly, silent brown faces make their way to the north, and maybe even south again, moving toward the beacon of light that promises a better life. Latinos are the masters of motion. Migrating between countries, languages, races, becoming everything and everyone as a means for survival.

This is the story of a migration for survival, of a people struggling to find a sense of themselves in an increasingly complex world. As America enters a new millennium, its fastest-growing minority, Latinos, is enjoying a level of visibility unparalleled since the days of the mambo fads of the mid-'50s. In urban centers like New York and Los Angeles, youth of all cultures are scurrying to take salsa-dancing lessons; film actors like Jennifer Lopez and Salma Hayek are starring in mainstream roles. In mid-'99, the Puerto Rican singer Ricky Martin broke through into the mainstream with a song called "Livin' La Vida Loca," instantly creating a Spanglish cliché,—appropriating a phrase that was used to describe Chicano gang life first in a book by Luis Rodriguez and a movie by Allison Anders. The title also had a strange double meaning because Martin has long been rumored as being gay—"loca," (crazy, feminine usage) is a currently favored term of self-description for Latin gay men.

But while the '50s fixation with Latin culture—which culminated with the enormous popularity of *I Love Lucy*, the sitcom that virtually invented the standard conventions of the genre—was a passing fancy, today's Latino mania is rooted in a demographic phenomenon. It is widely predicted that within twenty years Latinos will surpass African Americans as the country's largest minority, mostly due to an unprecedented wave of immigration that began in the '70s. These new tired, huddled masses are adding a numerical weight to the continual evolution of Latino culture within the U.S., which is entering its fourth and fifth generations.

So at the same time recent arrivals are changing the landscape from the lowest levels of the class structure (the greengrocer, the gardener, the domestic servant), new generations of English, Spanish, and Spanglish-speaking Americans are transforming U.S. society with their subversive, off-center point of view. A few years ago, an article appeared in the Sunday *New York Times* that attempted to explain why so many successful comedians come to the U.S. from Canada. Since the vast majority of Canadians live close to the border and grow up watching American TV, they develop an intimate knowledge of the culture without being part of it, thereby putting an automatic ironic distance on their interpretation of it. Imagine this seemingly isolated sociological quirk happening en masse, within the borders of the U.S., affecting a huge bilingual population that has lived in the New World for longer than Americans have!

More importantly, the continuing migration of Latinos to the north has the effect of reinforcing the Latin culture that we otherwise would have lost. Central to the process of "Americanization" is the loss of contact with people from the "old country." The U.S.'s Latin barrios are constantly being replenished by new immigrants, who bring with them the latest mores from their home countries, the latest music and dancing, reminding us what we are on the verge of losing, of the language and movement of our ancestors. Still, these immigrants are constantly striving to survive in an American landscape, adjusting to life here. The interaction between U.S. Latinos reaching back to their past and new immigrants grasping for their future is the central dynamic of Spanglish America.

Latinos have always been Americans in the sense that Europeans, Africans, and indigenous people are our ancestors. Both societies were created by explorers and frontier seekers that exploited people of color and imposed a European way of life on a continent far from home. Both democratized their societies in the late eighteenth/early nineteenth centuries, and their struggle for an identity involved rejecting the Old World and embracing the capitalism and mysticism of the new one. Most of Latinos' "American" ancestors go back as far, if not further, than North American bluebloods—we share with old-line Protestants a lack of affinity for the Ellis Island experience. So it follows that if America asked the European immigrants of the twentieth century to sublimate their old identities into an American one, Latinos would be much more likely to resist such a notion.

The problem for Latinos is that we are neither viewed as Americans—being consigned to a South of the Border ethos and all the foreign-tongued otherness that it implies—nor are we viewed as white, black, or even Asian in the American race hierarchy. Even now, as bipartisan politics recognize that the country must confront its racial divide, Latinos are made invisible through negation. *Neither black nor white,* says the discourse on race—a perspective some Latinos take as a positive assertion that they lack the historical baggage of either group. This blessing or burden of cultural multiplicity is one of the main reasons Latinos find it difficult to be represented by the mass media. In a society in which the lowest common denominator is favored, where the consumer profile—regardless of the proliferation of niche marketing through cable television or the Internet—needs to be as narrow and definable as possible, Latinos become indistinct blurs in the media mirror.

Many Latino icons in mainstream entertainment and the media are hidden and under-acknowledged. Actors like Martin Sheen, the late Anthony Quinn, and Jimmy Smits, while never denying their Latino-ness, are rendered shadow Hispanics by non-Spanish surnames and creative hair coloring. The most visible Latinos in America are the heroes of Spanish-language showbiz, like the late Tito Puente, Celia Cruz, Gloria Estefan, Julio Iglesias, and Ricky Martin. But while these cultural figures have great resonance for Latin America and the Latin American sensibility in the U.S., they are only predecessors to a new aesthetic that fuses the north with the south.

Spanglish is something birthed out of necessity. There is a need for Latinos to assimilate in the U.S., but we have always searched for a way to do that without losing what we are. In fact, generations of living in el Norte have allowed Latinos the space to begin to create a hybrid American culture that reflects the flexibility and absorptive ability of Latin America's. We do this when we speak Spanglish, which allows Anglo consonants to flirt endlessly with Iberian vowels (our fondness for vowels is also augmented by the African and indigenous languages that are uttered in our ancestral memory). We do it when we dress up to go dancing even though we are overbearingly down to earth. We feel it when our most profane sexuality takes us closest to our most sacred spirituality.

If, as Frederic Jameson writes, postmodernism is characterized by the loss of the modern subject, then Latin-ness has evolved from a culture where that subject, teetering on the edge of economic insecurity, has always been in doubt. To live in Spanglish is to engage in a radical doubt about North American existence, whose subject is a virtual consumer who is less concerned with worshipping the Judeo-Christian God than the profit-hungry machinations of multinational corporations. Many observers have noted that American culture is suffering from a fatal lack of originality—the superficial is on the verge of strangling what little literary and artistic tradition is left from the modern era. Latino culture is a much-needed infusion into a pop culture that has bogged down in its own market-driven formulas—it is a romantic return to a more organic sense of culture.

WITHIN YOU, WITHOUT YOU

Spanglish culture is not about segregation; its borders are permeable, but it has a strong core. If there is stability in the state of flux, it exists in a core that celebrates difference—permanently evolving, rapidly expanding difference. It's a dynamic, hyperactive state of absorption and re-creation that will inevitably change America from within. Within almost all Latinos is a dizzying array of genetic and cultural information. Every day I wake up and look in the mirror I see someone of a different race, a different social class, a different life philosophy. Sometimes I see an Egyptian, a fantasy brother to a seven-year-old boy I once sat next to on a flight from O'Hare to Kennedy. Another morning I see a high-yellow African American, wondering whether he's over the hill as a jazz saxophonist. Or sometimes, when I'm feeling really scattered, I see a Taino tribe member, ingesting the psychoactive drug called *cohoba* in search of the vertical shaft that leads to the Fourth Dimension. When I was younger I was sometimes teased as "China boy," and was embraced by Italian Americans, Jews, and African Americans as one of their own.

In the Information Age, Latinos have begun to crystallize their living idea of multiplicity. It's the extreme melting pot at a level that North America has never known, where samba meets salsa meets punk meets rap meets tango meets grunge. El Internet allows for cyber-Spanglish to flourish, Peruvian encounters Salvadoran and Dominican, and the soccer rivalries are beginning to break down. The globalizing imperative begun by the Clinton administration is trying to turn El Sur into a massive free-trade zone just as the Euro takes flight in the Old World. But although the time for a monolithic idea of Latino identity may have arrived, it's just rearranging its variability. It's just another new day for resolving contradiction. Because that's what we do best; every day we confront our own negation. It's the product of the culture clash that exists in almost every Latino family, where skin tones range from black to white and everything in between. It's a culture where the lightest skinned can insist on African and indigenous identity as their birthright. If Bulworth, the lead character of Warren Beatty's film, suggests the answer is for Americans to keep fucking each other until they're the same color, then America should understand that Latinos have about a four-hundred-year head start on them in this process.

Latinos are united by language, but divided into wildly varying nationalities with often-conflicting agendas. There are several borderlines between us. One between first-generation immigrants and American citizens of varying levels of assimilation, and more between Caribbean Latinos, who are more influenced by African culture, Mexican/Central American Latinos, who are more influenced by indigenous Meso-American cultures; and South Americans, whose societies tend to be more Euro-colonial in tenor.

In the U.S., control over the Latino agenda has long been a competition between Puerto Ricans in the Northeast, Cubans in Miami, and Mexicans in Texas and California. Within New York City, rivalries between Puerto Ricans, Dominicans, Cubans, and now Mexicans and Salvadorans are seemingly incessant. Among the youth, there is a schism between hiphoppers, rockers, and *salseros*. It is a big mistake to lump Latinos together, but there are important ways we feel like one people. They have to do with physicality (dancing, body language, suspension of reserve) and spirituality (that strange syncretism between Catholicism and African and indigenous religions that allows us to be sacred and profane at the same time).

For the purposes of this book, I will be focusing most of my analysis on the big three Latino groups: Mexicans, Puerto Ricans, and Cubans, primarily because of their longer and significant histories in the north. In the past ten years, the impact and accomplishments of immigrants from the Dominican Republic, Colombia, and other South American countries like Venezuela, Peru, and Argentina have become more important to the mix, as well as Central Americans from Guatemala to Panama.

While *Living in Spanglish* tries to cover the broad range of Latinos in the U.S., it can't begin to include all the varied contributions of all the Latinos who have made an impact. The construction of what I call Spanglish culture is not necessarily born out of a historian's impulse, but that of a sociocultural critic with a point of view that many may decide is coming from a left perspective. Certainly there are left themes in my analysis, including the basic assumptions that the European conquest of the Americas resulted in a grinding economic exploitation of the African and indigenous people that make up the majority population of the Americas. The seeds of Spanglish culture from Latin America to the north were carried primarily by the exploited, and the hybrid culture they created was a form of resistance against the dominant culture.

But the resistance to a certain prescribed form of assimilation that Spanglish symbolizes is not part of a culture of victimization—it is a needed counterbalance to the constricting monoculture of the north. It is a resistance that can only result in creating a new, united Americas that will finally fulfill the promise of human endeavor. The time for assimilation under duress is over. Toni

Morrison's famous statement about American assimilation being achieved on the backs of black people is undoubtedly a basis for this argument. The separatism of the African-American community to reinforce its sense of self was not only necessary, it was pre-scribed by the segregation that is imposed on Americans by social and economic forces.

The Spanglish idea rejects the halfhearted attempts by a litany of "multicultural conservatives" to promote assimilation as a way to — enhance progress in society. Multicultural conservatives are multi-cultural only in name and not in practice—their goal is to reinforce the monocultural majority. *Living in Spanglish* does not promote assimilation, but rather suggests that North America begin its long-overdue process of assimilation into the greater American hemi-sphere. In tracing Spanglish from a procreative act between Spaniards and their exploited operatives, I embrace the contradic-tion of miscegenation as a potential solution. This miscegenation is the true embodiment of the revolutionary dream that has always been at the root of the American psyche. With this book, I invite America to envision its inevitable Spanglish future.

Play the role you never played before. Be the thing that is most opposite to your sense of self. Imagine that nothing is foreign, and everyone could be a cousin to you. Listen to the music that follows the path of the Gypsy from India to Andalucía to Havana to New York. And above all, dance, dance, dance.

I.

THE ROOTS OF SPANGLISH

The Pachuco does not wish to return to his Mexican origin,
nor it would seem does he wish to blend into North Ameri-
can life.
— OCTAVIO PAZ, *The Labyrinth of Solitude*

Puerto Rico, 1974
This is not the place where I was born
— MIGUEL PIÑERO

Greater East Los Angeles, February 20, 6:30 P.M.
Home away from home away from home.
— LUIS VALDEZ

To be Spanglish is to live in multisubjectivity; that is, in a space
where race is indeterminate, and where class is slipperier than
ever. As an integral part of their history, Latin Americans engaged
in a mass experiment in racial miscegenation. Social class was partially determined by relative skin tone, although family standing,
the ability to trace lineage to Spain, and, of course, accumulated
wealth were important factors. But the economic instability of
Latin America made social class lines fluctuate wildly, and it didn't

take much for a family's standing to slip rapidly over a brief period of time. When Latinos came to North America, some were able to transfer their class standing into American categories. But the majority of us came into the lower portions of the labor pool, bringing with us a fluid sense of race and class, and we began to immediately create a new multisubjective sense of ourselves, which could be thought of as Spanglish.

Who are the Spanglish people and when did they appear? Legends of the conquest of Mexico point to La Malinche, a woman from the Maya nation that extended from Yucatán to Guatemala, who journeyed with the conquering Cortés into the heart of the Aztec empire as his translator. La Malinche, a.k.a. Doña Marina, served as an interface between Europe and the Americans, and has taken on all manner of criticism for "selling out" her own people and aiding the Spanish conquest of Tenochtitlán, the seat of Aztec power. She was said to have borne a child to Cortés, the first mestizo child of the Americas. Malinche's betrayal was real, yet inevitable. Her actions don't constitute an utter betrayal of Mexico's indigenous people, since there were several tribes to the south and east of Tenochtitlán that joined Cortés's army merely because of rivalry with Moctezuma's clique. But La Malinche set off a chain reaction of race-mixing that gave birth to the encroaching Spanglish reality of the twenty-first century, and it is most fitting that she accomplished this at the intersection of two languages, two cultures. In order to survive, she took on both, became both. That capacity, in a nutshell, is what Spanglish is all about.

To become Spanglish is to fuse the North American with the Latin American in a way that approaches the former with a healthy skepticism and takes care not to obliterate the essence of the latter. It is a sometimes violent, sometimes delicate rethreading of two parallel story lines, of long-separated siblings and hated enemies. Becoming Spanglish is inextricably linked with history and issues of race and class, and there are two tendencies that I consider central to understanding the process.

First, the great majority of migrants and immigrants from Latin

America to North America came from the lower classes, and tended to be of darker skin tone than the elites of their origin countries. Second, their class standing tended to be fixed in Latin America and seemed to have more potential to change in North America, while their racial oppression, which was more subliminal in Latin America, became overt in the U.S. The process of becoming Spanglish was fairly painful at first, like growing a thick callus to protect against the hostile dominant North American world. The first stage of this process was in many ways a desperate struggle that involved an increasing alienation from the homeland coexisting with a strong desire to return.

But the North Americanization process had its advantages for the darker Latin Americans: They were able to open their eyes to the subtle ways in which they were treated as second-class citizens in their homeland, and began to understand how to use North American laws to protect themselves. They became Americanized to the extent that they were leaving the semifeudal, postcolonial ways of their home countries at home. But just as Spanglish folks might have made a transition to a more conventional American identity, they pulled back and consolidated their position. They found a third option, the Spanglish way.

The way we conceive of Spanglish, the language, today is primarily from the point of view of the Spanish language, absorbing English words, giving it something of a modernity and some of English's inherent flexibility. But the emergence of Spanglish in the U.S. had its origins in the reverse process, that is, English absorbing Spanish. It began with the period of the Mexican War, which was resolved by the 1848 Treaty of Guadalupe Hidalgo. That treaty formalized the U.S.'s acquisition of Texas, California, Colorado, Utah, Arizona, and New Mexico. In the sense that this moment did not involve immigration, I consider it a prehistorical Spanglish phase in which North and Latin America's boundaries were still being drawn. The people of the Southwest have variously identified with

Mexico, Spain, and the U.S., and engaged in a proto-Spanglish project that is closely related to today's phenomenon.

What could have been a historical footnote in the treaty process turned out to be crucial to the future of Spanglish. Because of the fertility of the land between the Nueces and Rio Grande rivers, the originally proposed southern boundary of the U.S. as a result of its victory in the war, the U.S. negotiators insisted on its inclusion in its new territory. The acquisition of what became known as the Nueces Strip incorporated into the U.S. an area that was majority Mexican. By eating up this territory, America had irreversibly changed its internal makeup, and its culture.

According to historian Carey McWilliams, the meat of the revered cowboy culture of the Old West was copied from the Mexican vaquero style. Words like bronco, buckaroo, burro, mesa, canyon, rodeo, corral, and lariat, all steeped in heavy symbolism, were imported from Mexico. This means every John Wayne movie you've ever seen is in Spanglish. Like John Wayne himself, who married a Latina, many strategic land alliances between incoming Scots, Irish, and Germans, and local Mexican landowners were accomplished by intermarriage, creating one of the more miscegenated societies within the U.S. border. The roots of the Chicano movement are all in the Southwest, from the rebel persona of the pachuco, to the first lands rights activists of the '60s. The extremely important symbolic figure, the pop star Selena, had as her axis of power all the towns between Corpus Christi and San Antonio. The Nueces Strip was an important incubator of Spanglish in North America, but its remoteness from the rest of the country diminished its overall effect, and its Hollywoodization tends to obscure Mexican contributions, "assimilating" it into Anglo America.

Spanglish reality's formal beginnings can also be traced to the end of another war. In 1898, Spain ceded Cuba, Puerto Rico, and the Philippines to the U.S. following its defeat in the Spanish American War. Under the guise of keeping European interlopers at bay, the U.S. finished off the Manifest Destiny project by seizing the last remaining part of Latin America still owned by Spain at the turn of the last century.

An intellectual debate raging in Latin America about what the "other" America's role would be in the modern world at this time is an important root of Spanglish. Writers like the Cuban independence activist José Martí and the Uruguayan essayist José Enrique Rodó came up with some lyrical, if fairly inadequate, romantic notions about the differences between North and Latin America. Martí argued against racial categorization because he saw it as an attempt to diminish and obliterate the importance of indigenous and African people—the "natural" people were the soul of "our America." Rodó wrote a famous essay called "Ariel" in which he uses the characters of Ariel and Caliban from Shakespeare's *Tempest* as an allegory for North–Latin American relations. Caliban, which was originally read as Shakespeare's representation of the untrainable mulatto of the colonies, was used by Rodó to personify the U.S.'s crude, unthinking materialism, as exemplified by its rapid industrialization.

In the '20s, José Vasconcelos, a Mexican writer of Italian-Spanish parentage, came into the fray with his essay "La raza cósmica." He proposed the idea that Latin America's mixed-race population constituted a "cosmic race" that would lead humanity in a new direction by focusing instead on purely aesthetic concerns. Vasconcelos's ideas have been dismissed as a loopy overreaction to positivism. They have also been criticized because they favor the European component of the race-mixing. But despite the fact that he was European-identified, Vasconcelos had an archetypal Spanglish experience. As an adolescent, he and his family moved to a border region in northern Mexico and young José attended an English-language prep school in Eagle Pass, Texas. His revulsion for northerners was a major influence in his motivation to declare mestizos as the savior of civilization.

But Vasconcelos's, vision, though flawed, had a utopian excitement to it that feels like an antidote to North America's self-fulfilling prophesy of one-dimensional man. His idea, borrowed from many writers of his time, that humanity would eventually transcend physical labor, seems to be borne out by our increasingly technological world. And, as my increasing involvement with Spanglish culture tells me, the mixed-race future does seem to be coinciding with a humanity devoted more and more to self-development, yet mired in a North American culture wasteland severely in need of a shot of pure aestheticism. It is a culture happy to see itself endlessly reflected in the funhouse hall of mirrors in the last sequences of Orson Welles's *The Lady From Shanghai*, content to become virtual, soulless echoes of itself. Who will define the aesthetics of the high-tech future? What cultural force will break the postmodernist chain of repetition that makes the Police's "Every Breath You Take" the soundtrack for gangsta eulogy?

The end of the Ariel versus Caliban debate coincided with the failure of the Caribbean independence movement, interrupted by the last war of the U.S.'s Manifest Destiny period. It was a period when the first waves of Latino immigration came to the U.S., much of it spurred by refugees from the Martí movement. It was a period before the massive migration of Latin Americans to the mainland U.S. became strongly evident, before we were making a significant impact on communities and civil society. Although many of these immigrants came merely to better their financial situation, many were part of the fallout from the failed independence efforts. The Americas were slowly beginning to approach each other. They needed to get an idea of what each other was about. It was a period in which, at least on a symbolic level, America, through its nascent popular culture, began to become aware of "Latin-ness."

> "Yes, Mexico must be thoroughly chastised! . . . Let our arms now be carried with a spirit which shall teach the world that, while we are not forward for a quarrel, America knows how to crush, as well as how to expand!"
> —WALT WHITMAN, WRITING IN THE *Brooklyn Eagle* DURING THE MEXICAN-AMERICAN WAR

One early part-Latino immigrant played a major, if largely unrecognized, role in inserting the Ariel–Caliban debate into Modernist North American discourse. In Lisa Sánchez González's book, *Boricua Literature*, she contrasts the contributions of Arturo Schomburg, a black Puerto Rican migrant to the United States, and William Carlos Williams, whose mother was born in Puerto Rico and whose father was an Englishman raised in the Dominican Republic, a fluent Spanish speaker. Despite a clear Caribbean heritage, both men had their Spanglish characters elided by North American historical narrative: Williams became the link between Walt Whitman and Allen Ginsberg, and Schomburg a forerunner of African-American nationalism. (Adding to their invisibility was their lack of "Hispanic" surnames.)

Schomburg was important for embarking on a Pan-Africanist project similar to that of Marcus Garvey's, envisioning his Spanglishness as that of a black man set free from Latin American colonialism. But whereas Schomburg and his proto Harlem Renaissance stature tends to be lumped in with the discourse of the African-American "other," Williams engaged in the mainstream American debate, "passing" for an Anglo-American. As Sánchez González observes, Williams wrote "in a panegyric tone that clearly inscribes the authenticity of mestizo consciousness as the American consciousness" in his collection of essays, *The American Grain*. The bilingual doctor/poet from Paterson, New Jersey, inspired by Rodó's essay wrote in Ariel's voice, critiquing America's Caliban-esque tendency.

"The basic incapacity to touch, tenderly, the Other, is for Williams the definitive tragic flaw of Anglo-American cultural history," writes Sánchez González. "The juxtaposition of the United States' unparalleled power as a nation and its poverty of aesthetic-ethical (read sensual) grace is also an obvious thematic legacy of Walt Whitman's *Leaves of Grass*." Like Rodó and Vasconcelos, Williams contrasts the Roman Catholic "compassion" of the French and Spanish conquest with the genocidal furor of the Protestant colonization of North America.

And, like his Latin American predecessors, Williams ignores the African presence in his idea of "mestizo" consciousness in favor of the indigenous, creating a kind of new twist on Whitman's metaphor for the earth as woman. Whereas North Americans unapologetically raped the New World, the key to American happiness is the ability to seduce her. Just as Schomburg predicted the feelings of liberation an American city like New York gave black Latin Americans, Williams prefigured the flawed claim to absence of racism that—for many light-skinned Latin Americans, as well as Williams's beatnik heirs—would render their arguments inadequate.

FROM THE RIO GRANDE TO HOLLYWOOD

I am not an American
But I understand English
I learned it with my brother
Forwards and backwards
And any American
I make tremble at my feet
— "JOAQUÍN MURIETA," ANONYMOUS, CALIFORNIA
MEXICAN "CORRIDO" (FOLKLORIC BALLAD) C. 1850

In 2001, independent filmmaker Jim Mendiola made a short film called *Come and Take It Day*, which re-tells the story of the famous Robin Hood–style bandit Gregorio Cortez. Ironically, one of the contemporary characters in the film who lionizes Cortez finds that he is a distant relative of the Mexican American who turned the bandito in to the Texas Rangers—ambiguity and sometimes betrayal of the mother culture is one of the sticky problems of being Spanglish.

The role of social banditry in the early "Americanized" Southwest was an important seedling for Spanglish culture. Men like Cortez, who killed a lawman in the early 1900s, and Joaquín Murieta, a Californio (a Mexican living in California when it was taken over by the United States), were lionized by the corridos, or popular songs of the time. Since Mexican Americans were denied the right to acquire property and maintain political control over their destinies, banditry could be considered a legitimate form of social protest, and at once a symbol of the spirit of an oppressed people.

Paranoia about the presence of Mexicans in the Southwest produced their demonization in late nineteenth-century dime Western novels, which became the basis for the appearance of the "greaser" in silent films from the period 1900 to 1918. The originator of this genre was *The Birth of a Nation* director D. W. Griffith, whose *Greaser's Gauntlet* starred Tom Mix and "Bronco Billy" Anderson. In later years, Hollywood's crudity became more sophisticated, constructing the ideal type of the Latin lover. Pioneered by an Italian, Rudolph Valentino, the Latin lover came to symbolize the dark force of sexuality in the years immediately following Freud. The Latin lover is parallel to a vampire myth like Bram Stoker's Dracula, a count from an Eastern European country that was still struggling to find an identity "between" the Ottoman Empire and the Christian West, steeped in heavy sexual symbolism. That Dracula is so frightening yet seductive is a very Spanglish quality.

Valentino was a forerunner to the era of Ramon Novarro and Dolores Del Rio, two Mexican actors who successfully made the transition between the silent and talkie film era. Novaro, who played the spy in love with Greta Garbo in *Mata Hari*, clearly became identified with being Latin and sexual; Del Rio became the all-purpose exotic "face," the evocation of forbidden fruit. Her romance with Orson Welles in the '40s was a small Hollywood scandal, and she became a partial victim of the reprisals by the Hearst Company against Welles for *Citizen Kane*. Welles followed up on his Spanglish fascination with Del Rio by culminating his career with the bizarre *Touch of Evil* (1958), which starred Charlton Heston with a heavy tan, playing a Mexican in love with Janet Leigh (Hitchcock muse of *Psycho*). *Touch of Evil* is like a Diane Arbus photograph of a border town, presciently anticipating the importance of "border" in Spanglish culture, while at the same time acting as a vertigo-inducing antidote to *West Side Story*.

But by far the most important Spanglish story out of Tinseltown in this early stage is about Carmen Miranda, a woman who was born in Portugal and grew up in Brazil. Brazil's relationship to North America tightly parallels that of the rest of Latin America, but because it was settled by Portugal rather than Spain, it is somehow separate. Since Portugal's colonization process was so similar to Spain's, and it shared Catholicism, an Iberian history, and the languages are so close, it feels right to include Brazilian experiences in the Spanglish orbit, although their story is the subject of another book entirely. Carmen Miranda is significant here because she was recruited by Broadway producer Lee Shubert while on a trip to Rio de Janeiro, and she was subsequently chosen by Hollywood to represent all of Latin America. As part of the Good Neighbor Policy, which began in the '30s (designed by the government to promote relations with Latin America to dissuade them from falling victim to German propaganda), Miranda was propped up as one of the biggest movie stars of her time—she was the highest-paid woman in Hollywood at one point. She was given roles fronting large-scale Busby Berkeley musicals, modeling the famous absurd headpieces bursting with tropical fruit, a signifier of opulence during a time of war rationing.

The material she performed about Latin culture was a simulation of real Latin culture, a stitched-together patchwork of samba, mambo, and *son montuno* (the Afro-Cuban song form that is most widely known as "Latin" or "tropical" music. It is a remarkable fusion of complex African rhythms, Spanish folk melodies, and European waltz.), which actually made more of a reference to Spanish-speaking Latin America than Brazil. Miranda ultimately became a victim of the Hollywood star-making machinery—when the '50s came, elaborate musicals were going out of style, and Hollywood's fascination with Latins was also easing. But probably the worst moment for Miranda came when, at the peak of her career, she returned to Brazil and was rejected by her hometown Rio de Janeiro audience. In response to this, she wrote a song called "Disseram Que Voltei Americanisada" (They Say I Came Back Americanized), which she performed with varying responses. Miranda never got over this rejection and returned to Hollywood, one of the first large-scale victims of a classic Spanglish syndrome: Too foreign for America, too American for the folks at home. It is the prevailing trope for Spanglish, and it is a problem that we are only now beginning to understand how to solve.

THE FLOW TO THE NORTH

Spanglish dreams come directly from immigrant realities. The prevalent view of Latino immigrants is shaped by relatively recent phenomena—the gardeners of Southern California and the fruit and vegetable markets of Manhattan. But the movement of Latinos to the north goes much farther back. Early in the twentieth century, as the New York immigrant experience becomes legend for swarms of Europeans, there are simultaneous accounts by people like Bernardo Vega, who wrote a memoir about his life as a Puerto Rican in his teens and twenties. Vega's milieu was the lifestyle created by the tobacco workers, who established small communities in various areas in Manhattan and Brooklyn. His perspective—that of a committed socialist recounting the political history of Latinos in New York—allows us to see Gotham as a refuge for activists in the struggle against Spanish colonization. First there were those who were loyal to the Bolivarian dream of a united Latin America, fleeing to New York to regroup. Then, at the turn of the century, Vega recalls the shellshocked Puerto Rican intelligentsia hanging out in New York, depressed about the reality that they hoped would fade away: The Americans were really going to hold on to Puerto Rico, and José Martí's dream of free Caribbean nations would be dashed. Both the Puerto Rican and Cuban flags were designed in New York by pro-independence exiles. Even though Cuba was officially independent, it was already being carved up and bought out by U.S. investors, and there was little autonomous control of the economy or the foreign policy of that country.

In fact, Cuba had been in the process of exporting its labor and culture to the U.S., in particular places like Ybor City, Florida, a New Orleans–like area of Tampa, and the island of Key West, to set up cigar factories. Even more fascinating is the degree to which the island itself was becoming Americanized, not just with the penetration of land speculators but with things like baseball and consumer goods. As is well chronicled in Louis A. Pérez Jr.'s *On Becoming Cuban*, islanders were hot to buy Ford automobiles, soft drinks, and appliances, fueled by advertising that was designed to appeal to a middle-class tropical denizen. Cubans were busily constructing a parallel America and, by extension, immersed in the American zeitgeist even though their language and culture was something very different.

Bernardo Vega's world was filled with labor organizing, and ties to Samuel Gompers, who visited Puerto Rico and helped establish labor rights in the island. It was a world where Arturo Schomburg, a black Puerto Rican, was a major spokesman in the way Paul Robeson would become. Schomburg, a key figure in the Harlem Renaissance, went through periods when he identified more with African Americans and more with Puerto Ricans, but in the end he was said to have embraced both, changing his name from Arthur to Arturo. It was also a world where Rafael Hernández, also black, one of Puerto Rico's greatest songwriters, wrote "Lamento Borincano," the unofficial anthem of the island. The song was first recorded on vinyl in a New York studio. Black Cubans were coming north to play baseball in the Negro Leagues. In fact, some Negro League teams called themselves "Cubans" to deflect racist attention when they traveled to certain cities.

But folks like Bernardo Vega were just making their way through a foreign terrain, experiencing prejudice when they tried to live in better neighborhoods, trying to find a sense of home in Sephardic

Jewish restaurants in Harlem, because they served food that was the closest to the Spanish-style diet they were used to. Vega was a pioneer, representing a significant Latino presence in New York earlier than most people conceive of. Ruth Glasser's *My Music Is My Flag* documents a thriving community of Puerto Rican and other recent Latin immigrants in New York in the '20s and '30s. The hybridizing experiments of these musicians, and the crowds that came to dance, is a classic early form of Spanglish. "Just like black Harlem dances," says John Storm Roberts in his book *Latin Jazz*, "Puerto Rican dances featured a wide variety of music, Latin and Anglo. While Anglo rumba dancers wanted exoticism . . . younger barrio residents wanted something hip, which meant swing."

As Rodolfo Acuña documents in *Occupied America: A History of Chicanos*, Mexican Americans began to move from rural areas to the cities in massive numbers in the 1920s; Los Angeles and San Antonio were primary destinations. While Anglos feared that their increasing numbers would herald an attempt to repatriate the areas Mexico lost in their war with the U.S., Mexicans were merely trying to survive in a harsh economic environment. In the '20s, as returning to Mexico became a distant dream for immigrants, organizations like Los Hijos de America were formed to protect Mexican-American interests. These organizations were strongest in the San Antonio area. But the most important development for Mexican-American immigration occurred in the '20s, when Los Angeles surpassed San Antonio as the capital of Mexican America. This power shift would affect the evolution of the Chicano movement in the '60s.

In Southern California and Texas, however, Mexican American migrant labor was creating such a significant presence in cities from Santa Barbara to Corpus Christi that the Southwest began to develop a kind of two-tier experience, where language and sometimes class differences had the effect of creating slight separations between established Mexican families and more recent immigrants.

In Tuscon, Arizona, Lalo Guerrero, a singer who specialized in parodying American hits to reflect Mexican-American concerns, began his career as "The Father of Chicano Music." Guerrero, who was one of the first to write and record bilingual music, documented the rise of Spanglish from the pachuco to the Chicano, and also managed to write a song, "Canción Mexicana," that was recorded by one of Mexico's most popular singers, Lucha Reyes, and became an unofficial national anthem.

The early Spanglish people were having mixed results fitting into the polarized society of America in its postwar years. It was an atmosphere where the European ethnic melting pot ruled New York, and those who didn't conform to that model could raise suspicions. But Spanglish culture, in some ways incubated by the Good Neighbor Policy, was feeling its way into the mainstream. It was flaunting itself in the Palladium on Fifty-second Street on the West Side of Manhattan, vamping in the style of the Cuban immigrants in Oscar Hijuelos's novel *The Mambo Kings Play Songs of Love*, and finally exploding negatively onto the American scene in the Broadway hit *West Side Story*. The new culture emerged in a splash of bad publicity, a reflection of the racism that would greet its arrival.

In Texas, the stagecoach travel from the northern Mexican city of Monterrey brought the influence of German immigrants, the accordion, and a fusion of polka and ranchera (Mexican traditional) music. The pachuco, the penultimate Spanglish figure of resistance for Mexican Americans, is born in South El Paso, a border town with a much more fertile hybridization rate than its more famous cousin, Tijuana. On the West Coast, after a steady stream of agricultural worker migration at the turn of the century from Mexico into several cities in southern California, Spanglish was born in the flames of the zoot suit riots of the '40s. Mexicans who lived in Los Angeles dressed in outlandish costumes as if to mock their status of invisibility in a town some of their ancestors once settled. Their manifestation as "different" during a time of national conformity—wartime tends to reinforce xenophobia—was intolerable. The zoot suit, a flashy outfit originally worn by African Americans in Harlem, was extremely

44

important in establishing a Mexican American identity in Southern California. The clothes were looser, and the capability of the body to stretch in them and perform intricate dance moves made them popular. By adopting the zoot suit, Mexican Americans were staking their own claim to blackness—they were asserting a "most oppressed" status. Conversely, Los Angeles–area Asians and blacks wearing zoot suits were also harassed by the police because they were mistaken for Mexicans.

The problem for the zoot-suiters is that Los Angeles was home at the time to swarms of sailors on their way to the South Pacific to fight the Japanese. With the anti-Japanese internment process already in full swing, this Mexican affrontery was beyond the pale. The riots followed what was known as the Sleepy Lagoon incident, in which the death of a young Mexican American prompted a string of sensationalized newspaper accounts that branded the entire group as lawless savages. Inspired by the iconic figure of Cantinflas, a masterful Mexican comedian who parodied the vanity and arrogance of the upper class, East L.A. teens reinvented themselves as pachucos, immortalized in Luis Valdez's 1978 play *Zoot Suit*.

A native of Mexico City, Cantinflas became a major international movie star, earning the praise of his contemporaries in Hollywood. But though he was such a staple in the early '60s that even my parents, Puerto Ricans living in New York, were well versed in his material and brought me to his movies as a small child, Cantinflas's significance to Spanglish culture may have more to do with his methodology. As one of Mexico's leading intellectuals, Carlos Monsiváis, writes, "He makes visible the outcast's vocation for the absurd—in part disdain and annoyance for a logic that condemns and rejects him . . . To a lack of resources, Cantinflas opposes a happy combination of verbal incoherence and bodily coherence." In other words, Cantinflas became the hero for the outcast Mexican American, "verbally incoherent" because of the use of Spanglish, and bodily coherent—strong, smooth, confident, wearing those baggy zoot suits. Cantinflas was the prototype for the pachuco. His embodiment of the class struggle within Mexico, when imported north, becomes symbolic of the struggle between Chicanos and the disdainful Anglo majority.

Many pachucos tattooed their left hand between their thumb and forefinger, a practice that still survives in Mexican prison gangs. They spoke *chuco*, a mixture of Spanish, English, archaic Spanish, and border slang: The original pachucos are said to have originated in the border region of El Paso, Texas, in the '30s, just across the border from Ciudad Juarez, Mexico, where one of Cantinflas's comedic predecessors, Tin Tan, performed.

What makes Valdez's work definitive is his use of El Pachuco, a wraithlike, Greek chorus of a character, as the voice of *el nahual*, which is a Mexican indigenous spirit-form that represents "the other self." Like Mikhail Bakhtin's theory of inner dialogism, the duality that springs from *el nahual* allows the play's protagonist, Henry Reyna, to figure out how he's going to become a Spanglish American. It's the same principle that Valdez applies to Ritchie Valens in the film version of his life, *La Bamba*.

At the end of the play, the pachuco is literally stripped bare, recalling the practice of the rioting mob of sailors and civilians who invaded Chicano neighborhoods. That the symbolism of the zoot suit was so outrageous as to provoke a response like stripping is a tribute to its signifying power, and a reference to Spanglish, hybrid culture. If blacks were tarred and feathered, or had white paint splashed on them, pachucos had to be stripped of a look they had constructed, a fashion that was grafted onto their skin. The subtext of mixed race took on a literal meaning when the California Committee on Un-American Activities declared that Carey McWilliams, a journalist and lawyer who helped defend the Sleepy Lagoon defendants, had "Communist leanings" because he opposed segregation and favored miscegenation.

Havana in the '40s and '50s was one of the centers of a peripheral American culture, with its decadent club scene, prostitution, and some of the best music recorded in this century. But something was simultaneously happening in New York involving two Cuban musicians who were beginning to influence the entire sphere of popular music in America. Chano Pozo, a flamboyant conga player who enjoyed prowling the Spanish Harlem nightlife, and Mario Bauza, a more reserved, cerebral trumpeter-arranger, began teaching Dizzy Gillespie the intricacies of Cuban music. Cuban music itself was a fascinating process whereby elements of eighteenth-century French waltzes were introduced to Havana by free blacks who were able to join musical bands in Cuba because, as Alejo Carpentier writes in *La música en Cuba*, there weren't enough competent European musicians. The superior fluidity and interchange of culture between blacks and Europeans in Cuba enabled them to adapt a musical style from another European culture (albeit a Romance-language one) and gracefully graft on the essential African drum elements. By the mid-nineteenth century, Cubans had created a "rock and roll" that wasn't the fine line between sex and violence, one that had superior harmonic and rhythmic integrity.

The innovations Bauza and Gillespie made revolutionized the traditional rhythm patterns of American jazz, influenced the playing of the bass that laid the groundwork for funk and rock and roll, and perhaps even was the direct inspiration for that most inventive and idiosyncratic of African-American musics, bebop. Even though bebop became known as one of the quintessential expressions of African-American art in the '50s and '60s, it was also a hidden expression of Spanglish culture in the way it represented a moment when Afro-Cuban rhythm altered conventional jazz wisdom. It was a liberation from the march, the essential form of American popular music from John Philip Souza onward, a movement into a mystic way of being. The word itself, bebop, is a fusion of two words signifying existence and movement, emanating from an inner self-doubt, that combines African rhythms fused with European expressionism. Bebop is identity arrived at through utterance, melody conceived through rhythm.

Bebop has often been considered an outsider music, an anti-assimilationist music, a survival instinct of African-American urban culture, but it was informed by, and probably infused with, a shot of Afro-Latin culture. It was a parallel double consciousness with a doublespeak that went along with it, both drawn from the inevitability of the drum. In Yoruban culture, drumming was essential to art, spirituality, and community. Melody emerged from percussive tones, syllabic utterances that had the quality of language. Bebop emerged from the struggle to resolve African-American identity in an Anglo-American context, using a musical language parallel to Spanish.

> *El puente de Brooklyn ha de tocar tierra*
> *Brooklyn-Queens-Express-Way*
> — ERNESTO ÁLVAREZ-VALLE

When U.S. Latino writers began to write in Spanglish, they were merely reflecting the language the people were speaking; they were keeping the oral tradition in their literature intact. But they probably had no idea they were giving voice to a revolutionary utterance, a living metaphor of the future. There were rumblings from Puerto Rican poets in New York who were starting to slip the cold, industrial language of El Norte into their texts, like the above-cited Álvarez-Valle, and Clemente Soto Vélez. But their thoughts had been formed on the island, and their discourse was a migrant (immigrant would be used here but for the Jones Act) one. The most important early literary manifestation of Spanglish is the work of Piri Thomas in *Down These Mean Streets*, because he was a New Yorker—a kid from East Harlem who was trying to figure out what it meant that his blood came from Puerto Rico. The mixing of languages that occurs in Spanglish is a metaphor for the mixture of race; it allows for races to have different voices in the same language, eliminating the need to structure language, or thinking in terms of a racial category.

The encounter with the north is a metaphor for the exchange between races, as well as the clash between town and country. *Down These Mean Streets* anticipates a central aspect of Spanglish culture, a struggle to define its racial identity, ending in ambivalence. Thomas had the daunting task of trying to devise a notion of himself as a black Puerto Rican. His free use of Spanglish in the book, dropping Spanish words without translation in the midst of "black" English sentences was revolutionary. In one chapter, "If You Ain't Got Heart, You Ain't Got Nada," he tries to define the street code of *heart* that eventually finds its way to the center of another hybrid idiom, hiphop. In "Brothers Under the Skin," he wrestles with whether he can actually be Puerto Rican and black at the same time.

Spanglish identity from the beginning could be read as an attempt to find a free space outside the North American black-white racial dichotomy. The idea of race in North America contrasts greatly with Latin America in its absolutist tendency. The one-drop rule of American racial identity, in which blackness is immediately ascribed to anyone with any amount at all of African blood, conflicted with the nuanced race identity of Latin America. In Latin America, several drops of African blood do not disqualify you from the privileges of "whiteness." While there is always a premium for the authenticity of fair skin, blackness is only conferred to individuals who exhibit relatively undiluted African physical traits.

The confusion wrought by changed racial categories upon immigration to the U.S. is a central theme of Spanglish culture. Racism in Latin America is somewhat mitigated in that most countries make attempts to venerate or honor indigenous culture, and actually incorporate African culture into national musical traditions. When a Latino comes north, unless he is in the minority of fair-skinned immigrants, he has to choose whether to "enhance" his ability to appear white or identify as nonwhite, which immediately relegates him to a lower societal status. Given this choice, many Latinos, using fair skin and Catholicism as a bridge, try to assimilate. But many Latinos, particularly of Caribbean descent, go with their souls. It becomes impossible to betray the legacy of tropical swing, the inevitability of negritude.

> *Ay, ay, ay, that my black race escapes*
> *And with the white one runs to become dark*
> *To become the one of the future*
> *Brotherhood of America!*
>
> —JULIA DE BURGOS,
> *Roses in the Mirror*

Spanglish culture springs from a reaction to racism: in the case of the Caribbean Latino, like Puerto Ricans or Dominicans, there is a refusal to let go of an African identity; in the case of the Mexican or Central American, there is a profound anchoring to the roots of the indigenous soul. It is an attempt to allow for multiple identification with the cultures of multiple races. In the Caribbean case, the negritude movement of the mid-'30s, most often associated with Martinique's Aimee Cesaire, had a strong influence. The Puerto Rican poet Luis Palés Matos, whose work is undergoing a small renaissance since his 1998 centennial, is emblematic of the roots of Spanglish culture. Although his attempts to capture the African essence of Puerto Rican culture were at times awkward and steeped in what some might call racist humor, Palés Matos's work represented a direct attempt to incorporate Africanist discourse in the island's largely colonial narrative. It was an above-board acknowledgment of the essential part that African culture plays in the identity of the *jíbaro*, the archetypal Puerto Rican peasant farmer. Still, the "above" part is key to some Puerto Rican critics, who feel Palés Matos's work is condescending and trivializing of African-ness.

Ironically, in many island paradigms, the *jíbaro* (in Cuba, the guajiro) is often thought of as the light-skinned country farmer who lives in a kind of mestizo purgatorial vision of the yeoman Spanish peasant. He is opposed to the coastal, urban seaport culture that is dominated by African-based music and religion. But as the result of migration to urban centers in the twentieth century the *jíbaro* romanticizes the coastal blacks; his songs yearn for sexual union with the *mulata*, and he may be descended just as easily from an escaped slave who managed to move into the high country as he was from a Galician or Corsican yokel.

> *On his days off, Cesar did a lot of the footwork, going from club to club on Eighth, Ninth, and Tenth Avenues, and to the Bronx and Brooklyn and uptown, Harlem. He was always trying to set up auditions with jaded, tan-suited Puerto Rican gangsters who owned half of the mambo singers in New York. . . . It would help a lot that he was a white Cuban bolero singer like Desi Arnaz, what they called in those days a Latin-lover type, dark-haired and dark-featured, his skin being what was then called "swarthy." Swarthy to Americans, but light-skinned when compared to many of his friends*
>
> —OSCAR HIJUELOS,
> *The Mambo Kings Play Songs of Love*

Perhaps the clearest evidence of the emergence of Spanglish culture as reflected through the mass media was a television show named *I Love Lucy*. The show made direct use of literal hybridity, that is a marriage between north and south, which produced a Spanglish narrative as spoken by its two central participants. Desi Arnaz met Lucille Ball in the first place because of the popularity of Latin music, which was in one of its peak periods of appreciation in the late '40s.

What was extremely significant about *I Love Lucy* was that it helped define the American family in the '50s despite having an extremely unorthodox (i.e., racially mixed family) at its core. The reason it worked so smoothly (leaving aside the considerable talents and innovations of Arnaz as a producer) is the function the show had in the context of American society at the time. The fact that Arnaz was a "foreigner" who had successfully engaged in a respectable American marriage to Lucille Ball was only the subtext of the show. The dominant idea behind *I Love Lucy* was to reestablish the woman as inferior, laughable, frail, and dependent on a dominant male. The country was still emerging from a postwar situation in which women, having been used heavily in the work force with their husbands away in World War II, needed to be put back in their place. What better way to reestablish the ideal patriarchal American family than to employ a macho man from Latin America to at once belittle her and put her on a pedestal. This was a theme that ran through the American situation comedy in shows like *The Honeymooners, The Burns and Allen Show*, and others.

The absorption of imported macho attitudes in the '50s was also demonstrated by Ernest Hemingway and John Wayne, both of whom had Latina spouses and had a kind of reverent view of Latin culture because it allowed them to assert themselves without compunction. In *Slouching Towards Bethlehem*, essayist Joan Didion tells the story of the Brat Pack who enjoyed themselves so enormously in Mexico City and Havana because they were allowed to be as outrageous as they wanted to be. In *Guys and Dolls*, a venerated Broadway work, the perfect paradigm of macho dating is played out in Havana.

But the mid-century Cuban manifestation of Spanglish culture is strongly influenced by a vastly different set of circumstances from the Puerto Rican and Mexican varieties. The Cuban context was dominated by the strong involvement of that island's elite in adopting an American lifestyle since the early part of the century. The relatively extensive development of Cuba in the late nineteenth century—it had a railroad network and telegraph machines before Spain did while it was still a colony of Spain—strongly influenced Cubans to look toward the U.S. as part of their cultural liberation from the mother country. The yearning for independence grew simultaneously with an almost erotic desire for union with America, an idea that is elaborated on with great elan by Gustavo Perez-Firmat in *Life on the Hyphen*.

Perez-Firmat's take on *I Love Lucy* focuses on Desi Arnaz as the subject (an empowering position, flipping around the role of the other) and Lucy as the object of desire. Pérez-Firmat argues that the show's interpretation was focused on trying to reassert the primacy of the American TV viewer as the true lover of Lucy, and therefore the owner of her sexual power. Since history seems to support this notion, relegating Arnaz to, at best, a transparent surrogate for American sexuality, and at worst, a buffoon, "beard" husband for the purpose of a crude vaudeville skit, it would seem that this particular Cuban attempt at Spanglish was ineffective. Arnaz's legacy is one of the man who fails to receive credit for many of the directorial ideas that made the show a success, whose careful stance of not asserting himself as a dignified subject relegates him to sideman status. And while there are stories about the couple's marriage that point to Arnaz's infidelity as the cause of its disintegration, there is little speculation about his adulterousness having to do with his insecurity about the public's accepting him as Ball's true love.

As the '50s era of social conservatism began to give way to the exigencies of the '60s, on the West Coast there was a strong cultural movement of Mexican Americans who began to understand that they were too brown to be American and too Anglo to be Mexican. During the Zoot Suit riots of the World War II years, they began to find an identity that was born out of the tough streets of East Los Angeles and Boyle Heights, one that forged mystical ideas of their indigenous origins and the bitter realities of any American immigrant on the bottom rung of society. Luís Valdez, who was a radical organizer for the United Farm Workers Union, began to write plays in the '60s that explained the origins of the Chicano branch of

Spanglish. Instead of becoming a translator of his culture, rendering it intelligible to Anglo culture, he chose to become a translator of his culture to his own people.

Luís Valdez addressed the Sleepy Lagoon case in 1942 as a landmark case, like the Scottsboro Boys in the '30s, in which minority kids were put up en masse for a criminal trial. For Valdez, the two cases were similar because they disregarded the individual identity of the accused and put them on trial as stereotypes. *Zoot Suit* was Valdez's attempt to dramatize this in a way that would be palatable to a paying public, by making it a musical. The zoot suit itself was an outgrowth of the swing and big-band music of the era. Duke Ellington's "Perdido," a work based on his flirtation with Latin-based rhythms, is the play's opening number, but despite its Spanglish nature, it is primarily a prototypical piece of big band jazz. "This was the first generation that embraced all aspects of the culture—the music, the dance styles, the slang, they were bilingual," Valdez said.

The sudden manifestation of pachuco consciousness, and the starkly unapologetic repression in reaction to it, is at the root of the Chicano movement that would prevail in the '60s. The Chicano was less a stranger in a strange land, as Caribbean immigrants were in New York, but an outcast in his own land. The entire milieu of the Southwest has the extremely strong genetic and cultural feel of "home" for Mexican Americans, but the last 160 years of U.S. history has made it into a hostile territory for them. If Cubans were the closest to Anglo-American culture, Mexicans are the closest to "real" American culture, the culture of the Native American. Their Spanglish was not the rapid-fire semi-Yiddish spewing of New York Latinos but the words that fit the landscape of the Rio Grande Valley and the Camino Real. Most of all, the pachuco represents the mestizo, the mixed Spanish-indigenous Mexican too "European" (or "American") to be Aztec, Toltec, and so forth, and too indigenous to be "European" or "American." The pachuco is not only a symbol of mixed race, but also of a certain class sensibility. The pachuco can never be one of the ruling, light-skinned elite of Mexico, nor the white working-class citizen of the U.S. Two of the important contributions to Spanglish culture were made by Mexican Americans in the '50s: the novel *Pocho*, by José Antonio Villareal, and the music of original rocker Ritchie Valens.

> *They had a burning contempt for people of a different ancestry, whom they called Americans, and a marked hauteur toward Mexico and toward their parents for their old-country ways ... The result was that they attempted to segregate themselves from both their cultures, and became a truly lost race. In their frantic desire to become different, they adopted a new mode of dress, a new manner, and even a new language. They used a polyglot speech of English and Spanish syllables, words, and sounds.*
> —JOSÉ ANTONIO VILLAREAL, *Pocho*

Pocho's subject matter is very much the same as the rest of Spanglish literature, treating themes such as the modernization of culture, the industrialization of the working class, and the disintegration of the patriarchal family (and its attendant feminist critique). Most importantly, it establishes the in-between ground of Mexican American, and by extension, Spanglish culture. *Pocho*'s great accomplishment was to locate the estrangement of Mexican Americans from the mother country in a contradictory site of progress (in the sense of participating in the modernized, industrial society) with guilt and self-negation. There is always a classic moment in the life of every Spanglish person, when one realizes that by adapting or assimilating to the dominant culture, there is a feeling of satisfaction and a profound inability to return to where one came from. The word *"pocho,"* which means faded or pale in coloring, suggests the nausea of transmigration, the onset of vertigo from being pulled back and forth across the border by a desire to embrace a dynamic North Americanism while retaining the deep spiritual sentimentality of the South.

A similar experience is felt by Ritchie Valens, who is trying to emerge as a lower-middle-class rock musician, like many of his fellow Americans, while trying to retain the sensibility of Mexican American culture. Like many Spanglish cultural figures, he experienced assimilation first, simply trying to "fit in" to the Southern California lifestyle by speaking English and forming a rock band. (Abraham Quintanilla, Selena's father and the mastermind of her career, made his children sing in Spanish and play traditional *norteño* [northern Mexican] music because his attempt to play rock was rejected by intolerant Texans.) But, as shown by Luís Valdez in his remarkable movie *La Bamba*, Valens had a roots experience that influenced him to return to his Mexican identity. The highly dramatic sequence in the film shows Valens awakening as he hears the traditional version of "La Bamba" being played in a Tijuana cantina, then experiences a vision of his future through a *curandero*, or shaman seer. The assimilation/return to the roots experience is replicated in many Spanglish arts careers, including that of salsa musician Willie Colón, salsa singer Marc Anthony, and writers Abraham Rodríguez and Junot Díaz.

As if on cue, with the more frequent appearance of Puerto Rican images in the national discourse, a trend began in the media that involved a preponderance of negative manifestations. The film *Blackboard Jungle*, released in 1955, while criticized by conservatives like Clare Boothe Luce—who successfully boycotted the Venice Film Festival until it agreed to remove the film—had a mixed message in its portrayal of youth rebellion. Although Sidney Poitier and Vic Morrow were drawn as subversive antiheroes, the small part of "Morales" (ironically, the same name as a character that became a hero of the Broadway play *A Chorus Line*) is a weak, stuttering role that has the effect of infantilizing Puerto Ricans, (and by extension Latinos) as inept followers. As the '50s continued, films like *Cry Tough* (with John Saxon as a Puerto Rican hood) and *The Young Savages* reinforced the idea of Puerto Ricans as illiterate, oversexed, knife-wielding thugs.

Then came *West Side Story*. The film, disguised as fair treatment of an under-acknowledged group in society, became the hallmark for Puerto Rican stereotypes, the measuring stick by which much future discourse on Puerto Ricans would be based. My parents refused me permission to see it out of disdain, and the New York City public school system banned it for fear of reviving ethnic rivalries. In fact, each time it was shown on national television, the following day the playgrounds were abuzz with challenges between Sharks and Jets.

The Puerto Ricans were depicted in typical fashion as hotheaded and largely unintelligible, except for the occasional grunt from their leader, and the alternately high-pitched (Carmen) and passive (Maria) women. At best, the movie/play championed tolerance for intermarriage, but the underlying message was that Puerto Rican culture was dangerously exotic and needed to be reined in, and perhaps was not suited for intermarriage. In some ways, the movie may have had a subliminal effect on Latinos (and by extension other "ethnic" Americans) to indulge in the romantic fantasy of intermarriage as a way of assimilating. But it also seemed to predict the stubborn refusal of Puerto Ricans to do this on a large scale.

My generation and successive ones have suffered under the "I Like to Live in America" diminution of our experience. *West Side Story* made only passing references to the fact that Puerto Rican emigration to the U.S. is profoundly ambivalent and painful, and there was no attempt to characterize the life that was left behind except for references to the tropical climate. Being reduced to a cartoonish spectacle of dancing figures with childlike voices straining to speak English was deeply embarrassing. The casting of Natalie Wood as Maria was a strong hint at the narrative that would come into play in my own assimilative experience: The "good

Puerto Rican" syndrome. Although we are supposed to suspend our awareness that Natalie Wood is not, in fact, Puerto Rican, or any stripe of Latino, her virginal passivity and lack of ethnic charge is a kind of hot-button eroticism for Euro-ethnic Tony. Tony would never have been attracted to Rita Moreno's Carmen, an obvious "other," which is reinforced by the fact that Moreno is the only real Puerto Rican in the cast. By presenting Maria as the "good Puerto Rican" who has a possibility of assimilating into America, *West Side Story's* liberal perspective can then condemn bigotry by the Jet mob who cannot accept the liaison. The message: Urban Ethnic America must turn its back on bigotry and learn to tolerate "good Puerto Ricans" like Maria. Carmen and those who insist on retaining their ethnic character will die off eventually.

But how to read "I Like to Live in America"? There are two meanings, which of course apply to all American immigrants, but have a particular twist for Latinos, Puerto Ricans, and ultimately Spanglish people. First, it is true that we *like* to live here; there's an adaptation survival mechanism at work in this proposition, but there is also increased access to consumer goods and a slight rise in wages. On the other hand, we miss our homeland, so there is a bittersweet aspect to it, just like the Italian or Irish immigrants who might miss their respective countrysides, cuisines, or dancehalls. But we not only *like* to live in America, *we* like to live in it, meaning the Spanglish *we*, the we that is still part of our homeland and is now transferred here—the accent, the dancing, the food, even now, the *casitas*. Even now, *casitas,* small wooden houses that are replicas of island homes, are dotting the urban landscape of New York City.

The "I Like to Live in America" chant is a statement about a people that refuses to assimilate and who also happen to be grooving on their surroundings. They are escaping the colonial attitude of Latin America a little bit, and are slowly falling in love with the unsentimental streets filled with intrigue, romance, and the power of being onstage in those streets. But a glaring, gaping hole in *West Side Story* undermines its entire message of assimilation. There were no black characterizations in the movie. The assimilation drama of Puerto Ricans is not just tied to whether they can accept whiteness—they must also reject blackness as part of the bargain.

The White Negro as a Pseudo-Spanglish Persona

So it is no accident that the source of Hip is the Negro for he has been living on the margin between totalitarianism and democracy for two centuries.
— Norman Mailer, "The White Negro"

Ever since I first read *On the Road* and its passages luxuriating on the exotic Mexicans that Kerouac wrote about, I felt the link between the hipster ethos and Spanglish reality. While Norman Mailer made his awkward theories on hipsters and the "other" explicit in the famous 1953 essay, "The White Negro," there has always been a Spanglish subtext to the entire history of postwar bohemia. Mailer correctly locates the African-American consciousness in an "in-between" site parallel to that of Latinos. But by proposing the crude grafting of whiteness onto the hyper-sensual, rather gross desecration of the "Negro," Mailer makes probably his most grotesque attempt to explain American culture through sexual metaphors. In some ways it is a simple restating of the blackface and minstrelsy that is at the root of vaudeville and, by extension, American popular entertainment. In fact, like most self-serving bohemian tracts of the period, Mailer's is merely updating a phenomenon long existent in American culture, trying to lay claim to it as if it were a new development. By positing a bohemia born of the social collision between alienated, nihilistic bohemians (whom he at times openly describes as psychopaths) and noble savage street blacks, Mailer ignores the fact that despite its pervasive racial segregation, America has always been a mixed-race society in denial.

"The White Negro" is obviously a poor attempt at Spanglish dynamics—in Spanglish culture, the White Negro occurs in an infinitely more fluid, organic fashion. The White Negro was an absurd construction based on an underlying racism, which was more of an attempt to kidnap black culture for American whites still struggling with the transition from nineteenth-century Victorianism, trying to account for the vitality of the early twentieth-century European immigration. While manifestations of this idea outside of Mailer's puerile constructions have yielded positive advances in literature and music, the "Negro-ness" at the root of his idea disappears and becomes folded into a whitened idea of American culture. Far from perfect in its distillation of mixed-race culture and art, the Spanglish milieu allows for the veneration of African- or indigenous-origin influences, and a more seamless fusion of personalities and attitudes. The Afro-Cuban jazz of Mario Bauzá and Chano Pozo, masterful fusions of European traditions with African rhythmic structures, were opportunities for American jazz musicians like Dizzy Gillespie and Charlie Parker to expand their craft without losing any of their identity or prominence.

Elvis Presley was a "white Negro"; the Beat poets spoke a kind of Spanglish in their transmutation of black prison dialect to their high/low world of Columbia University and hobo hitchhiking, MoMA and heroin addiction. It seems fitting that William Carlos Williams, whose somewhat noble yet inadequate attempt to rein-terpret Whitman, wrote the introduction to Paterson, New Jersey, native Allen Ginsberg's "Howl," the seminal Beat poet text. The entire culture of rock and roll, the juvenile delinquent, and finally the hipness of the '60s counterculture was a crude form of Span-glish. There were numerous intersections between the bohemia spawned by variations on the White Negro and the emerging Span-glish culture: Oscar "Zeta" Acosta's intimate involvement with Hunter Thompson, producing gonzo journalism; the prominence of Carlos Santana and the part-Spanish Jerry Garcia in the San Francisco rock scene; the rapprochement between William Bur-roughs and Miguels Piñero and Algarín of the Nuyorican Poets Café movement. But North America's racial divide prevented the cultural intercourse from bearing fruit: Whiteness eventually swallowed rock music whole, and African Americans strove harder to develop dialects and slangs that would become passé almost instantly, to ensure that the ghetto would always control its use. White Negro was doomed to failure, and in some ways destined to succeed, from the start.

Historian Winston James has written: "[Spain's] imperial nonchalance provided a level of de facto autonomy for the inhabitants [of the Caribbean islands] that they otherwise would not have enjoyed . . . there occurred a level interaction between the [free] black and white population that was prolonged and unparalleled in the New World."

> *I am a human being*
> *Of multiracial and multinational*
> *Ancestry*
> *The loveliness to come*
> *Embrace my song, lose yourself*
> *In my tropical jungle*
> —SALVADOR AGRON

In Caribbean islands like Puerto Rico, Hispañola, and Cuba, a different kind of interaction between "white" Spaniards, mixed-race islanders, and Afro-Latinos allowed for an entirely different dynamic in the formation of miscegenated cultures. The Afro-Caribbean culture began to make itself felt in '50s New York, and *West Side Story* became one of the first mainstream works to try to represent it. *West Side Story* was a fantastic spectacle of the sudden manifestation of Spanglish culture, but it, like *The Tempest*'s Ariel-Caliban paradigm, was based on a work of Shakespeare. Perhaps more importantly for our postmodern Spanglish culture was how it was represented in the tabloid-media apparatus. Right around the time of the premiere of *West Side Story*, a true-life drama was unfolding around a mixed-up teenage kid who became known simply as "The Capeman."

In 1998, Paul Simon found it worthy to dramatize the story of Salvador Agron, a quintessentially Spanglish juvenile delinquent, in a musical called *The Capeman*. The play suffered from narrative dysfunction and lack of dramatic tension; if you weren't already familiar with the story, you could have sat through the play and wondered what exactly was taking place. But these problems don't exist because the play was a gratuitous glorification of a mindless Nuyorican street thug. *The Capeman* was problematic because it attempted to take on as its subject matter an extremely complex young man who was in many ways deeply involved with the changes that took place in postwar America.

There were objections from both the families of the victims of Agron's misguided violence, as well as apprehension from New York's Latino community, fearful of more stereotypes. But Agron's story, like that of Raskolnikov in *Crime and Punishment*, is one of redemption, one provided by an inventory of the self and the understanding of identity and historical forces, rather than a moral lesson from the church. This radical idea, combined with the relative ineptness of Simon's production team, is what doomed the play to failure on a Broadway tamed by the atmosphere created by neo-conservative mayor Rudolph Giuliani.

The true story of "The Capeman," or Salvador Agron, the "bad Puerto Rican," is not simply the story of a mentally ill, chronically violent serial killer or cult leader. Born in Puerto Rico in 1947, Sal Agron was in many ways the quintessential baby boomer, whose life in prison allowed him to extensively educate himself in the feverish Marxism-Leninism of the post-Vietnam era '70s. He quoted everything from *The Communist Manifesto* to Hegel's *The Phenomenology of Mind* in his writings, and became a poster boy for many obscure radical groups like the Socialist Workers' Party. One *International Worker's World* newspaper that appeared in the mid-'70s trumpeted "Salvador Agron has been in prison for 16 years . . . and Richard Nixon is still free!"

Agron was part of the big wave of Puerto Ricans who emigrated to New York in the '50s. He was a child who spoke very little

English—still, he was a product of his era. Although he suffered through a miserable childhood, including a stint in a sadistic orphanage, he quickly became a New Yorker. During his adolescence, Hollywood was busy generating a series of movies about juvenile delinquents, many of which starred Agron's idol, Sal Mineo, as a tortured Hispanic gang member. (Chicano comedian Cheech Marin has argued that many of the styles and attitudes of the motley crew of *Rebel Without a Cause* were inspired by Mexican-American delinquents in Southern California.) Agron came to know and inhabit the styles and codes of New York's streets, which held the seeds of an emerging culture of resistance that would later manifest itself during the civil rights era, the anti–Vietnam War movement, and Afrocentric hiphop culture of the '70s. While he is often described in reports sympathetic to him as "illiterate," he once wrote—in a socialist newspaper while in prison—that he was trained by the streets to engage in "the Dozens," a game of competitive wordsmanship that is seen by many as one of the roots of rap music.

Agron grew up fully a part of the postwar explosion of media images, bilingual coding, rock and roll, and disenchantment with government and authority that everyone from the Beats to Carlos Santana did. With a little luck, if he had only wounded someone on that fateful night, or managed to avoid the confrontation altogether, he might have become Freddy Prinze or Geraldo Rivera. But Sal represented the poorest strata of the Puerto Rican experience, coming from a culture that had almost no material wealth, but an enormous store of mythic and spiritual beliefs, albeit entwined with a backward rural Christianity.

Desperately trying to free himself from a childhood of oppression and ignorance, Sal envisioned himself as a powerful, mythic figure that combined spiritualism and the Hollywood bad boy. Because of his involvement with the Capeman murders, Agron became one of the first tabloid media villains, a predecessor of Son of Sam, Ivan Boesky, or Patty Hearst. His crime occurred while *West Side Story* was on Broadway, already sensationalizing teenage gangs and interethnic tensions in New York. But what most accounts of this era leave out is the hostile environment that migrating Puerto Ricans found in the city. Salvador Agron, considered by many to have given his people a bad name, was trying to function in a society that had already given him a bad name.

The details surrounding the night of the murders are fuzzy and often further obscured by the hysteria surrounding Agron. He had been chummy with Luis Hernandez, who became known as the Umbrella Man, with whom he formed a gang that was not into serious violence, but pursued the inevitable fisticuffs with other groups the way any New York peer group organized around turf would. The context for these gangs is well documented in several books, notably Emmet Grogan's *Ringolevio*. Throughout the postwar years, various ethnic groups had been engaged in turf battles that merely reflected the perils of growing up lower class in the center of the industrial machine, New York. The mid to late '50s were a time when many Puerto Ricans were threatened by Irish and Italian gangs—everyone from my own father to journalist/ author Juan Gonzalez (as he describes in *Harvest of Empire*) has his story about fending off violent attacks, especially from Italian gangs in El Barrio.

The murders occurred on a hot summer night; Salvador and Luis showed up at May Matthews Playground on West Forty-fifth Street—there are many alleged reasons. Some say it was a drug deal gone bad, others say it resulted from a cry for help about an impending gang collision. Two white teenagers were stabbed to death and Sal and Luis were captured several days later and paraded before photographers. Sal delivered his famous sound bite, "I don't care if I burn. My mother can watch me."

The startlingly eerie thing about watching Agron's appearance on the local news on the Kinescope tapes from so many years ago was the look on his face, which seemed to indicate that he understood he was being turned into a media image at a time when the concept was in its infancy. Sal was engaging in a very postmodern practice, seizing the spectacle of urban criminality to make a kind of narcissistic political statement, something very much like the "performance art" of the late Tupac Shakur.

> *The smile is not the smile of a psychotic criminal, but it is*
> *the reflected smile of a drunken public . . . they saw their*
> *social apathy, their very own souls and ignorance and they*
> *screamed in horror.*
> — SALVADOR AGRON, PRISON WRITINGS

Salvador Agron was a kind of wannabe radical revolutionary figure in the mold of the Black Panthers and Young Lords, and his prison-culture socialization gave him a lot in common with the gansta rappers of the '80s and '90s. His involvement with left-wing politics while in prison, where he was supported prototypically by radical lawyer William Kunstler, made him into a kind of minor celebrity among New York leftists. The continued attempts to have his parole expedited anticipated what happened in the early '80s when Norman Mailer successfully got prison author Jack Abbott released, only to have him horribly murder an East Village restaurant waiter.

Agron was finally released in the late '70s, partially as the result of efforts by the cultish New Alliance Party, but was never able to adjust to living outside prison. He was a pioneer of the Nuyorican experience, which combined the shock of transition from peaceful but poor tropical island to the hard streets of the world's most renowned metropolis. He was aware of his standing within the street culture that produced the language of prison and resistance. He also educated himself with texts that elevated him to an almost upper-middle-class world of leftism. To an outraged public, his "Watch me burn" statement was an act of extreme barbarity, but it was probably a bizarre attempt to reconcile his island naïveté with the onus of being the trash tabloid media star of the moment. In the Kinescope images, Agron is fighting back at the gaze of the mainstream media, which kept him invisible, only to shine its glar-

ing lights on him at the moment of his almost inevitable criminalization.

When I visited Agron's surviving relatives in the North Bronx,
they were a typical Spanglish family. They were schoolteachers,
auto insurance salespeople, students. They were dark skinned,
light skinned, and olive skinned; they were religious and they liked
salsa music and rock music. His sister, Aurea, was a striking survivor who was very much an average American, except she believed
in magic. Amid the stacks of papers and files and mementos she
kept in an office reserved for her brother, she told me, her eyes
tearing, that Agron had spoken to her from the dead and approved
her trust in Paul Simon. The *espiritista* belief in communication
with the dead had survived the horrible orphanage they had grown
up in, the one that may have turned him into a murderer, and was
still keeping them together in the Bronx, as the millennium drew to
a close.

The late '50s was a crucial moment for Spanglish culture. The first
large wave of Puerto Rican immigrants in New York were in the proc-
esses of class differentiation, choosing, when able, modes of assimilation usually along racial lines. Lighter-skinned, better-educated
Puerto Ricans were beginning to establish themselves in areas bor-
dering Italian neighborhoods, while darker Puerto Ricans were on
the verge of a long-lasting cultural alliance with African Americans,
largely through the bugaloo/Latin soul fad in music. White ethnics
are heavily participating in the mambo shows at Midtown spots like
the Palladium. *I Love Lucy* was still wildly popular. Movies like
West Side Story, although condescending and oversimplifying, as
well as distorting through plot and bad casting, were almost
embraced as acknowledgment of the presence of Latinos in the
U.S. Even Fred Astaire had to dance the way we do. Puerto Ricans
began making alliances with both African-American and mainstream figures, indirectly influencing developments on both sides
of the racial divide.

In Southern California, Chicanos were helping to popularize rock and roll by providing a mass audience for the music. Music acts like those of Ritchie Valens and Cannibal and the Headhunters helped to aid the transition between r&b and doo-wop music and the surf music of the '60s. But with the exception of a single shining moment from Tijuana native Santana, the nature of rock culture would ultimately diminish their contributions. Cesar Chavez would strongly influence the '60s milieu of organized protest, and a writer named Oscar "Zeta" Acosta would be at the root of what would become known as gonzo journalism.

Something was about to happen in America that would change everything. The "advances" Latinos made in the American consciousness would be exposed as the products of a false integration. African Americans would challenge the status quo of America's popular culture and effective social segregation. The arms-length "acceptance" of Latinos would be exposed, and the triumph of the baby boomers would create an era of social change that would coincidentally obscure the civil rights movement and establish a new kind of white cultural hegemony. And with that white hegemony, the whole perception of racial conflict would become a rigidly black versus white question, with little room for other factors.

We could no longer gather on an El Barrio rooftop, dance to Rafael Hernandez's "Preciosa," and celebrate being able to see the stars, as Puerto Rican writer José Luis González did in his crucial short story, "The Night We Became People Again."

It is the moment that Spanglish culture, which felt as if it were about to take its rightful place on the main stage of "American" cultures, was forced underground.

2.

SPANGLISH GOES UNDER-
GROUND TO REINVENT ITSELF

The decade of the 1960s has been canonized as an era of tremendous social change, the logical culmination of social forces brewing since the end of World War II, a kind of double-barreled attack on American normalcy from the African-American civil rights movement and the white middle-class antiwar movement. But there isn't much attention paid to what was going on in the Spanglish world, where there was also great upheaval influenced by both sides of this societal explosion. The Spanglish world was strongly influenced by the civil rights movement, forming organizations like the Brown Berets and the Young Lords that took the Black Panthers as their role model. U.S. Latinos also let their freak flag fly high, through music groups like the California-based Santana, which gave one of the most stunning performances at Woodstock, and the psychedelic experiments of New York *salseros* (salsa musicians) like Ray Barretto and Eddie Palmieri.

The '60s was a period when America began to confront the idea of a possible multiracial culture, a notion that began with the substantial contributions of white college students to the civil rights movement in the early part of the decade. The brief overlap between black and white musicians in the milieu of rock and roll and the early stages of the counterculture were also important beginnings for multiculturalism in America. But by decade's end, rock music was well on the way to becoming an exclusively white form, the multiracial antiwar movement coalition began to fall apart, and the idea of a rainbow American culture was consigned to advertising images.

Puerto Ricans, Cubans, and Mexican Americans spent the '50s and '60s coming to grips with their bicultural nature, their apparent neither-here-nor-there positioning in North America. They had engaged in literally speaking in Spanglish as a rite of passage that didn't quite fade away in the strongholds of Southern California, Texas, New York, and Florida. The period of the brief opening of the door of possible assimilation, something made possible by the postwar ethnic solidarity consensus, the Latin ballroom dance fad, and especially in the West Coast, the centrality of Latinos in the development of rock and roll and cool jazz, was over. Except in the case of the Cuban exiles, the possibility of assimilation existed only through denial of Latino identity. The neither/nor problem could only be solved by a sense of transnationalism, that is, a willingness to accept a transitory status in North America. The ability of Spanglish identity to imagine itself as continuing to exist partly in the psychic space of the home country while at the same time becoming North America was how we survived the '60s.

The use of English in Puerto Rico had been proliferating since the U.S. takeover in 1898, so the great wave of island migrants that arrived in New York in the '50s were already a little bit American. Since Puerto Ricans are born American citizens and can move back and forth between the mainland and the island without passports, we have been engaged in what has been called a "circular migration," one that may be prescient of a more fully developed social movement in the next century. The Nuyorican Journey has laid ground for what has come to be known as transnationalism, a lifestyle that has been at the core of my identity since the beginning. Nuyorican transnationalism anticipated today's global economy, and it was key to the ability of Spanglish to survive underground.

The prototypical Nuyorican transnational experience was very much like that of my parents, who came to the U.S. in the late '40s, fully expecting to become Americans, only to find their sense of themselves blunted by their journey. Their assimilative experiences changed them, modernized them, enriched them, but they did this in a way that I feel was pushed underground. My father grew up in Cubuy, a *jíbaro* town on the western side of the mountains, and my mother in Mameyes, at the northern mouth of El Yunque. Depression babies who never met on the island, they were destined to meet at an East Harlem party in the early '50s. My parents were part of a massive emigration to the U.S. in that decade as the result of Operation Bootstrap, an economic policy that introduced large scale agriculture and rapid industrialization to the island, which suffered more in the Depression than the mainland had. The plan entailed the displacement of many islanders, who were beckoned into recruitment offices where they were given cut-rate tickets to New York on old military planes. My parents had been struggling along the lower rungs of the service sector when they met at a party in Manhattan Valley, and like so many other '50s couples, married in their mid-twenties and had children.

Many of my parents' generation believed, if their skin was light enough, they could attain the status of European ethnic groups in New York. They were young lovers at a time when the Palladium, a club in the West Fifties, was a Roseland-like mecca of the Manhattan melting pot. It was a time when *I Love Lucy* was one of America's most popular TV shows and even the average Midwesterner knew how to do a little cha-cha-cha. The gringo world drank and danced to popular music in essentially the same way Latinos did— dressed to the nines in suits and ties, swing-dancing to big bands. Mambo orchestras led by the two big Puerto Rican stars of the day, Tito Puente and Tito Rodriguez, were just the latest style that the Americans shared. If Americans liked pizza and Frank Sinatra enough to accept Italians as "white," it was only a matter of time before they would absorb rice and beans and Tito Puente into the pop culture canon.

But things changed drastically as a result of the Cuban revolution and the advent of rock and roll culture. The Cuban revolution could be seen as the official end of the Good Neighbor Policy, which the U.S. established in the 1930s to positively interact with Latin America. When Havana—which was the Las Vegas of the Caribbean, and the primary exporter of Latin culture to America— went over to the side of the Soviets in the tensest period of the Cold War, it was no longer cool to be Cuban, or any other Latino. As the poster children of the evils of juvenile delinquency, Latinos were scapegoated as rock and roll culture began to mature. As the American mainstream moved off the ballroom dance floor and into the discotheque, they moved away from traditional Latinos.

But as Spanglish culture was forced underground, it was evolving in very contemporary and exciting ways. In the late '60s in the South Bronx, a first-generation Nuyorican named Willie Colón was starting a band with his best friend, Hector Lavoe, an enigmatic vocalist recently arrived from Puerto Rico. Colón's concept was innovative: He would take the trombone, a little-used instrument in Afro-Caribbean dance music, and put it front and center in his band, creating an image of hilarity and daring. Lavoe's distinctively nasal inflections fused cutting-edge island folkloricism with the slang of the Bronx's hard streets. The *jíbaro* that was Puerto Rico's romantic troubadour emblem was conflated with the neo-gangster violence of city living.

Colón coveted his nickname "El Malo" (the Bad Guy) as much for record sales as protection from the vagaries of playing salsa clubs in tough neighborhoods. But as much as his bad-boy stance was a shield from the increasingly violent inner city, it was an aggressive, unapologetic arrival in American culture. A precedent for Colón's proactive posturing was the zoot-suit pachuco movement of Mexican Americans in Los Angeles during the mid-'40s. Exaggerated dress and provocative posturing was a way for that group of U.S. Latinos to break the mold of submissive immigrant behavior.

But El Malo was more than just a lawless riff on how to be Nuyorican in the late '60s; it was an expression of the deep-seated nationalism and highly sentimental nostalgia for island culture. One of Puerto Rico's fascinating contradictions is that it is at once a winner, for being the middle-class miracle of economic development that produces a standard of living higher per capita than anywhere in Latin America, and a perennial loser because it has been a colony for over five hundred years. Even as the U.S. closed in on the island as part of the booty for winning the Spanish American war in 1898, Puerto Rican legislators had just won its nominal independence from Spain. Independence lasted for about a month, and once again, Puerto Rico was a colony.

The combination of Puerto Rico's legendary lack of self-determination, the classic immigrant homesickness for his home country (a verdant and gentle-climed paradisiacal one at that), as well as some *tristesse* left over from the particularly brutal Depression years, imbued the '60s Nuyorican with a highly sentimental desire for national identity. A song written in the '30s by Puerto Rican composer Rafael Hernández called "Lamento Borincano," became the unofficial national anthem for Puerto Ricans on and off the island. "Lamento" told the story of a subsistence farmer who suddenly finds his crops can no longer support his family. It was an image I could envision quite easily, since my own maternal grandfather made his living by growing crops like coffee and fruit and taking them to the town to sell. It was a collective trauma that was relived in New York as the tens of thousands of new Puerto Rican migrants found that the industrial sector of the economy was falling apart, and the jobs they dreamed of were vanishing into thin air.

While America was reeling from the civil rights movement and the intensification of the Vietnam war, Colón and his buddy, the legendary vocalist Hector Lavoe, were busy inventing a subcultural music that reflected the "cultural schizophrenia" of being Puerto Rican in New York. Colón brought a unique jazz-oriented sensibility to Latin dance music, along with a very unusual instrument, the trombone. He was a slight, short teenager with a carefully cropped mustache, playing a huge cylindrical instrument; he was loud, proud, and sensual. Colón grew up in a South Bronx neighborhood that was making the transition from white-ethnic to black and Latino in the early '60s. He grew up speaking mostly English, until he caught *bugaloo* fever. *Bugaloo* was a unique urban music that fused Latin styles with African American soul music; it became an important signifier for the interlocking of black and Latin urban culture in the '60s.

Colón began to feel it was important for him to return to his roots and he retaught himself Spanish. He entered the world of Latin music at a time when it was losing Cuban influence because of the Cuban revolution. The end of the long dominance of the Cuban style had the effect of opening up the music to a wide variety of influences. By the end of the decade a new sound was coming together that we now know as salsa. The music was a quintessential Spanglish phenomenon, since it represented the crystallization of a transnational culture in New York that mixed influences from the existing North American urban culture as well as bringing together influences from different Latin American countries. Salsa could have happened only in New York because of its cauldron of different Latino nationalities. Colón melted together the sounds, fusing *murga* (from Panama) with *bomba* (from Puerto Rico) and throwing it in a *guaguancó* (from Cuba). In the end, the edgy lyrics of the nascent salsa style reflected a new urban reality for Latinos. Ulti-mately, Colón would find melodic ideas in Beatles' records. Colón's own partnership with Rubén Blades—the vocalist who starred in Paul Simon's 1998 Broadway musical, *The Capeman*—even took on some qualities of the Lennon–McCartney partnership and sub-sequent feud.

But Colón and his aesthetic—somewhere between the faux-gangsterism of the Rat Pack and ultra-realist hiphop gangsta rap—belonged to the South Bronx. The salsa of Colón and his counterparts Johnny Pacheco, Ray Barretto, and Celia Cruz drove the emotional energy of hardcore Latino barrios. But Spanglish forces, particu-larly from the West Coast, were playing a major part in the devel-opment of rock, the music of the counterculture. Through Chicano artists like Ritchie Valens and the participation of East Coast Lati-nos in doo-wop, the development of rock had strong Latino roots. Until the end of the '60s, rock music was a multiracial enterprise, with crucial participation by musicians of color. The fact that three of Woodstock's most memorable performances—that of Jimi Hen-drix, Sly and the Family Stone, and Santana—were carried out by Latinos and blacks is a little-developed notion about the great festi-val of the counterculture. In another Spanglish, transnational move, Carlos Santana, a Tijuana native, moved to Oakland, California, and successfully incorporated the Afro-Cuban sounds that were the basis of Colón's salsa into the day's psychedelic acid rock. It was no coincidence that one of Santana's smash hits, "Oye Como Va," was a Tito Puente song, one of the classic big Latin band standards of the '50s.

Santana played music that combined the mores of the counter-culture—that is, wild acid-tinged guitar solos—with the elemental Afro-Cuban *son montuno*, but their style was just an explicit example of the Latin influence on rock. The rock-ballad style developed by Brill Building songwriters for groups from the Dixie Chicks to the Beatles (especially in songs like "And I Love Her") had Latin roots, and this carried over to groups like the Moody Blues and Crosby,

Stills, and Nash. The preeminence of black rockers like Jimi Hendrix (whose fascination with his Native American roots resonated with both the counterculture and my Latino self-identification) and Sly Stone gave the counterculture an urban feel that was inclusive.

There did exist a bohemian underground among Spanglish folks, which was associated with the Chicano movement in California and what eventually became known as the Nuyorican Poets Café in New York. It is only natural that the beginnings of a hybrid consciousness is expressed through literature, because it is the fluid convergence of English and Spanish as vocalized by Nuyoricans and Chicanos that defines the cultural overlap. Some of the early Spanglish writing dealt with the typical problem of hybridity in New York: The dull shock of relocation to a harsh industrial city packed around an island and a great harbor, the adjustment to new class- and race-based prejudices exhibited by Americans, and the attempt to make one's way with a kind of coolness like the one expressed by African Americans through jazz and literature.

Much of this era of cultural nationalism developed in conjunction with the political movements of the time, which were personified on the East and West Coasts, respectively by the Young Lords and the radical Chicanos. It can be argued that the true first epoch of Spanglish happened when the Treaty of Guadalupe Hidalgo was signed by the U.S. and Mexico in February 1848, ending a two-year war between the two countries. The signing of the treaty, which Chicano activists still believe was illegitimate, in view of its administration by a corrupt Mexican official, effectively ceded about half of Mexico's territory, including California, Texas, New Mexico, Arizona, Colorado, and Utah to the U.S. Along with the Louisiana Purchase, the Treaty was a crucial in creating the U.S. as we know it today, laying the ground for the Manifest Destiny ideology that would ultimately justify America's continuing incursion into Latin American territory.

Nourished by the spirit of the times, which favored national liberation movements, the Chicano movement was primarily a nationalist movement. But it wasn't a unified national entity; it was a series of separate actions waged by organizations, most famously, the Brown Berets, the Chicano Moratorium Committee, and La Raza Unida Party. During the early Chicano movement in the 1960s, New Mexico land rights crusader Reies López Tijerina and his Alianza movement invoked the Treaty of Guadalupe in their struggle. In 1972, the Brown Berets youth organization also invoked it in their symbolic takeover of Catalina Island, off the Southern California coast. Corky Gonzales, ex-boxer and author of "I Am Joaquín," also referred to the treaty. The Chicano movement was a cultural awakening for Mexican Americans, who felt betrayed by the false hope raised by Viva Kennedy clubs that enlisted large numbers of Latinos to support the 1968 presidential campaign of Robert Kennedy. The word "Chicano" was chosen because it was a pejorative name given to working-class Mexicans; this attempt to empower the scorned resonates with other cultural liberation movements. The Chicano movement was not a monolithic consensus; rather it was the sum of many regional movements that shared the idea of identification with indigenous people, the de facto colonization of Mexican Americans within the United States, and a desire to protect Chicanos from race discrimination.

> We are free and sovereign to determine those tasks which are justly called for by our house, our land, the sweat of our brows, and by our hearts. Aztlan belongs to those who plant the seeds, water the fields, and gather the crops and not to the foreign Europeans.
> — EL PLAN ESPIRITUAL DE AZTLAN (1969)

El Plan de Aztlan was presented at the first National Chicano Youth Liberation Conference in Denver, Colorado, March 1969. Coincidentally, representatives of the Young Lords also attended this meeting. The presentation of El Plan was a turning point for Chicanos, combining a long-brewing discourse about internal colonialism and a kind of progressive mythology about a theoretical homeland for the original Mexicans (the prevailing theory is that they later moved to the south to engage in land rivalries that eventually produced the Aztec civilization).

Like the mythic origin epics of Roman, Hebrew, and German cultures, Aztlan is a place that allows Chicanos to claim their own territory—in their case within the U.S.—as well as allowing many Mexican Americans who are descended from indigenous people north of Mexico an ancestral homeland. Its actual location has been theorized as being in the flat arid expanse east of San Diego, the mysterious Anasazi lands home to several national parks in Arizona, and sometimes even China. The map included as part of the Treaty of Guadalupe Hidalgo includes a reference to the "Ancient Home of the Aztecs," situated in the Utah segment of the Four Corners area.

The choice of Aztlan (which has been ironically translated as "the place of whiteness") as a political rallying point for Chicanos was significant for contradictory reasons. Because Aztlan was theorized to have been the original homeland of indigenous people who set out on a nomadic journey to the south, Aztlan became a symbol for Chicanos that "Mexicans" had originated in the area within the "lower forty-eight" states of the U.S. But at the same time, because of that very nomadic tendency of the original inhabitants of Aztlan, it became a place of the heart that existed wherever someone who identified with Aztlan brought it. The idea of Aztlan as an independent "state of mind" is very parallel to ideas ultimately popularized in the Nuyorican world by poets like Miguel Piñero.

The introduction to El Plan de Aztlan was written by a poet named Alurista (Alberto Baltazar Urista), a native of Morelos, Mexico. Alurista was one of the first Chicano poets to have his work published in both English and Spanish; his transnational life experience forced him to define himself in the middle of the most intense period of Mexican American self-definition. "We do not recognize capricious frontiers on the bronze continent," Alurista's introduction reads. "With our heart in our hands and our hands in the soil, we declare the independence of our mestizo nation." At once defining Chicanos as multiracial and transnational, Alurista sets the standard for the Spanglish idea of erasing political boundaries; when racial miscegenation encounters the idea of '60s empowerment, national borders break down.

Many of the backers of El Plan de Aztlan broke with Vasconcelos's cosmic race idea because of his Eurocentrism. His central take on miscegnenation painted it as a bonanza for Latin America's indigenous population because it lifted their culture up to Spanish standards. But the radical Chicanos still proclaimed that their new nation was mestizo. The denial of Spanish culture is understandable because the conquest was a brutal, genocidal process, but it is unrealistic because it ignores the fact that the Spaniards, through the writings of monks like Bartolomeo de las Casas, were the only European conquerors who produced an internal critique of the conquest and made attempts to humanize it. In addition, there were many oppressed people of Spain in the New World who fled because of the Inquisition and did not always interact with the indigenous as oppressors. The process of the conquest was inextricably tied to Spain's own ethnic cleansing, which dumped a multiracial group of Moors, Jews, and Gypsies into the Americas.

Still, in much of the Southwest there were many descendants of Spaniards who insisted on segregation from indigenous people, and the mythological creation of Aztlan was necessary for Chicanos to claim an American identity. There have been attacks on the idea of Aztlan because it is a fragile concept that is hard to prove through anthropological study. But its fleeting nature and mythic status make Aztlan the quintessential heterotopic space for the imagining of what Spanglish might look like. Aztlan is where

Spanglish is dreamed, where it takes root, and where the effects of Manifest Destiny, and the colonization of the Southwest, can be reversed.

> The conquest of the Southwest created a colonial situation in the traditional sense—with the Mexican land and population being controlled by an imperialistic United States. Further, I contend that this colonization—with variations—is still with us today. Thus, I refer to the colony, initially, in the traditional definition of the term, and later (taking into account the variations) as an internal colony. The parallels between the Chicanos' experience in the United States and the colonization of other Third World peoples are too similar to dismiss.
>
> —RODOLFO ACUÑA, *Occupied America*

According to University of California San Diego professor Ramón Gutiérrez, the theory of internal colonialism was first used by Chicanos through the writings of Berkeley sociologists Robert Blauner and Tomás Almaguer. The theory first came about in the 1950s, as an attempt to explain the "development of underdevelopment" in Africa, Asia, and Latin America. The internal colonial theory had a great influence on black radical thought in the years that witnessed the transition between the civil rights movement and the radical Black Panther era. In 1965, Kenneth Clark in his book *Dark Ghetto* proposed that the political, economic, and social structure of Harlem was essentially that of a colony; a model Stokeley Carmichael and Charles Harris employed explicitly as internal colonialism in their 1967 book *Black Power*. The Chicano use of internal colonialism coincided nicely with Puerto Rican activists' critique of the island's more obvious colonial situation. Such an analysis is crucial in the Spanglish break from "melting-pot" theories of ethnic assimilation, placing Latinos in a historical role more parallel to that of African Americans.

In 1967, the Chicano movement seemed to explode through discrete local organizaions in Texas, California, Colorado, and the Southwest. The separate identity of Chicanismo was epitomized by a poem written by boxer-turned-activist Corky Gonzales, who headed an organization called Crusade for Social Justice, based in Denver. The poem, "I Am Joaquín," was a call for identity that, while claiming multicultural and multivocal roots, refused to assimilate. Gonzales outlines the predicament of the Chicano in the '60s—searching for an identity, wondering how the Chicano can take part in twentieth century America. He uncovers the tangled nature of his multicultural roots, recognizing conqueror and conquered alike:

> I am Joaquín,
> Lost in a world of Confusion,
> Caught up in a whirl of a
> gringo Society,
> Suppressed by manipulation,
> And destroyed by modern society.
> I am the sword and flame of Cortés
> the despot.
> And I am the serpent of
> the Aztec civilization.
> I owned the land as far as the eye
> could see under the crown of Spain,
> and I toiled on my earth
> and gave my Indian sweat and blood
> for the Spanish master
>
> I ride with revolutionists
> against myself.
> I am the masses of my people and

I refuse to be absorbed.
I am Joaquín
My faith unbreakable
I am Aztec Prince and Christian Christ
I WILL ENDURE!

In "I Am Joaquín," Corky Gonzales demonstrates a remarkable awareness of the crisis of modernism as faced by an emerging Spanglish consciousness. He understands that his *raza* has undertaken a long, nomadic journey, from its multiple indigenous beginnings to its mixing with Spanish conquerors to become "Mexican," and finally finding itself in twentieth century North America as an outsider. For Gonzales, Chicanismo is born out of both victory and defeat—the pride in his indigenous blood remains at the cost of his economic subordination.

Invoking the Aztec emperor Cuauhtemoc, as well as the Mayan prince Nezahualcoyotl, Gonzales must also admit he carries the blood of the conqueror, Cortés. Gonzales alludes to a more generous understanding of *raza* that is inclusive of many variations of mixed-race strains. The reference to Christ supports the notion of a dynamic syncretism in Mexican culture, where Catholicism and indigenous beliefs coalesce, as they did in the form of the brown-skinned Virgen de Guadalupe, one of Mexico's strongest symbols of miscegenation. By including Pancho Villa and Zapata in his pantheon of spiritual predecessors, Gonzales shows how the spirit of rebellion can rise up even among a people who are aware of the contradictions of their history. After recapping centuries of turmoil in a single poem, Gonzales dares to face the internal anguish of his mixed-race past in the twentieth century and offers a vision of hope and triumph. "I Am Joaquín" also functions as a polemic that took its place alongside the tracts used by liberation movements of the Third World that were happening at the time. Most important is the couplet: "I am the masses of my people and/I refuse to be absorbed." The Spanglish determination to remain a transcendent option in America's race debate is at the root of all its definitions.

Young Lords and Nuyorican Resistance

> *I was raised in East Harlem, and my first models of resis-*
> *tance were Puerto Rican men. I saw Puerto Rican men*
> *stand up to the Italian gangs, oblivious to the fact that*
> *these guys might put a hit on them. I saw them stand up in*
> *swarms: short men, tall men, fat men, thin men, black*
> *men, white men, trigueños, in-between—stand up, in T-*
> *shirts, with pegged pants and curly hair coming down*
> *their foreheads.*
>
> — Felipe Luciano

The late '60s was a period of tremendous social upheaval in America, as the antiwar movement and the civil rights movement, frustrated by the lack of response from a conservative Republican government, became even more radicalized. During this period groups like the Black Panther Party and the Weather Underground began to arm themselves and distribute newspapers and pamphlets that represented a far-left analysis of foreign and domestic policy, and a point of view that urged people to prepare for what was seen as an inevitable popular revolution. In this atmosphere of increasing turmoil, inspired by these groups and their own need to identify themselves as a people, a small group of New York Puerto Ricans formed the Young Lords Party.

The New York Young Lords Party was originally an offshoot of a Chicago street gang with the same name. The politicization of the street gang was one of the central motifs of the so-called liberation groups of the counterculture era. Over a two-year period between 1970 and 1972, the Lords, whose peak membership was in the hundreds, staged several militant activities—twice occupying a neighborhood church and setting up free lunch and education programs à la Black Panthers, commandeering a TB truck to demonstrate the lack of health care for the Puerto Rican community, and staging a sit-in at Lincoln Hospital to expose its conditions of squalor. The

Lords became a kind of local legend that garnered them much media attention and a fierce loyalty from neighborhood residents. Most importantly, the Young Lords gave people who were having trouble fitting into the assimilation paradigm something to identify with. The Young Lords were the first to manifest a defiant attitude by Puerto Ricans, who had suffered a period of ineffective political clout for a variety of reasons.

While Puerto Ricans had organized, first as tobacco workers in the '20s and ultimately as garment workers in the '40s and '50s, their most powerful base in electoral politics resulted from the representation of the enigmatic Vito Marcantonio, whose territory included East Harlem. East Harlem at the time was shared by Puerto Ricans and Italian Americans, many of whom were political holdovers of the socialist era of the turn of the century. But when Marcantonio lost in the mid-'50s, the demonization of Puerto Ricans began. It was a period in which street gangs were common, and once Puerto Ricans were blamed unjustly for Marcantonio's electoral loss, much racism was directed against them, including routine beatings. Puerto Ricans, like Chicanos on the West Coast, were forced into a position where the only aggressive resistance they could manifest was anarchic gang activity. In fact, the Young Lords appropriated the Chicano slogan "Viva la Raza," universalizing their mestizo consciousness. While there was obviously an attempt to recover the African roots of Puerto Ricans in the Young Lords' ideological framework, their philosophy was also inclusive of lighter-skinned Puerto Rican "creoles," acknowledging their discrimination as "spics."

The Young Lords tried to politicize young men who were in and out of prison, but a small cell of New York Puerto Ricans quickly appropriated the dynamic name and although the Young Lords grew into a '60s-style resistance movement patterned after the Black Panthers, they were never the gun-toting, super-militant band that caused the FBI to crack down with violent tactics. Their movement was eroded by a protracted campaign of infiltration and psychological warfare, a campaign that had the effect of eroding the mental stability of the American left as a whole.

One of the unique traits of the Young Lords is that they were founded at the beginning of the '70s, at the dawn of the feminist movement, which enabled them to incorporate a sensitivity to women's issues and feature several women leaders, an extraordinary achievement coming from a macho-dominated culture. The original members of the Young Lords were mostly students in their late teens and early twenties who felt their studies were irrelevant during a time when their energies would be best directed toward organizing their own community. The original members were archetypal Spanglish citizens, incorporating a newfound American street sense with a disposition to incorporate varied influences from different liberation groups.

From its inception, the New York chapter of the Young Lords was a Spanglish hybridizing phenomenon. The Lords were a much-needed joining of Puerto Ricans who had identified themselves as either white or black, but had neglected their Puerto Rican identity. Pablo Guzmán, the Minister of Information, and Felipe Luciano, the group's charismatic leader were "Afro-Ricans" who had originally affiliated themselves with the radical black underground. Juan Gonzalez, the Lords' strategist, was a key organizer in the Columbia University chapter of the white-dominated SDS (Students for a Democratic Society). David Perez came from the politically oriented Chicago street gang, which had coined the name Young Lords, while Micky Melendez and Richie Perez were New York Puerto Ricans who were inspired by the history of Puerto Rican nationalists. After a meeting with the leaders of the Chicago group in late '69, this group received permission to use the Young Lords name, although over time they eventually disaffiliated themselves from Chicago.

In November '69 the Young Lords began to interrupt services at the Second Methodist Church in East Harlem, demanding space to operate free breakfast programs for the community. "The message of Christianity is to serve poor people," said Juan Gonzalez as he addressed the congregation. "To turn your back on them is to be un-Christian." They were met by fierce opposition from the church's reverend, who called the police to have them violently ejected. On the weekend between Christmas and New Year's Day, the Lords entered the church and set up an occupation that lasted several days and attracted media attention, until they were finally evicted by the police. The image of the group being led from the church, outfitted in berets and raising fists in the familiar Black Panther salute, immediately established them as players in the growing array of radical groups across the country.

The Lords also featured strong women leaders like Iris Morales and Denise Oliver. "There used to be only four choices for the Puerto Rican woman," said Morales in *Pa'alante,* the party's newspaper, distributed on streetcorners in much the same way that the Black Panthers' was: "Housewife, prostitute, drug addict, and worker. Now there's a new choice open to her that threatens the existence of the family and the state itself: the Revolution." As much as they could during a time when women were only beginning to assert themselves in radical politics, the male Lords took the issue of feminism seriously. "Because of the frustrations that Puerto Rican men have gone through under the capitalist system, a lot of them have turned their anger inward upon themselves and the women in their lives," said Richie Perez in another issue of *Pa'alante.*

In the summer of 1971, Young Lord Julio Roldan was arrested on a minor charge and imprisoned in the Tombs, which had been experiencing a large degree of unrest due to its intolerable conditions. A few days later, Roldan was found hung in his cell, a death that the police called a suicide. In those days of high militant drama, the Roldan death was met with anger: At the funeral, which featured a group of beret-clad pallbearers and a casket draped in the Puerto Rican flag, the Lords openly expressed their belief that Roldan was murdered. The Lords then staged a second takeover of the Methodist church, for the first time packing weapons. The siege lasted several days, and the Lords emerged triumphant once again, with growing defiant support from the community.

But many Lords say that this incident was the beginning of the unraveling of the party. "I don't know exactly when the party decided to hurt itself," says Feliciano, "I do know that for me it happened when the second church takeover occurred. There was a lot of posturing and grandstanding."

At this point the Lords were taking themselves more seriously—the revolution was no longer a game. This time they brandished weapons. "We felt that a proper response then was to raise the ante a little bit and show them the weapons," says Pablo Guzmán. "When we did that, the police surrounded us and to this day they haven't figured out how we got the guns past them when we worked out the truce, and the reason why we did it was because we were all organized in our community and those weapons were broken down and little old ladies had them in their coats and just walked right past the cops . . ."

The legacy of "revolutionary" liberation movements was one of COINTELPRO (counterintelligence program) infiltration, sabotage, and a kind of inner self-destructiveness driven by the left's obsession with Maoism. "The group that had been so welcomed by so many Latinos had taken a narrow, 'movement' path of dogmatic 'correctness,' said Pablo Guzmán about the waning days of the Young Lords in an essay published in *The Village Voice*. "We were on the verge of acting like . . . a gang—of beating down anyone in our ranks who disagreed."

Soon after the Julio Roldan incident, Luciano was purged from the party, which cited "extreme opportunism" and "male chauvinism" as the reason for his departure. The party began to deteriorate as intensified pressure from COINTELPRO, agent provocateurs and infiltrators created an atmosphere of extreme paranoia and recrimination. "The party began to move away from its strength," said Guzmán, "its relationship to the community."

Deviation from the party line was not tolerated, and members who tried to leave were reported being violently attacked in their apartments—some incidents of torture have long been rumored. The ultimate symbol of the party's ineffectiveness was a disastrous trip to Puerto Rico, where the Lords, ignorant of local movements, attempted to establish themselves as leaders of the Puerto Rican independence movement. In retrospect, many ex-Lords have commented that they deeply regretted their attempt to export revolution to an island that already had a well-developed leftist independence movement.

For many years, the members of the Young Lords went through a painful process of readjusting to the changing times. They were often mistakenly hounded by the New York City police for being affiliated with the violent Puerto Rican nationalist group, the FALN, which was responsible for several bombings in the New York area. But the core members of the Young Lords were survivors, and what's more they have reemerged in New York as high-profile professionals. Pablo Guzmán is currently a newscaster at WCBS TV, Juan Gonzalez is a columnist for *The Daily News,* Iris Morales is an attorney, Sonia Ivany is an assistant director at NYS AFL-CIO, Luis Garden Acosta runs an enormously successful community resource center in Williamsburg called El Puente, Richie Perez is an activist à la Al Sharpton, pioneering the movement against police brutality in New York, and Felipe Luciano is currently hosting talk shows on Fox 5 and WLIB radio.

The Brown Berets and La Raza Unida were also damaged by government-sponsored COINTELPRO campaigns, which many activists of the period blame for the deaths of Black Panthers and Malcom X. In some cases, the radical activity of Puerto Rican Independence group FALN was used as justification for the harassment of Chicano leaders. Warring between factions of Brown Berets, which mirrored the recriminations between Young Lords members, were blamed for its demise. While there has been an admirable period of nostalgia about the Young Lords and Brown

Berets, one that has been seized upon to inspire a new generation of Latino youth, radical political groups were only part of what was happening in the Spanglish revolution of the '60s and '70s. The Spanglish underground, like its countercultural counterparts, also spawned more playful, art-inspired activity. José Montoya's Royal Chicano Air Force was a key contributor to this aspect of Spanglishness. The California-based Montoya personally helped uncover proof, through unearthed government documents, that pachucos were the victims of persecution by government and media. On the heels of the zoot suit riots, first lady Eleanor Roosevelt headed a commission that issued a damning report, "The Government Riots," blaming the disturbances squarely on the government and the media.

In the 1970s, in the process of operating a barrio art school for street youths, Montoya's group sent community kids to the state library where, through archives, they helped uncover the searing report. They also found that during World War II, state legislators had plotted to open up concentration or "work" camps for pachucos. Montoya's group was originally called the Rebel Chicano Art Front, but when people confused the letters with the acronym for the Royal Canadian Air Force, Montoya and his fellow officers capitalized on the misunderstanding and adopted the name Royal Chicano Air Force. This new identity found its way into their wardrobe, as well as their highly successful silk screen poster program, which began to disseminate the World War I aviators and barnstorming bi-winged planes as icons. Following the tradition of double-edged humor established by Cantinflas and Tin Tan in the creation of the pachuco identity, the RCAF banked on outrageous humor to fuel the message in their fine art posters, murals, and community activism. Montoya was a proponent of what became known as *rasquache* art, that is, art made with materials available to a relatively unschooled, working-class person. To be *rasquache* is to fearlessly mix media and materials in sometimes embarrassing fashion. But it is the same principle behind the development of *norteño* music, which threw together accordions, polka, and *ranchera* music, salsa music, and even hiphop. Montoya himself adopted the aviator's cap, goggles, and jacket, promoting his "tortilla art" as a fundamentally *rasquache* form of cultural sloganeering. One of his enduring legacies is the work of his son, Richard Montoya, one-third of the political-cultural theater comedy troupe Culture Clash.

A New York counterpart to Montoya was Eddie Figueroa, a conceptual artist and director of plays who had been the driving force behind New Rican Village, a space down the block from the Nuyorican Poets Café in New York's East Village. Figueroa was a disaffected Young Lord who felt betrayed by the group's revolutionary dreams. Although he was the archetypal anarchist who was naturally predisposed to be hostile toward organized political movements, Figueroa's grounding in the arts and the spiritual represented what was missing in the Young Lords.

In what is now the Pyramid Club on Avenue A, Figueroa's great experiment was a showcase for the cutting edge in Puerto Rican theater, music, and poetry, featuring names like Puerto Rican Traveling Theater director Miriam Colón, Latin-jazz pioneer Jerry Gonzalez, and poet Pedro Pietri. He was thoroughly obsessed with two ideas that are central to the developments of Spanglish during its underground era—that Latinos were a multicultural rainbow people and that there was no space for us in the conventional world, and we had to invent an imaginary space to allow us to gel.

Figueroa was completely caught up in the notion of self-creating identity, and the overlapping proliferation of everything. He'd insist on his belief in magic, the belief in a multidimensional universe, simultaneous eternal time, the navigation of an inner spirit. Figueroa was a Spanglish mystic, a guy whose job it was to turn the gibberish at the intersection of the material and spiritual world into a kind of street logic of liberation. He insisted he was visited in his dreams by *espiritistas*, mystic priests of his mother's church. The *espiritista* doctrine speaks of perpetual change and transformation, of another world behind the perceptible one. The idea that the Puerto Rican psyche can contain a nonlinear, nonrational component predisposed to what is popularly known as New Age thinking is intriguing. "New Rican is an open-ended idea to unify our identity," Figueroa explained, "Our culture is the culture of the future . . . life doesn't proceed in fuckin' straight lines, you know."

Toward the end of his life, Figueroa became involved in a project with Pedro Pietri and photographer Adal Maldonado called the Puerto Rican Embassy, which evolved later into the Spirit Republic of Puerto Rico. "The Puerto Rican Embassy is a concept, it's an idea, it's not a physical location," he said. "We're dealing with concepts that are beyond geography, beyond three dimensions. With the Puerto Rican Embassy and the conception of the Spirit Republic of Greater Puerto Rico, we're declaring our independence. The spirit republic is a free place. To win this fight we don't need weapons, this is the weapon that's going to win [points to heart]. The revolution is here, man."

Figueroa's assertion could be dismissed as the rants of a dying '60s burnout. But he was asserting the primacy of a new kind of identity that transcended physical location, and nationalism. In doing this, Figueroa was not abandoning the efforts of Lolita Lebrón, who was among a trio of nationalists who fired on the House of Representatives in 1954 in a desperate act to gain attention for their cause. He was moving into a world of pure aesthetics, which was only concerned with celebrating the mixed-race beauty of his people.

At one of Figueroa's last benefit concerts, Fort Apache Band leader Jerry Gonzalez was introducing the members of his group. "Larry Willis on piano, this is my brother Andy on bass," Gonzalez muttered, pausing for a moment, "and I'm trying to be two people at once." Gonzalez was referring to his unusual decision to reconcile his love for North American jazz with the Afro-Caribbean traditions of Puerto Rico by playing both horns and congas, but he was also acting out the continually expanding hybridism Spanglish folks feel defines them. As the unflinching narrator, a deranged seer, Ed Figueroa does makes it a little easier for Puerto Ricans to be several people at once, in several places, looking backward from the future into the past, deeply in love with an eternal, kissed-by-the-sun tropical present. It is an idea that is no longer as bizarre as it seemed.

Figueroa was part of a generation of Nuyorican idealists that had occasional interaction with Chicanos through the visits of poets like Jimmy Santiago Baca and José Montoya, and there's a good possibility his idea of Puerto-Rico-in-the-heart, or wherever one chooses it to be, was influenced by Alurista. Alurista's collection of poetry *Timespace Huracán* was structured on the idea of three levels of "time-space" within which all individuals live and function. The first level is a historical or collective time-space that describes reality as recorded by a consensus of people; the second, a personal, individual, psychological time-space; and the third, a mythological time-space that unifies the personal and historical time-spaces. Figueroa's notion of "simultaneous eternal time," which he felt had a connection to Jung's synchronicity, may be parallel to Alurista's.

As the '70s came to a close, fleeting images remain of Spanglish's underground period. The draping of the Puerto Rican flag over the crown of the Statue of Liberty at once shocked and inspired me. The nasty FALN bombings, including a fatal one at Fraunces Tavern in lower Manhattan, reminded me of the despair of a movement still determined to bring independence to Puerto Rico by force. On the West Coast, Oscar Acosta was disappearing into the Mexican night, and Chicano rock and rollers were beginning their foray into the roots of L.A. punk. A crew of American label executives were visiting Cuba for the first time, ready to uncover new treasures, and a boatload of undesirables left the port of Mariel for Miami, turning the stereotype of the Cuban exile inside out. I was back in New York after college, and I was about to enter into one of the primary sites of Spanglish hybridism in a dark café on the edge of one of New York's most dangerous neighborhoods.

3.

SPEAKING IN SPANGLISH

*... Puerto Rican history has shown that language can be the
site and theme of historical action.*
— JUAN FLORES, *From Bomba to Hiphop*

Somewhere around the time that Puerto Ricans began to prolifer-
ate in New York and pachucos began to claim the territory of East
Los Angeles, Tejanos began feeling their oats in Houston and San
Antonio, and Cubans made their way up from Havana to Tampa
and Miami, Latinos were looking up at the street signs and advertising slogans, struggling to pronounce the strange English words.
In that moment, Latinos who came to the United States began to
rewrite their history in a new language, Spanglish. Spanglish is the
ultimate space where the in-betweenness of being neither Latin
American nor North American is negotiated. When we speak in
Spanglish we are expressing not ambivalence, but a new region of
discourse that has the possibility of redefining ourselves and the
mainstream, as well as negating the conventional wisdom of assimilation and American-ness.

Speaking in Spanglish became a necessity for survival not only
in our communities, but a bridge to survival in the mainstream

world. Just as Latino laborers learned to express fragments of their thoughts in English, their bosses slipped in a word or two of Spanish to add emphasis to their orders. The earliest Spanish words to seep into the American language were most likely used in conjunction with commands, like *pronto, comprende, hombre,* and *rápido.* But as Latinos became more adept at English they began to combine the two languages according to an internal rhythm that reflected at once their transplantation and their re-created homeland in the U.S.

While the ghettoization of immigrants is a constant in American history, the dissolution of the European ethnic ghettos was a function of their eventual acceptance into American society. This acceptance often coincided with continued redefinitions of whiteness, with that racial categorization expanding to accommodate previously stigmatized, "darker" ethnicities. The Irish, Italians, Russians, and Jews were all at various times considered "less than white." These groups were bilingual, but increasingly separated the use of English and their native language over generations and social situations that brought them closer to the mainstream. But because Latinos are so relentlessly multiracial, no amount of intermarriage within the group to "lighten the race" could allow for the expansion of whiteness to include Latinos. We rejected the separation of English and Spanish and began to construct a new identity in which languages and cultural affiliations overlapped and blended.

While Spanglish speaking began informally in barrios and along the southwest borderlands, it gradually became part of the living cultural history of Latinos in the U.S. An oral history, expressed in Spanglish, became one of the central characteristics of a new body of literature that had a more populist character then the more European influenced writing from Latin America. It is a literature that reflects different social class concerns, but it retains one of the distinguishing characteristics of the Latin American literature boom. It is strongly related to magical realism in the way that it conveys the indigenous and African spiritual postures of Latin America, as well as retaining the kind of journalistic quality that Gabriel García Márquez, who began his career as a reporter in Barranquilla, Colombia, so often claims as his fundamental methodology.

The literal speaking of Spanglish is a survival mechanism, a way of importing the tongue of the adopted country while retaining the mindset of the old one. While English words are more and more freely internalized in the Latin American lexicon, especially with the advent of the high technology of the information age, the process is turned around by U.S. Latinos. This time Spanish words are imported into English prose, giving the Spanglish reader a sense of grounding in a newly created space while forcing the English reader to accept the presence of Latinos. The dropping of Spanish words into a stream of English ones functions much like the ubiquitous presence of Latin music, coming out of moving cars and the open tenement windows. In this sense, it's not surprising that Spanglish "letters" emerge from a public setting, where music and dance are not far behind.

My personal involvement with the Spanglish experiment began in the late '80s, when I began reading my work at what has become an institution of Spanglish "letters," the Nuyorican Poets Café. The café became such a media magnet that in the mid-90s, I was part of a touring group of poets who traveled around North America and Europe spouting a new, "hybrid" form of poetry. But although we came out of a milieu that is on the surface a Latino institution, our touring group featured only three actual Latinos along with three "white" Americans and four "black" Americans. This caused some confusion for us, but what became increasingly clear to me was that the café, a Spanglish institution, had created a group that was multiracial, spoke mostly in English, and had a kind of arresting, subversive effect on the dominant culture. In short,

— the café could be understood as a working model for the way Spanglish culture could work in twenty-first century America.

The Nuyorican Poets Café began in poet Miguel Algarín's living room in the mid-'70s because a growing number of New York Puerto Ricans, from the same generation as the originators of salsa, were writing in both English and Spanish about the neighborhoods they were raised in. The Lower East Side was going through the same kind of economic convulsion that afflicted many urban cities across America. White ethnics were moving out, eroding the tax base, and the housing stock began to fall apart or be literally burned to the ground by unscrupulous owners looking to escape their financial burdens. The Nuyorican Café, which eventually moved out of Algarín's living room and into a nearby storefront, featured poets like Miguel Piñero, Miguel Algarín, Tato Laviera, Sandra Maria Esteves, and Pedro Pietri—the literary arm of East Coast Spanglish culture.

"Reverend" Pedro Pietri (of the Church of the Mother of Tomatoes) can be spotted on the streets of the Lower East Side, as well as his Uptown turf, carrying a briefcase stuffed with reams of his poetry. Long before the outbreak of the AIDS virus, Pedro Pietri was one of the first to stand on street corners advocating the use of condoms. A Vietnam war vet from the early '60s, Pietri was concerned about less fatal sexually transmitted diseases like syphilis and gonorrhea, and used the condom thing as a kind of performance art; comedy prop. In 1963, Pietri, who had grown up on the Upper West Side and known contemporaries of Salvador Agron, the infamous Capeman murderer, and had once aspired toward a career singing doo-wop music, wrote one of the first Nuyorican poems, "The Puerto Rican Obituary." An epic about the fate of the faceless Puerto Rican worker who came to the U.S. for a better life but found only disappointment, "Obituary" struck a chord in a new political underground. By the time the Young Lords were formed in the early '70s, Pietri was their house poet, appearing in a notorious Third World newsreel documentary reading his signature poem.

Here lies Juan
Here lies Miguel
Here lies Milagros
Here lies Olga
Here lies Manuel
Who died yesterday today
And will die again tomorrow
Always broke
Always owing
Never knowing
That they are beautiful people
Never knowing the geography of their complexion
PUERTO RICO IS A BEAUTIFUL PLACE
PUERTORRRIQUEÑOS ARE A BEAUTIFUL RACE
— PEDRO PIETRI, "THE PUERTO RICAN OBITUARY"

"The Puerto Rican Obituary" struck a chord because it not only lionized the Nuyorican underclass, it signaled the "death" of Puerto Ricans in New York and the subsequent birth of the Spanglish-speaking Nuyorican. The Nuyorican was class-conscious, darkly humorous, and aware of a mixed-race heritage. Through the inaccuracies of cultural history and criticism, Pietri has come to be known as one of the Nuyorican poets, but in fact he was reading and writing before the emergence of the Nuyorican Poets Café in the mid-'70s. He could have been categorized as one of the late "Neo-Rican" poets like Julio Marzán, Puerto Rican poets who began to experiment with English in the '40s and '50s. Nuyorican Spanglish began as a way of establishing a presence in a cold, unfamiliar world, as a way of conversing with strange surroundings. Then it became a complaint, a litany of regret over the emptiness of the new world and the rejection by the old one. Finally, as in Tato Laviera's classic "Ame-rican," it was an assertion of Puerto Rican–ness in New York, a pure Rican-ness that in some ways was more Puerto Rican than the culture on the island.

It was the oral testimony of a poor underclass that had been swept up and redeposited in a hostile ground. "Ame-rican" broke ground for the idea of Spanglish Nuyoricans transcending the limitations of colonial Latin American culture without submitting to assimilation.

Nuyorican Spanglish became the emboldened speech of a lower-class consciousness that had been sophisticated and elevated by inhabiting the city at the center of multinational capital. The conflict between Nuyorican and Puerto Rican was a conflict between a hyperculturized urban poor and a plantation-style southern gentility. Puerto Rico's obsolete colonial attitudes, once used to pull rank on Nuyoricans, faced a serious challenge. By the time the Nuyorican Café was reborn in the early '90s, Pedro Pietri was a regular Friday-night fixture, showing up in the middle of the slam competition as a moment of comic relief, as well as to recall the legacy of classic Spanglish poetry. Pietri hated the slam competition, but thrived in the atmosphere, and deservedly gained many new fans, many of whom were white bohemians. The ability of Pietri gained this new audience by performing in a space nestled deep in the heart of a Puerto Rican barrio is an archetypal Spanglish story.

> Only a multiculture pueblo can understand
> El adentro y the outside of the dynamic
> Culturally, we possess ritmos y sueños que no se
> Pueden sacar de our essences
> They are reflected in our speech and our manner
> No matter what language or banner we choose
> Freeing us from being aquí o allá, here, there, everywhere
> Mixed race is the place
> It feels good to be neither
> It's a relief to deny racial purity

We're amused as America slowly comes to see
The beauty of negritude and the Native American attitude
We've been living it day-to-day since 1492
    —ED MORALES, "Rebirth of New Rican"

In the early '80s, the far East Village was a crumbling, dangerous neighborhood dominated by Nuyoricans. Heroin and crack cocaine were hawked by street dealers up and down the blocks of what real estate speculators called Alphabet City. One infamous crack super-market, called the Rock, would have constant lines of customers at its storefront window, addicts lined up like baseball fans waiting to buy World Series tickets. The Nuyorican Poets Café, once the site of a flourishing Spanglish-speaking cultural community, was closed for renovation.

In a year or two the Great East Village Art Explosion arrived, and kids from Rhode Island School of Design, Bard College, and New York's own School of Visual Arts began to move into the per-ilous precincts of Alphabet City. While these young artists brought some interesting and politically charged work into the neighbor-hood, they also brought the seeds of gentrification. Their mere presence made the neighborhood more palatable for outsiders. One club, located on Second Street and Avenue B, was called the S.I.N. Club, which stood for Safety in Numbers. The flyer that advertised S.I.N. advised visitors to approach from Houston Street, and not chance walking down Second or Third Streets, which at the time were controlled by the drug networks.

A small literary scene, anchored by Joel Rose and Catherine Teixier's *Between C&D* magazine, and reading spaces like the Life Café and Neither/Nor, sprouted around and between the art galleries, hardcore punk dives like A7, and the drugs. Bimbo Rivas, a follower of perhaps the father of Nuyorican poetry, Jorge Brandon, had written a poem called "Loisaida." Loisaida was a conflagration of "Lower East Side" and Loiza, a town in Puerto Rico that is widely acknowledged as the heart of African culture on the island. Brandon, who read at the Nuyorican Café in the later years, was an expert improviser using the form of *decima*; it was a kind of spontaneous rap/poetry evolved from seventeenth century Spain that was parallel to the improvisations of a salsa singer during the percussion "bridge" of a song.

A couple of Pedro Pietri's plays were produced at Life Café, and Pietri began a reading series with Bob Holman of the St. Mark's Poetry Project. The mid-'80s were the last days of Miguel Piñero, a self-styled junkie gangster poet who helped found the original Nuyorican Poets Café with Miguel Algarín. Piñero, who called himself "junkie-Christ," mesmerized listeners with lines like "*la metadona esta cabrona*/methadone is a bitch." Piñero was in many ways an éminence grise of Spanglish culture and the Nuyorican ideal. He was fiercely proud of his Puerto Rican identity but experienced the cold shoulder from island literary luminaries when he gave a reading there at the height of his career. His experiences in prison enabled him to exploit the crossover between black and Latin cultures—long before wiggers in the Midwest, Piñero saw it fit to embrace the term "nigger" in the '70s, claiming the African-American identity of the streets. Piñero's body of work is a late twentieth-century fusion of bluesman Robert Johnson and pioneering French prison writer Jean Genet, underscored by the same kind of rural/urban influences that helped shaped the songwriters of the golden age of New York salsa.

The gentrification of the Lower East Side was a slow, painful event involving the displacement of thousands of Puerto Ricans. As the art scene ebbed and flowed, and various attempts were made to crack down on the drug trade, there was a steady turnover in apartments as older Latinos died and young Anglo-American painters with orange and blue hair moved in. Nuyorican multiculturalism flourished in the Lower East Side, as it did in San Francisco's Chicano-dominated Mission District, because of the Spanglish tolerance for many races. It was an atmosphere that was ripe for bohemian infiltration, a ready-made environment for imagined hip fantasies about race transcendence that were still unattainable for white bohos. If you rightly allow for the huge influence of prison behavior on hipsterism, then the following passage from Miguel Piñero's *Short Eyes*, spoken by a white character, takes you into the subliminal East Village–Lower East Side mindset:

> It's okay to rap with the blacks, but don't get too close with any of them. Ricans, too. We're the minority here, so be cool . . . Ricans are funny people. Took me a long time to figure them out, and you know something, I found out that I still have a lot to learn about them. I rap spic talk. They get a big-brother attitude about the whites in jail. But they also back the niggers to the T.

Piñero's last days were spent in the back room of Neither/Nor, a gloomy coalescence of post-Beat and Loisaida Latino avant-garde arts. He had spent most of the money he had made as a part-time actor in *Miami Vice* and his health soon went into a tailspin. He died of a variety of ailments, like liver cancer in the fall of 1987, after the first wave of the neighborhood's gentrification had receded. A year later, in August 1988, there was a momentous riot in Tompkins Square Park, a place in the middle of the neighborhood where homeless people had set up a tent city. The issue of gentrification was thrust violently into the forefront, but the political fragmentation of the neighborhood would eventually leave it vulnerable to its transformation into a high-rent hipster Disneyland. But before that, another "art" movement, performance poetry, took hold in the Nuyorican Poets Café, newly reopened as a response to Piñero's death.

There was a spectacular turnout for his wake in a Lower East Side funeral home and an unforgettable ceremony in which, in memory of one of his favorite poems, his ashes were scattered in a vacant lot. But the shooting and robbing and drugging that Piñero longed to be close to was going to disappear quickly. Piñero's death seemed to signal the death of the old East Village. The images of the riot, in which TV cameras caught scores of policemen pummeling green-haired punks and anarchists with their nightsticks, was fresh on everyone's mind. The activists were protesting a curfew that would be imposed on the park, which many homeless slept in at night. The police riot, which occurred ironically during the administration of African-American mayor David Dinkins, eventually drove the homeless and anarchists out of the park, a goal on the agenda of neoconservative Nuyorican City Councilman Antonio Pagán. There would be a new Lower East Side with cleaner, crime-free streets and a new version of the Nuyorican Poets Café. At Miguel Piñero's funeral, a conversation between Bob Holman and Miguel Algarín resulted in a new commitment to reopen the café.

Flash forward to 1990, when Pietri is lurking inside the café because he's doing a featured reading right before the poetry slam begins. Pietri hates the poetry slam because he thinks it's turning the café into a media circus. On this night, there are cameras from MTV, the BBC, and local news outlets jamming the room, spurred on by a cover story in *New York* magazine, and a major feature in *The New York Times*. Poetry slams, in which audience members rated poems from one to ten, were attracting widespread attention as a new entertainment form because they were harnessing the raw energy of restless youth by merging literature, music, theater, and performance art. In New York's Lower East Side, poetry slams were special because they combined the inputs of the Downtown arts scene, which drew aspirants from all over the country, and local kids just out of high school, trying to tell the story of their wild city lives.

Pietri was a little off that night, but had a credible righteousness in his disdain for the slam. It was the reaction of a countercultural Nuyorican who had inculcated the values of the '60s and its liberation movements. His condom-poetry street performances had a carnival atmosphere that fit into the '60s aesthetic. So for his generation, art was a communal thing, to be given freely, like a marijuana joint being passed around a roomful of strangers.

Several years earlier, the poetry slam had been invented in Chicago by a well-meaning working-class poet named Marc Smith, as a vehicle to get out his inner angst. But it became a monster in New York reflecting the worst of the hustling hucksterism of Gotham. Like some *Gong Show* idea of bohemia, poetry slams had the stench of commerce attached to them, the feel of advertising language. They even wound up having an effect on advertising culture, most notably poet Max Blagg's Gap ad, that aired in the early '90s, in which he reads a poem that describes an idealized woman wearing Gap jeans. Many slam poets were trying to communicate the desperate desires of marginalized youth to "get over" in a society that was cutting back on the largesse of social programs. These street poets were commodifying themselves for record deals, tours, and movie appearances.

The weekly poetry slams—festive, raucous affairs—spotlighted a small crew of spunky poets. MTV taped an *Unplugged* segment, *New York* magazine ran a cover story, and the rest of the media followed suit. Soon the neighborhood was safer, and the poets were going on national reading tours, and many went on to book and recording contracts. The Friday night slams were run by ringmaster Bob Holman, who held sway over a ragged swarm of East Village artist types and NYU students. There was much rhetoric, diffused primarily by Holman, about the unimportance of the scores, but the event itself generated a feeling that they were the bottom line. The café was becoming a workshop for the new self-made poetry star whose ambitions were to wind up making a name for himself or herself on MTV. While there was a great deal of Spanglish on display at the Nuyorican, the whole feel of the readings was moving away from the creation of a new transcultural identity and toward a kind of multicultural urban/suburban Americana.

But there was some truth to the multicultural myth of the café. The fusion between hiphop culture and the vestiges of the White Negro beatnik scene, carried out through a Spanglish institution, was startling. Hip-hop poetry was employing more and more Spanglish, and some African-American poets were digging into Spanish. Having been inspired by her stint working at the Caribbean Cultural Center, a museum/community space that celebrates the African diaspora througout Latin America, Tracie Morris captured the spirit of Nuyorican with her poem "Morenita." A description of her ambivalent identification with Latin-ness, "Morenita" was one of the few attempts by café poets who were not of Latino background to take on Spanglish.

Not Latina. Morenita.
Negrita chiquita
De Estados Unidos
Ese país
Same world, different world
Black. A compliment or curse.
I, a girl from this country
At peace with one identity

While Nuyorican poets going back to Piri Thomas and the island tradition of Luis Palés Matos invoked African-ness as a way of calling attention to the race issue in both North and Latin America, Morris took the initiative to engage in Spanglish culture from outside and invoking the transcultural option. But the essence of the new Nuyorican poets was allowing varied voices that represented that early '90s moment in the Lower East Side to speak, side by side, like a community speaking in tongues. Maggie Estep was essentially an East Village postpunk poet with a background in the beat mecca, Colorado's Naropa Institute, who tried to romance

106

the entire Downtown underground while taking revenge on her ineffectual lovers by documenting their inadequacies in print. I suggested that her name was a variation of the Hispanic Estepa and she said that her father once mentioned a possible Iberian ancestry. Paul Beatty incorporates memories of his Chicano friends into some of his poems and novels. Reg E. Gaines, whose poems were always formally based in hip-hop delivery, infused Spanish into some of his recitations, again concretizing the crossover with African identity that is present in the basic construction of Nuyorican-ness.

The hype that surrounded the spoken word scene didn't benefit everyone equally. People like Edwin Torres, who made the cover of *New York* magazine in the spring of '92, and Tracie Morris, Grand Slam champ of the following year, had to scrape together their own money to put out independent "chap" books. Willie Perdomo had a book published by Norton Press. He imagined himself as a descendant to Langston Hughes; in the late '90s, Perdomo became a central figure in an attempt by young Nuyoricans to bring about an East Harlem Renaissance. He was the Charlie Parker of our group, and when he read it was like jazz on the street corner.

Perdomo's signature poem, "Nigger Reecan Blues," was a brilliant reformulation of the groundbreaking work done by Piri Thomas in his book *Down These Mean Streets*. When Perdomo openly questioned whether his identity was Puerto Rican or African American, he was exposing the latent racism in Latino society as well as confronting the manifest intensity of North American prejudice. His languid fluctuation between Spanish and hiphop English helped put "Boricua" on the lips of African Americans, even though he concludes that "his friend" is right when he says, "You ain't nothin' but a nigger." The strange valence between "*negro*," the word the Spanish were the first to give to New World slaves, which can also mean "dear," and "nigger" packed an unprecedented charge, and explained quite bluntly the difference in approach between two European colonial powers.

The emotional bloodshed and economic triumph engendered by the café is permanently intertwined with the phenomenon of Spanglish, and another misunderstood condition of postmodern urban society, multiculturalism. Societal movements happen when they move out of the realm of theory (linguistics and sociology) and inhabit people and places. Two fiftyish poets, Bob Holman and Miguel Algarín, embodied the Spanglish and multicultural ideas, and the success and ultimate failure of their relationship weighed heavily on the café.

Undoubtedly, there have always been philosophical disagreements between the two men who were at the core of the guerrilla poetry revival in the early '90s. Algarín, the son of Puerto Rican migrants who teaches Shakespeare at Rutgers University, helped to invent the notion of a bilingual literature from the streets. Holman, a product of the Midwest, and the literary tradition of the Beats, found a spiritual home in the Downtown performance art world. While Holman's smash success as ringmaster of the Friday night slam competitions was welcomed by the café, which was reopened in 1989 after being closed for eight years, there was always a delicate question of turf involved. Holman had come in and made Algarín's house popular, but Algarín would soon take it back.

The café, which had been closed because of various bureaucratic snafus, was reborn out of a tragedy. As Algarín wrote in his introduction to *Aloud: Voices From the Nuyorican Poets Café*—an anthology published at the height of its revival—Holman had approached him at a wake for Miguel Piñero, one of the original Nuyorican poets. "It's time to reopen the café . . . Miky is insisting upon it," whispered Holman. Piñero had once written a poem asking that in death his ashes be "scattered thru the Lower East Side." Out of Piñero's ashes, and a political restlessness that had climaxed in the 1988 Tompkins Square police riot, a new artistic movement was born.

From the start, the alliance between Algarín and Holman worked to iron out differences for the sake of a fascinating multicultural experiment. At first, there was a violent struggle about what to name the place. Algarín didn't want to call it the Nuyorican because founding fathers like Piñero and Lucky Cienfuegos had died. But it became clear that the public wanted to hear that name again, and so did institutional funding sources.

There was always an uncertainty about exactly what the Nuyorican Poets Café movement was about. Was it bona fide literature, or theater, performance art, comedy, rap? The resurrection of the Beats, or a multicultural version of the Harlem Renaissance? MTV's attempt to synthesize aspects of hip-hop, alternative rock, Dennis Leary, and jazz into a new international pop product? Even though only four of the fourteen-member Nuyorican road show were actual New York Puerto Ricans, there was a metaphorical rationale for the sobriquet. Like poetry from other people of color and oppressed groups, Nuyorican poetry leaned heavily on identity search. But since our identities bore so many contradictions, our identity poems were precursors for the crises of postmodern America, busily engaged in the process of cultural, and to an extent, genetic, miscegenation.

The Nuyorican Poets Café movement began to embrace the idea of using the experience of Latinos, who celebrate a mixed-race heritage, as a metaphor for muliticulturalism. Both Algarín and Holman began to speak about "the generosity of the Puerto Rican experience" in absorbing a diversity of cultural referents. The new Nuyorican tradition included African-American poets like Morris and Gaines, who inflected their poems with Spanish, and Hal Sirowitz, author of *Mother Said*, a litany of laments about growing up with an overbearing Jewish mother. "Everyone can be Nuyorican," Holman would say, paraphrasing the Irish-American claim uttered every St. Patrick's Day.

It was a noble sentiment, but by transferring the Latino model into post–Tompkins riot East Village, the café was marginalizing the Nuyorican voice, just as the neighborhood's gentrification did. The Holman-run slam, though sometimes denounced as Pulp

Poetry, was fulfilling its mission to bring a new, raucous, in-your-face poetry to a wide audience. The all-important slam nights had few Latino voices, and valued the theatrical and the controversial. The other powerful trend that blossomed in the slam theme was a convergence of performance art and rap.

The power of the poets, who reveled in their difference, seemed to resolve all the contradictions of the thorny issue of East Village gentrification. They challenged the old paradigm of lily-white artists who had come to drive up rents and force out the ethnic workers. The café's best poet, Paul Beatty, whose *Big Bank Takes Little Bank* had just been published by its own in-house press, was an African American who'd grown up in Los Angeles and lived around the corner. At one point, Beatty's one-time professor, the late Allen Ginsberg, was quoted as saying "The Nuyorican Poets Café is the most perfectly integrated place on the planet."

But Beatty's was the only book published by the café, which abandoned its forays as an independent house and, as its detractors claim, focused its energies on the performance aspect. In 1992, buoyed by the throngs that showed up for the Friday night slam, Holman teamed up with former hip-hop publicist Bill Adler to start a new series at the Fez, a glitzier venue that acted as a showcase for spoken-word entertainment. The hype came quickly, and there was soon controversy. The *New York* magazine cover story featured a picture of Edwin Torres, a New York–born Puerto Rican who happened to look goofy and wear a goatee. The headline said, "The Beats Are Back." Torres, whose work is kind of a Spanglish retake on the Russian Futurists, had never hitchhiked in his life and was resoundingly antidrug. Tracie Morris, who had not been chosen for the MTV special, objected strongly to the café movement's being compared to that of the Beats, and believed poets were compromising their artistic integrity to get corporate entertainment approval.

As the Nuyorican poets live phenomenon burgeoned, some poets were beginning to clash with slam master Bob Holman. Reg

E. Gaines was one of the first to leave the touring group and secure a recording contract. He complained that Holman and Adler had recorded him without his permission, and the tape wound up being played in dance clubs in San Francisco. Holman claims that the tape was a demo distributed to some magazine writers and was never sold for profit. In almost nightly discussions in the hotel rooms, poets wondered if they were being paid enough for their work.

In 1994, as an attempt to prove that the café was a real literary movement, Algarín and Holman published *Aloud: Voices From the Nuyorican Poets Café*, with Henry Holt. The book became a standard text in universities all over the country and is probably the single greatest thing the café has produced. But the appearance of the book almost coincided with the beginning of a serious rift between the two editors. Miguel Algarín was not asked to be in the touring group, something that increased his alienation from Holman. One night Algarín called me at home and played a phone message tape from a woman whose son went to school at UCLA. Holman had arranged a reading at the school, and the publicity materials said he was the founder of the Nuyorican Café.

Algarín began to feel that Holman was no longer an ideal representative for the Nuyorican Café; his faith in the "We are all Nuyorican" motto began to waver. Meanwhile, Holman forged on with his massive United States of Poetry TV project, a filmic catalog of new and older poets reading their work, which aired on PBS in the fall of 1994. He had taken a leave of absence from the slam nights to work on that project, and he continued to run afoul of Algarín over a variety of irregularities, which were procedural and financial.

The promise of the original Nuyorican poets, who had used Spanglish to express their transnational reality, had been swallowed up in an artificial attempt to create a "multicultural" arts community. In the spring of '97, Holman was officially severed from the café by its board of directors, which refused to work out an agreement for him to return to his duties as slam MC after a yearlong leave of absence. "*Nuyorican*" was no longer an inclusive enough term for Holman. A form of Spanglish-inspired multiculturalism appeared to have failed.

But years after the Algarín/Holman fallout the Nuyorican Café still thrives, and increasingly promotes voices from the Latino community, as well as remaining the center of slam poetry, albeit a particularly hip-hop–influenced version. Perhaps inspired by Willie Perdomo, whose work and life has had such resonance with Miky Piñero's, and DJ Bobbito Garcia's "All That" series, there is a growing Latino presence at the café. And a new generation of hip-hop poetry is evolving. The failed educational system in New York has turned its back on most of its students, who have in turn concentrated on their oral skills to develop themselves artistically. The hip-hop tradition of "battling," channeling aggressive energy that would otherwise result in gang warfare, fuses easily with the slam format—rhyming becomes a competition that encourages a different form of "literacy."

But the café's final stage of poetic jousting has begun to resemble the original goal of the Nuyorican poets, by telling ghetto stories that represent a way of life more in tune with the still-struggling neighborhood. Many of the late '90s slam winners have been "hip-hop theater" pioneers like Sarah Jones. And although they are not centrally based at the café, a new crew of Nuyorican poets like Mariposa, La Bruja, and Emmanuel Xavier have blossomed, greatly inspired by Perdomo. But to understand Perdomo's significance, you have to come to know the Nuyorican style pioneered by Miguel Piñero.

In a corner of the café where you enter is a small altar for Miguel Piñero, whose life force is the essence of the warm chaos that flows through the café. His memory is kept alive through Miguel Algarín, who has grown as an entrepreneur of community-based theater

and performance. Piñero was a great inspiration to a new generation, a classic, extremely flawed hero of the streets. He took parts in
movies and television that reinforced a very negative image of
Puerto Ricans. In *Fort Apache, The Bronx*, a movie that earned
much vilification from progressive elements in the community,
Piñero appeared as a soulless junkie who wound up shooting up a
hospital emergency room during a senseless robbery. In *Kojak*, he
played a ruthless murderer, and in *Miami Vice* a pseudo-pimp
denizen of the dark.

Piñero loved the taste of life's cruelty; it liberated him from pos-
sessions and status, sending him into an almost Buddhist junkie
calm. In a way he was a martyr for the Lower East Side: subcon-
sciously, the Tompkins Square Park riots encapsulated his rage and
defiance. The '80s hippie-anarchist chapter of the park, which
began with a clash between hippies and Puerto Ricans over turf in
the '60s, had ended in flames, with the yippies and the Nuyoricans
both on the verge of extinction. The cell phone generation Z film
deal makers were on their way. Still, in a strong way the café has
returned to its original intent in the last few years. Taking a cue
from Piñero's love of the streets, while discarding his despairing
self-destructiveness, the Nuyorican Café continues to incubate the
dreams of art and rebellion.

> *Code-switching is viewed as the tragic convergence of two*
> *nonstandard vernaculars, and thus is assumed to epitomize*
> *the collapse of the integrity of both. . . . Rather than com-*
> *pensating for monolingual deficiency, code-switching often*
> *signals an expansion of communicative and expressive*
> *potential.*
> —JUAN FLORES, *Divided Borders: Essays on*
> *Puerto Rican Identity*

In many ways, the café has moved on with the rest of the world,
and maybe the lack of fanfare about it in recent times has helped it

evolve gracefully. Maybe there was too much of a claim to newness about the place that never quite fit. It's not as if poets stopped reading their work aloud before the existence of the café, and it's certainly not going to end now that the media spotlight doesn't shine quite as brightly. The new hip-hop poetry for the most part has so much integrity in its journalistic grounding that it transcends the slam format. As far as what the meaning of Nuyorican really is, maybe multiculturalism is too big a concept to be solved by a bunch of slam poets with big hearts, as well as the need to make a name for themselves.

But then again, maybe not. What the café showed, and continues to show, is that a Spanglish-based institution served as a staging ground for one of New York's most viable multicultural happenings. The idea of taking a traditional art form—the oral declaiming style of the Puerto Rican *décimas*—and applying it to an urban setting that was completely out of context for that style, was a Nuyorican form of adaptation. As Juan Flores points out in his essay "Que Assimilated Brother, Yo Soy Assimilao/The Structuring of Puerto Rican identity in the U.S.," there are four definitive moments in the awakening of Nuyorican cultural consciousness. The first three, according to Flores, are as follows: 1) "The here and now, the Puerto Rican's immediate perception of New York," 2) "The state of enchantment, an almost dreamlike trance at the striking contrast between the cultural barrenness of New York and the imagined luxuriance of the Island culture," 3) "Looking at New York, the Puerto Rican sees Puerto Rico, or at least the glimmering imprint of another world . . . [he sees] a transposition of cultural background. . . ." The café represented the second stage of the fourth moment, "a selective connection to and interaction with the surrounding North American Society."

In its initial incarnation, the café was essentially a place for New York Puerto Ricans to express the relocation of their island selves in the context of the hard (yet sexy and exciting) city streets. After being closed for most of the '80s, the café redesigned itself to project outward into the surrounding neighborhood, which had been rapidly gentrifying over the previous ten years. Of course the personal vagaries of café founder and owner Miguel Algarín figured into this. As a Rutgers professor and a writer caught up in his own projects, Algarín was too distracted to do anything but let the café lie fallow during this period of bureaucratic difficulty. Also, Algarín saw the gentrification of the neighborhood as an opportunity to turn a profit from his dues-paying residence in the area. In an article about the twenty-fifth anniversary of the café, Algarín is quick to mention the early visits from Beat writers like William Burroughs—his emphasis was clearly on the café as a racially integrated part of Americana.

The best work produced at the café has incubated a new generation of poets like Mariposa and La Bruja, two Nuyoricans who take off from writers like Sandra Maria Esteves, and Universes, an Afro-Latin quintet of poets whose 2000 work, "Slanguage," speaks to the experience of the streets. Spanglish is spoken as a way of preserving part of an identity, moving back and forth between North and Latin American consciousness. Mariposa in particular has articulated the sense of identity regardless of place with her famous line "I wasn't born in Puerto Rico, Puerto Rico was born in me."

Mariposa is declaring not only her ability to create a new, American identity for herself without leaving behind her *puertorriqueñidad*—through the body of her work she is also announcing an evolution, a growth spurt, if you will, that Nuyorican consciousness has made over the traditional island mindset. By emphasizing her African-ness, she exposes the racism behind the common Spanish phrase *pelo malo*, (literally, "bad hair") which refers to Negroid hair. Mariposa's Nuyorican identity celebrates African identity where her island culture, outside of a lot of leering salsa and merengue songs about "mulatas," failed her. In José Luis González's landmark 1980 essay, "El país de cuatro pisos" ("The Four Story House"), he makes a case for the notion that Puerto Rican culture is essentially a Caribbean variant of African culture.

"The first Puerto Ricans were black Puerto Ricans," he avers, noting that the early Spanish presence was Spain-identified. The Nuyorican embrace of African-ness, without losing its feel for the standard rice-and-beans signifiers, demonstrates the hybridizing principle of Spanglish. The diasporic African element in Mariposa recombines with the African American culture of New York and revitalizes Luis González's Puerto Rican four-story house in an urban setting.

Chicano Spanglish literature is influenced by different conditions than Nuyorican poetry: A small core of '60s activists and artists began to be absorbed into the state college system, giving Chicano literature more of an acadmic-style canon, and the subject matter dealt less with race issues than with the problem of marginalization. Riding the bus every day to clerical jobs in the municipal sector of Los Angeles, Marisela Norte paints a lucid portrait of Chicana alienation. Her fluid Spanglish captures the speech rhythms of her native East Los Angeles, a self-contained Mexican American barrio that is a prime incubator of hybridity. Her most striking and available work is not a book but a CD recording of her poems, *Norte/Word*, which accentuate the impact of her Spanglish. *Word* plays like a soundtrack of the image of an ordinary Chicana riding a bus through the least privileged areas of Los Angeles County, observing the people who are not heard. Norte's poems illuminate the marginalization of working Chicanos and more recent Latino immigrants, who have to rely on substandard public transportation, working at marginal jobs. The suffocation of women in these jobs, and their lack of access to automobiles, is contrasted with Norte's inner voice of yearning for independence, as well as control of her own sexuality.

But one of *Word's* most penetrating works is "Act of the Faithless," in which she describes the act of crossing the border from Ciudad Juárez, Mexico, into El Paso, Texas.

It was a Holiday Inn downtown El Paso
where she crossed the line daily
paso por paso mal paso que das
al cruzar la Frontera
step by step mis-stepping
as you cross the border
There was the work permit
sealed in plastic like the smile
she flashed every morning
to the same uniformed eyes

Norte's narrator works cleaning hotel rooms, and in this poem she demonstrates the existence of a "Second Border," the one imposed on Latino immigrants by mainstream North Americans because of difference. Even though the formal border line is a heavily policed affair, both borders are patrolled, and the presence of authority is often used to threaten and criminalize immigrants. The border primary region is essentially "Aztlan," that is, the U.S. states of Texas, New Mexico, Arizona, Colorado, Nevada, California, and to a smaller extent, Utah, and the Mexican states of Coahuila, Sonora, Chihuahua, Tamaulipas, and Baja California. El Paso is an epicenter of this shadow nation, the last link of the Camino Real connecting Mexico City with Santa Fe.

Some argue that El Paso was the birthplace of the pachuco, as well as one of the contemporary Chicano cultural art forms, low-riding (the practice of revamping '60s and '70s vintage American-made cars so that they can be driven low to the ground, including the use of shock-absorbers to achieve a wiggling effect). The idea of border as the center of Spanglish culture is exemplified by Guillermo Gómez-Peña, who is one of the foremost practitioners of spoken Spanglish. "I speak Spanish therefore you hate me/I speak in English therefore they hate me/I speak in English therefore I hate you/*pero cuando hablo en español te adoro*/but when

I speak Spanish I adore you," he announces, in his guise as Border Brujo.

Gómez-Peña is a self-described "child of border crisis . . . part of a new mankind/the Fourth World, the migrant kind." Like Oscar "Zeta" Acosta and Alurista, who hails from Morelos, Gomez-Peña is one of the central Spanglish archetyphes, the Mexican who comes to the U.S. in his youth and creates a new "in-between" identity. Having educated himself at Cal Arts, where he was exposed to the cutting edge of the performance art scene, which was preoccupied with using the body as canvas, Gómez-Peña decided to use his corporeal self as a cipher for a Spanglish action hero. Like many Chicano border artists, he uses Mexican wrestler masks to both hide and reconfigure his identity. Gómez-Peña also embraces both the North American counterculture and Latin American boho chic: His Merry Prankster/Karen Finley ethos merges seamlessly with Catinflas canniness, and the liberation theology of *nueva canción* protest singers like Silvio Rodriguez.

Gómez-Peña often works with, and nurtures the careers of, partners like Cuban academic-performer Coco Fusco, "cyber-vato" Roberto Sifuentes, who hails from the emerging Chicano middle-class areas of the San Fernando Valley, and journalist-performer Ruben Martinez, whose pieces for the *L.A. Weekly* were groundbreaking meditations on the transnational inevitability of being Latino. Half-Mexican and half-Salvadoran, Martinez grew up in the comfortable suburb of Glendale with dreams of becoming a Spanglish bohemian Beat poet. His confrontations with his dual-Latino genetic information, especially the idea of both of his national identities being rocked by major earthquakes and catastrophic civil wars, set him slightly apart from the Chicano agenda. His journeys to visit Mexico and Central America began a new stage in Chicano-Mexican relations, and his participation, with Gómez-Peña, in art encounters between Chilangos (a nickname for natives of Mexico City) and Chicanos are an important basis of the Spanglish discourse of the future.

Still the idea of motion is crucial to the idea of the border, a place defined by an arbitrary line that cannot stop the movement of people and capital. Spanglish can't escape the idea of new space, of movement, just as the literal cognate of translate, *trasladar*, in Spanish, means to move to a new place. One of the most important poets of the border region of El Paso, José Antonio Burciaga, illustrates this in his poem "El Juan From Sanjo":

> *Sabes que, ese?*
> I'm a loco from the word go,
> In the purest sense
> Of the word *loco*,
> From the Latin,
> Loco citato,
> The place cited,
> I know my place, *ese*,
> I know my location,
> My station
> *Es aquí!*

In the new millennium, we are at a new level of Spanglish use. One of the most important writers using Spanglish right now is not a rapper, although he probably should be as time goes on; he's a Dominican who was raised in the postindustrial periphery, central New Jersey. When I got past the painstakingly crafted, starkly emotional stories in his collection *Drown*, the most striking thing about Junot Díaz is his measured use of Spanglish. It's not the code-switching that Chicano theater pioneered, which was often just direct translation of lines in dialogue, it's a rather direct, unapologetic injection of Spanish into an English narrative.

> Take it easy, nena . . . Coño, muchacho, why did you eat?
> Working at a fabrica will kill you before any tigre will.

Díaz did suffer what his book jacket characterizes as a "hard-scrabble youth" in the Dominican Republic and the dystopic underbelly of New Jersey. "We lived in the designated low-income community zone on the periphery of the periphery," Díaz said with perceptible irony. He shows an unusual virtuosity in telling *Drown*'s eleven stories—shifting gears from the sultry tropics to the New Jersey hood, he crafts a fluid text of heartfelt, artful sociology. The reigning bard of the litttle known Dominican migratory experience, Díaz possesses a riveting, conversational voice that's not afraid to drop hiphop, Spanish, or old school New Yorkese:

When the bar begins to shake back and forth like a rumba, I call it a night and go home, through the fields that surround the apartments. In the distance you can see the Raritan, shiny as an earthworm, the same river my homeboy goes to school on. The dump has long since been shut down, and grass has spread over it like a sickly fuzz, and from where I stand, my right hand directing a colorless stream of piss downward, the landfill might be the top of a blond head, square and old.

The key to Díaz's success lies in his near-assimilation experience in middle-school New Jersey, something he drew away from as a conscious decision in his adolescence. He resisted assimilation enough to concoct a voice that combines Spanglish urban dialect with Caribbean tin shack realism and he has managed to take the prescribed route to literary success: the MFA creative writing program. When asked about this, Díaz shows an unexpected vulnerability. In his telling it, staying at Cornell was an almost superhuman effort. Being suddenly yanked from a supportive, black-Latino peerage at Rutgers and thrust into remote, ivory-tower Ithaca made him terribly homesick. "One time I drank so much," says Díaz, "that I blacked out and when I woke up I was in Atlantic City, sitting there, not knowing how I got there."

But Díaz persevered. He sold a short story to *Story* magazine and, after he did a reading for them at the East Village's KGB bar,

The New Yorker pounced. At Díaz's book auction they bought "How To Date a Browngirl, Blackgirl, White Girl, or Halfie," and "Drown." Both of these stories suggest enough awkward sex that Bill Buford recently included Díaz with A. M. Homes, Rick Moody, Mary Gaitskill, and other high-profile writers in a *New Yorker* illustration themed "Really Bad Sex," an appearance akin to an MTV buzz clip. "I was surprised; there's such little sex in my stories," says Díaz. "The stories that were selected for *The New Yorker* were not really representative of the rest of the collection," said Díaz. "The collection is deeply about family, and what it means to be a part of a community."

Díaz's writing can be described as a cross between the working-class simplicity of a Raymond Carver and the visceral, tropical-urban mania of Piri Thomas, but in truth, *Drown* lacks clearly identifiable precedents. Díaz's literary influences aren't from European and American literature, but from the small world of Latino and black writers that make up the multiculturalist curriculum—the poetry of fellow Caribbean American Martin Espada is an important model for its content, if not literary style. "My writing is directly from the Dominican experience, which is simply an extension of the larger African diaspora. The truth is there's huge tracts of our experiences which haven't been spoken to, haven't been talked about."

Díaz experienced the typical culture shock of an immigrant child in acquiring a new language. "I learned to read English long before I could speak it," he remembers. "I started to lose my Spanish when I went into high school 'cause that's when the first serious waves of adolescent self-hate begin to roll in." Although he lived in a low-income corner of Parlin, New Jersey, he was bused to school at elite Oakbridge. He found he could play the assimilation game to an extent. In retrospect he interprets this as self-hatred, but even now, his acculturation bleeds through into our conversation. There are several languages, accents, and attitudes that make up Junot Díaz, and their intertwining is what makes his prose so fascinating.

Díaz's suburban homeboy narratives, which take some cues from and improve on Abraham Rodriguez's South Bronx stories

(*Spidertown, The Boy Without a Flag*), have drawn an unusual audience that is a bizarre meeting point between *New Yorker* gentility and ghetto poetics. His capturing of the bleak peripheral existence of suburban people of color is groundbreaking: His characters never wallow in self-pity even while jumping headfirst into love affairs with hopeless crackheads, palling around with alienated pool-table delivery boys, and surviving porno-driven adolescent sex encounters.

In more recently published short stories, Díaz has begun to dig deep into the contradictions of the Dominican Republic's racial dynamics. Sharing the same island with Haiti has driven the Dominican elite to a staggering self-denial as to the African component of its people. "Leticia, just off the boat, half-Haitian, half-Dominican, that special blend the Dominican government swears no *existe* . . ." he rambles on, continually ascribing blackness and Haitian-ness to annihilation in the popular consciousness of Dominicans.

Díaz's characters have been almost entirely drawn from the lower classes, and bring up a thorny problem in Spanglish literature, which is that it is considered most authentic when a certain class perspective is predominant. Spanglish literature faces a similar dynamic to the art created by African Americans—the art that celebrates the barrio, or the ghetto, becomes prioritized by well-meaning Latinos, refusing to leave touch with their roots, and mainstream gatekeepers and readers, whose need to identify with people of color is one-dimensional. Most of the classics of Spanglish literature, like Piri Thomas's *Down These Mean Streets*, Luis Rodriguez's *Always Running*, and even Sandra Cisneros's *House on Mango Street*, bring to light the voices of the less fortunate. A feature about Cisneros in the *San Antonio Current* in 1999 went out of its way in accusing Cisneros of moving from Chicago to San Antonio for the purposes of slumming in her own community to produce a voice that publishing companies want to hear. While Thomas and Rodriguez are authentically out of the barrio experience, a younger writer like Díaz and Cisneros may be under undue pressure to reproduce a certain narrative.

But the detractors of Cisneros's prose and poetry may have more of a problem with her persona, which tries to capture a Tejana voice that at times sounds childlike, bitchy, or in some way not corresponding to a preconceived expectation. Cisneros's characters project an apparent naïveté while simultaneously retaining a kind of homespun, survivor wisdom. *House on Mango Street* is somewhat true to Anzaldua's directive, encouraging Chicanas towards survival-oriented identity structures, the heterotopic spaces of self-invention. There is a kind of Southwestern Madonna aspect to her, a cranky funkiness that recalls the Material Girl in more substantial ways than Selena did.

Cisneros finds herself at the center of a struggle within Spanglish writing. The earlier narratives of ghetto existence, which ranged from Piri Thomas's frank street slanguage to Nicolasa Mohr or Denise Chavez's self-contained tales of community struggle, have given way to more overt hiphop values of "realness." There is something of value to be gained when a writer with a certain level of education doesn't use it to write abstract narratives that have nothing to do with Spanglishness. For the time being, at least, to be Spanglish is to nurture the underclass that remains within you, to allow the barrio experience to continually aestheticize itself and explore new truths. That truth, becoming more and more firmly established, will find a way to incorporate broader experiences, and continue to produce stories rich with the forbidden fruit of Spanglish. But there is no limit to the use of Spanglish, and the binary dynamic of the two languages it incorporates will ultimately never restrict it to prescribed formulas or renditions of lived experience.

The way that Spanglish allows the "inner barrio" in all of us to survive serves a similar purpose to the culture of resistance that grassroots hiphop culture implies. The neoconservative argument that hiphop culture has made anti-intellectualism a monkey on the backs of African Americans ignores that anti-intellectualism is one of the driving forces in mainstream America today. It is a form of class identification that is central to the self-image of macho Americans, who perceive of things European as effiminate and anti-American. It can be said that the anti-intellectual obsession of commercial hip-hop is softened by the use of Spanglish. Spanglish allows some European "high" literacy to filter through with its Latin-based vocabulary, while at the same time retaining the class loyalty to the Spanish-language barrio ("ghetto").

In some ways the transmitting of Spanglish through literature and the new oral tradition makes it impervious to the attacks on bilingual education by the center-right. Bilingual education, once widespread in German-English form at the turn of the nineteenth century, was demonized during the onset of World War I by an American public fearful of too much identification with an enemy power. If too many people were speaking German, then they might side with the Kaiser politically. The same kind of thing took place during the '80s, through an organization called U.S. English, led by Lynda Chavez, once the highest-ranking Hispanic (and I do mean Hispanic) in the Reagan administration. U.S. English was formed to pass a Constitutional Amendment making English the official language in this country. On its board of directors were Jonathan Singlaub and Adolfo Calero, two central figures associated with the counterrevolutionary army known as the Nicaraguan *contras*. There was little doubt that the Reagan administration was concerned about too many people retaining Spanish in the U.S. and identifying with a country that could possibly become a military enemy (not even mentioning Cuba).

The continuing fight against bilingual education has been folded into the well-known centrist policy of cutting back on federal expenses and defunding programs for "special interests." While bilingual education programs appear to be inefficient in many cases, that is probably due more to the general failure of public education than anything inherent to bilingual ed. But despite the erosion of such programs, Spanglish, which is a more organic

124

phenomenon that is rooted in the lived experiences of Latinos rather than their formal education, is under little threat. In fact the emphasis on separation between the two languages in a formal bilingual education program would inhibit the use of Spanglish.

The way people speak is a primal way of defining them, but the way they see themselves is also crucial. The representation of Spanglish people in the entertainment media is a battleground that serves to define what we are. There is a comforting notion in the fact that there are so few Spanglish faces on the big and small screens—this way we are a little bit freer to imagine who we are.

4.

LA FARÁNDULA DEL NORTE:

The Chameleon Syndrome

I see Al Pacino   fake Latino on the screen
And I scream   That's not me!
If Hollywood   would only wake up
And break the Anglo monopoly
On portraying mi gente as generic,
Semi-European honorary Italians
I might overlook   the I-like-to-be-in-A-mer-reek-a
Last Minstrel Picture Show
Now playing at a theater near me
Armand Assante fue muy galante
Como rey mambo
But I know   his ass was nothing near
A devera rice-and-beans eatin'
Pachanga congero with his heart in Spanish Harlem
Panama hat wearin' peg pants billowin'
Pendejito bonito he was supposed to be

You know Carlito's mujercita could only be a gringita
And Tony Montana es-Scarface de Cuba
Was chingando Michelle Pfeiffer, tu sabes?
I mean, let's be real—
What if Spike Lee cast Melanie Griffith
As Nola Darling
With Tom Hanks on his knees
Saying please baby please baby please?
What if Winona Ryder and Julia Roberts
Slanted their eyes, put on yellow dye
And made like the sisters in The Joy Luck Club?
What if Spielberg made a movie about the Holocaust
And centered it around a Christian man
Oh, sorry, he did do that
The point is, as long as you got your tanning machine
Work on your accent, you can fake Latino
Our stories are so universal
You can sell the idea of Jeremy Irons
And Glenn Close as aristocratic Hispanics
To Universal
Or Tri-Star
Or Paramount
Or Warner Hermanos
The last blackface,
Al Jolson singing
Mamacita, donde esta Santa Claus
Is a disgrace
How can we pay our $9.50
While they deny us our history?
        — ED MORALES, "THE LAST BLACKFACE"

What does it mean to be a Spanglish star? Most likely it means being misunderstood, mistaken for something else, or being the ever-popular chameleon. When Spike Lee's oeuvre began to take off following the success of *She's Gotta Have It*, there was a brief discussion surrounding the cinematographic techniques that had to be used in order to justly render African American skin into the light. While there is no doubt a manifold number of methods to "make up" the Latino appearance, the mystery of the Spanglish chameleon begins in front of the camera.

The entire trajectory of the Spanglish manifestation on the screen is defined by uncertainty, disguise, shifting tones. Spanglish movie and TV stars are often something other than themselves, and many non-Latino actors can play Latino characters without affecting the all-important suspension of disbelief. When I think about a Latino face on a movie screen or a television set I see John Leguizamo becoming Asian, Jewish, black, female, Jerry Lewis. Or I think of Natalie Wood, of Eastern European extraction, as Maria, which is my mother's name, which is my sister's name, which is almost every Latina's name. Marias who never escape *West Side Story*, or John Wayne's consort on *la frontera*. The history of Spangish folks on the big or small screens is like one long metaphorical exercise, where self stands for other and other for self, you are I and I are you and we are all together.

Since the early days of Hollywood, many non-Latinos have been cast as Latinos, most notably Paul Muni as Benito Juarez in *Juarez* (1939). Ironically, Muni had previously starred in the original version of *Scarface* in 1933, a role that was rewritten as a Cuban refugee, which was in turn acted by another non-Latino, Al Pacino, who also played a Puerto Rican in *Carlito's Way*. The free-flowing chameleonesque cross-identification that allows non-Latinos to play Latino parts is one of the most obvious metaphors for our hybrid Latino identity. If we resemble a European, a European can play our character; if we look Asian, an Asian (as Lou Diamond Phillips, a Filipino who played Ritchie Valens in *La Bamba*) can play us, and if we look African, an African American can play us.

So what happens when real Latinos become recognized names in the entertainment world? More often than not, they are relegated to roles in unremarkable movies (Jimmy Smits, *The Old Gringo, Price of Glory*), encouraged to play non-Latino roles in some kind of weird affirmative action move (Andy Garcia in *Hero, Ocean's 11*) or drag queens and freakazoids (John Leguizamo, *To Wong Foo, Super Mario Brothers, Spawn*). The Hollywood system of typecasting and Latinos' lack of visibility has put us out of focus. Adal Maldonado, Nuyorican photographer, made a literal interpretation of this idea in his series *Puerto Ricans Out of Focus* a few years ago. The constantly shifting, mutating idea of Latino, of Spanglish identity, makes it all the more difficult to present Latino characters that correspond to the idea of character type. This fuzziness of identity inspires many in the business to go for their art first and leave identity politics behind to languish in a gutter.

One of the most crucial factors that prevent Latinos from taking control of their image on the big screen is a lack of successful directors. So when Robert Rodriguez's *El Mariachi* debuted in the early '90s, it seemed that there might be hope for an inventive Spanglish cinema created by U.S.-born directors. Rodriguez's film *From Dusk Till Dawn* seemed intent on celebrating our beloved Latin dark humor, the kind we revel in when we try to explain the Mexican Day of the Dead, or the Argentine preoccupation with necrophilia (witness *Santa Evita*, Tomás Eloy Martinez's best-selling novel about the travels of Evita Peron's exhumed corpse). It's the reason a film like Pedro Almodóvar's *Matador*—climaxing with a couple's shared obsession with sex and murder—is a morbid turn-on.

But, as Rodriguez himself has put it in several interviews, this film turns out to be "trash." While the director apparently intended to play with the elements of *rasquachismo*, or the highly stylized low-brow aesthetic that defines a certain truth of Chicano culture, he wound up contributing to the cartoonish vision of just-over-the-border Mexico that is found in films like *Three Amigos* or *The Mex-*

ican. After he made the amazingly charming low-budget classic *El Mariachi* for seven thousand dollars and boldly remade it as *Desperado*, turning Antonio Banderas into a major box-office star in the process, Rodriguez lapsed into a Latin exploitation mode that makes *West Side Story* look like a superrealistic documentary.

Granted, Rodriguez has worked to make a difference in the problem that faces Latinos in the film industry — its skewed casting habits. By casting Hayek in *Quasimodo*, an HBO movie he made in between *El Mariachi* and *Desperado*, he primed her to be acceptable to Hollywood execs for her role opposite Banderas, avoiding their inevitable demands for an Anglo starlet. The most pleasing thing about *Desperado*, whose Tarantino-fication made it vastly less seductive than its predecessor, was the rare sight of two Latinos (for all intents and purposes, Banderas's Americanization qualifies his Spaniard self as an honorary Latino) playing the romantic leads. It's safe to say that such a pair is unprecedented in major studio releases.

The lamentable litany of Latinos' presence in Hollywood film is as staggering as it is largely unnoticed. With the recent renaissance in African-American filmmaking (Spike Lee, the Hughes Brothers, John Singleton, Charles Burnett, etc.) and a smattering of Asian-American films (*The Joy Luck Club, The Wedding Banquet*) it was certainly a propitious time for Latinos to become a major force in the cinema. But Latinos still lack young directors and presence in Hollywood's decision-making boardrooms, and consequently, most films about Latinos are still cast with non-Latinos in the lead roles. Add to these factors the reality that Latinos are a multiracial people who can be portrayed in metaphorical "brownface" by Anglo (and even African American) actors who are the right shade of skin color to "pass" for Latino.

From as far back as *Blackboard Jungle* and *West Side Story*, Latinos have been historically portrayed as ignorant, unrefined, hot-blooded, lazy people who can dance extremely well, by actors whose vaguely Mediterranean looks allowed them to continue the

Hollywood tradition of white actors like Sidney Toler portraying Charlie Chan and the blackface routines of actors from Mickey Rooney and Bing Crosby to Al Jolson. A brief examination of recent Hollywood films about Latinos makes this case quite clearly. Mira Nair's *The Perez Family*, a film about Cubans in Miami, starred Marisa Tomei, a Brooklyn Italian American, Alfred Molina, an Englishman of Spanish descent, and Angelica Huston, the daughter of Anglo-American director John Huston, as Cubans. You'd think Mira Nair, who made *Mississippi Masala*, a very sweet and affecting movie about the Indian diaspora in Africa and the southern U.S., would be somewhat sensitive to portraying Latinos—after all, "We people of color have to stick together" was *Masala's* unspoken mantra.

Rosie Perez was bitter about her audition for one of the roles in *The Perez Family*. She recounted this story: "After I auditioned for the part, I met with the director and she said, 'God, you have the heart and spirit of the lead actress; too bad I can't cast you because you don't look anything like a Cuban,' and I said, 'Huh? what are you talkin' about?' and she says, 'Well, you're not black enough and you're not white enough.' And I said, 'Wait a minute; have you seen Castro? He's a yellow man with an Afro; What are you talkin' about?' "

Although it's true that the cast was peppered with Latinos, mostly Miami-area Cuban actors, the lead actors of any production are the ones who convey the essence of the film. The unrestrained coochie-coochie harlot portrayed by Tomei is frankly an insult to any Latina who considers herself a modern woman. There is little to distinguish this portrayal from what film scholar Lillian Jimenez has characterized as the "historic representation of . . . Latino sexuality . . . as licentious, immoral, promiscuous, and therefore degenerate."

If we are to believe Perez's accounts of Nair's objections to her, perhaps the reason she didn't get the role is because she didn't possess the kind of dark Mediterranean stereotype that the Latin spitfire has meant since Katy Jurado in *High Noon*, Pilar Del Rey in

Tropic Zone, a movie so offensively literal about a "banana republic" that it could only star Ronald Reagan. Perez's chameleonlike
looks, her high yellow with an Afro, slight-nosed, green-eyed atypi-
cal appearance may not have been convincing in a part that needed
to strike a responsive chord with viewers conditioned by someone
who appears more like Marisa Tomei, who wound up playing the
role. It was those same looks that landed Perez her breakthrough
role in Spike Lee's *Do the Right Thing*.

According to Perez, she wasn't quite Latin enough for Lee,
either. She recounted a story about Lee spending hours trying to
get her to speak in the accent he thought he needed, only to finally
give up and allow her to more or less be herself. Perez was
extremely significant in the Spanglish *farándula* because she is very
much a Nuyorican type—"project princess" perhaps, street girl
with designs on a middle-class life, who once told me she went to
college in San Diego so she could study marine biology. While she
has been criticized unfairly for reinforcing stereotypes, Perez did
much more to break them. She was more African American than
anything else, the first Latin star to work that riff, and she has a
kind of Woody Allen presence in her comedic acting.

But alas, Rosie was just about the only Latino actor Hollywood
used for used several years after her debut. While employing actors
like Armand Assante in *The Mambo Kings*, and Al Pacino in *Carlito's Way* reprising his over-the-top Latino gangsta of *Scarface*, is
in itself not a moral crime against humanity, it does take away from
the authenticity of the characters they play. It's not so much that
Pacino and Assante play stereotypes (which, to an extent, they do)
but their function as stars playing opposite even more Anglo characters (Sean Penn as Carlito's best friend, Elizabeth McGovern as
his girlfriend in Carlito's way, and Marushka Detmers as Assante's
love interest in *Mambo Kings*) while relegating John Leguizamo
and Luis Guzman to almost forgettable subplot roles. Assante also

played a Puerto Rican drug dealer in *Q & A,* which demonstrates that it's easier for non-Latino actors to get typecast in negative Latino stereotypes than Latinos themselves.

Sensitivity to stereotyping is at such a fever pitch in the Latino community that when a film like *I Like It Like That,* made by Spike Lee alumnus Darnell Martin, portrays Latinos in a somewhat diverse and thoughtful way, it can still be subject to criticism for representing familiar urban poverty situations. Martin's lead character Tina, played by the Afro–Puerto Rican actress Lauren Velez, is written to illustrate the dilemma of the modern Latina: She is torn between furthering her career and her responsibilities as a wife and mother. Her defiant response to her husband's philandering and her relationship with her children, all played out in the loud, coarse setting of her Bronx apartment building, provoked some accusations of stereotyping.

But such objections raise interesting questions: Will we really be happy if all Latinos in movies are successful doctors and lawyers with problem-free families? If a lower-class Latino character is portrayed with depth and realism, is this stereotyping or accuracy? What if some of us like the idea, as *I Like It Like That* actor Lisa Vidal once told me, that Latinos are a "loud people"?

This debate is similar to the one taking place in the African-American community over the years, namely, "Who, as a people, are we?" In the answer to that question lies a significant reason why our representation in entertainment and the media is so problematic. We are *so many* different things, different people, that it is hard to portray us accurately, somewhat easy to rely on stereotypes. Latinos are as European as the characters in the movie based on Chilean novelist Isabel Allende's *The House of the Spirits,* a fact that made the casting of Jeremy Irons and Glenn Close not as inaccurate as some might guess. Latinos carry indigenous/Asiatic traits, which made it easy for us to believe that Lou Diamond Phillips, a Filipino/Hawaiian/Chinese/Cherokee/Scot/Irishman could inhabit the role of Chicano rock star Ritchie Valens in *La Bamba.* And

Latinos are light- and dark-skinned black people, a fact that made it easy for the producers of blaxploitation classic *Superfly* to cast African American Ron O'Neal as Priest, who was Puerto Rican in the original novel the movie was based on.

In the mid-'90s, a National Council of La Raza report called "Don't Blink: Hispanics in Television and Entertainment" pointed out that although Hispanics comprise nearly 10 percent of the U.S. population, they represented only 2 percent of all prime-time characters during the 1994–1995 television season. While the report showed that "negative" portrayals of Latinos had fallen by 18 percent, 55 percent of Latino characters were poor or working-class, and only 18 out of the 139 prime-time network series had a continuing Hispanic character. When the 1999 Screen Actors Guild report "Missing in Action: Latinos In and Out of Hollywood" appeared, the situation hadn't changed much. For the fall of the 1999 season, only Martin Sheen, who is only vaguely recognizable as a Latino, had a starring role in a television series. These kinds of stats also extend to the black and Asian communities, and this became the focus for some concessions from the television world in the late '90s when a coalition of organizations, including the NAACP and Asian groups as well as Latino groups, staged a boycott, known as a "brownout."

While the face of Spanglish is still lacking in most major movies and television shows, there has been a slight improvement since the Ricky Martin–led Latin music explosion of the late '90s. A summer 2001 report by the Screen Actor's Guild shows that Latinos captured 4.9 percent of the total TV/theatrical roles cast, which is the highest percentage since the Guild began tracking these statistics in 1992, and up from the previous high of 4.4 percent in 1999. This figure is still far short of the 11.4 percent of total U.S. population that Latinos represent. Still, the slight increase in visibility was sometimes enough to capture the mainstream imagination. The ubiquitous Jessica Alba is one of Fox TV's most recognizable stars; the Hispanic Martin Sheen (of Spanish heritage) stars in *The West Wing*, one of the major networks' elite programs; *Saturday Night*

Live has added a token Hispanic, Horatio Sanz; and even the much-lauded *Sopranos* features a half-Cuban actress playing Tony Soprano's irreverent daughter, Meadow.

With the possible exception of actress-singer Jennifer Lopez, there is still no transcendent figure in the entertainment world that rivals Desi Arnaz, no Spanglish star that dominates the mainstream and presents a quintessential picture of what we are. Before the '90s, Latino stars either played stereotypes or obscured their Latinness so they could play according to their skin tone; they could either pass for white, like José Ferrer, or be shrill and incorrigible, like Rita Moreno or Ricardo Montalban. There were very few Latino actors who could play something that approached themselves—figures like Raul Julia or the late Anthony Quinn, mildly accented, obviously olive-skinned men who were neither passing nor shuffling.

In the '90s a small group of grassroots talents began to develop that insisted on presenting Spanglishness au natural, that is, in all its unpredictable forms, making a case for the multisubjective identity of U.S. Latinos. Actors like John Leguizamo and Jesse Borrego, directors like the late Joe Vasquez, Jesus Treviño, and Miguel Arteta, were creating vital, urban images of bilingual, multiracial Latinos living in New York and Los Angeles.

Joe Vasquez, a now-forgotten director whose efforts may never be recognized the way they deserve to be, was born and raised in the Bronx by a Puerto Rican father and an African-American mother. As a child, he picked up a used Super 8 camera and subjected everyone in his neighborhood to his new hobby. Other than his filmmaking, he had the same profile as many "underclass" kids of the '70s: father left home, barely got through school, played basketball, was a bit of a hood.

But Vasquez, who went to City College in upper Manhattan, found a way to use the school's dilapidated equipment and make his student films. After a sloppy but sincere attempt to depict life in the gang lane with *A Bronx War*, Vasquez finally got his chance with Fine Line Features to make *Hangin' with the Homeboys*. A landmark urban film, predating *Boyz N the Hood* and *Straight Out of Brooklyn*, and starring then-unknown performance artist John Leguizamo, *Homeboys* had a rare narrative that linked the black and Latino experience in New York.

In *Homeboys*, Vasquez used a common fictional device by dividing different aspects of his own persona into four characters, reflecting the diversity that he saw around him growing up, as well as the different racial characteristics he inherited from his parents. The characters in *Homeboys* are ambitious, lazy, frightened, and bold when it comes to work, the streets, and the women they meet. Two characters are African American, at times trying to fit into a world of salsa-dancing and bilingual turns of phrase. One Latino character is so ambivalent about his identity that he poses as an Italian American. This is a ploy that indicates a lack of certainty that the character, Vinny, would be accepted by his darker friends as much as it does a desire to pass for white.

A spiral of drug use and psychological problems sent Vasquez into a downward spiral that resulted in his death from AIDS in 1994. Another factor in his demise was the dissolution of his friendship with monologuist/comic actor John Leguizamo. Leguizamo was Vasquez's contemporary, and shared with him an unusual combination of street smarts and self-taught intellectualism. He began to capture attention in the early '90s with his one-man show *Mambo Mouth*, in which he synthesized aspects of Jerry Lewis, Lily Tomlin, Desi Arnaz, and Freddy Prinze into a cavalcade of Latino personalities.

Many of *Mambo Mouth's* skits have penetrating societal critiques with political implications. A Latin man claims to have found success and acceptance by "assimilating" as a Japanese man, an immigrant explains how society uses him up as a worker and grants him only basic rights, and others merely project an attitude of defiance. Importantly, Leguizamo also displayed his facility in his drag interpretations of barrio women, which also earned him criticism from academics like Coco Fusco.

Leguizamo grew up in Jackson Heights, Queens, a neighborhood that became central for the Colombian community he is a part of. Different social forces in the area pulled him in different directions. While Jackson Heights had its share of drug and criminal activity, it's not quite the South Bronx or East Harlem. There are many Central and South American groups in the area, but although many came to the U.S. to escape poverty, there was a higher middle-class component in their immigration. Leguizamo cared a great deal about his street credibility—in early promotional materials and press, he was identified as being of Puerto Rican origins. This is because of his belief that his great-grandmother was of Puerto Rican ancestry. Whether or not this was a mistake, he did nothing to correct the impression. Eventually, his press releases admitted he was only half Puerto Rican. But finally, after his success with the Broadway revue *Freak*, he has finally acknowledged his Colombian purity.

Leguizamo went into performing at least in part to steer him away from minor adolescent troubles with the law. His desire to have street credibility on the block, and then as a performer, induced him to allude to an adopted Puerto Rican-ness, which he no longer needed when he became an established act. Still, the Puerto Rican community, which is still the dominant Latino community in New York as far as numbers and cultural influence are concerned, gladly accepted him, because he was indistinguishable from them. Certain aspects of the street Latino persona become universal, and national origin becomes less important when English and the ways of the street become the dominant lingua franca.

Another influence on Leguizamo was the burgeoning gay community of Jackson Heights. The largest one in New York outside Greenwich Village, Jackson Heights gays may have provided the models for Leguizamo's peerless transvestism, later showcased in *To Wong Foo*. His stunning *Mambo Mouth* drag performances earned a nickname I often heard used among his confidantes, Johnny Leggs. Leguizamo is an adventurous character, always willing to stretch boundaries and incorporate the worldview of almost any persona that comes into his head at a given time. His drag routines are demonstrations of his acting ability, but also reinforce the chameleon role Latinos are willing to play in multicultural melting pots like New York. They point out the possibility of considering drag as a metaphor for the Latino experience. Just as Latinos embody the presence of European, African, and indigenous genetic and cultural heritage, the drag persona contains masculine and feminine.

Leguizamo created a small controversy over the title for his second one-man show, one that was pivotal—*Spic-O-Rama*. Many older critics and intellectuals did not understand the revival of a word that is almost as offensive as "nigger." But Leguizamo had reclaimed *"spic,"* just as hip-hop had reclaimed "nigger," and the gay movement had reclaimed "faggot" and "queer." The characters in *Spic-O-Rama* angrily lobbied for a place in society, but revealed many flaws. A mother in a laundromat is frank and incisive about her quotidian slavery, but selfish and unscrupulous. An actor is so obsessed with not getting stereotyped, and thereby having access to preferred roles, that he dons blue contact lenses, a blond wig, and affects a British accent, denying his true identity. The central character, who holds the truth, is a preadolescent boy.

Through the boy, Miguelito, Leguizamo aligns himself with the hip-hop or rock-and-roll adolescent as hero, rebel without a cause persona, propelling himself beyond criticism of "political correctness." He also allows himself to inhabit the role of one of his heroes, Jerry Lewis—Miggy's buck-toothed idiot savant isn't far off from Lewis's infantile caricatures. But the cost to Leguizamo, and the integrity of his art, is reinviting the specter of stereotypes, which as his movie career progressed, he found hard to avoid playing.

Spic-O-Rama opened to rave reviews in the fall of 1992. At the opening party at the Coffee Shop in Union Square, a table that included Samantha Mathis, Brooke Shields, Richard Edson, and Leguizamo's collaborator, David Bar Katz, glowed when an aide rushed in with a fresh *New York Times* review. With a bit of a restrained rave, reviewer Ben Brantley, otherwise known as the Butcher of Broadway, officially welcomed Leguizamo to the fold of respected theater.

John Leguizamo has never quite become the major star his talent dictates, but has been fairly successful as a major star in *La Farándula del Norte*. Although his roles in movies like *The Fan, Super Mario Brothers*, and the vastly underrated Spike Lee opus *Summer of Sam* have received relatively little attention, to his credit Leguizamo stayed with his one-person show formula and made a major splash with *Freak*.

Freak was an extremely successful show, a phenomenon that stood out even more because it drew large, consistent crowds and favorable reviews in the wake of Paul Simon's *Capeman* fiasco. It was as if Leguizamo were proving that (despite a significant collaboration with his friend David Bar Katz) if Latinos are allowed to control the content and direction of a play, it can do better than works about Latinos that are primarily conceived of and directed by non-Latinos.

It's undeniable that the most essential trope in *Freak* is Leguizamo's attempt to reconcile his negative feelings about his father—a device that made the play dramatically powerful. Even though Spanglish narratives are filled with difficult fathers, variations on the black rage theme, albeit infused with the bizarre arrogance of colonial machismo, I even felt somewhat purged by the experience of watching Leguizamo's play. But what spoke to me even louder about *Freak* was something else. In describing the movement of his family from one neighborhood to the next, he was describing the development of multi-identifying Spanglish behavior. His ability to inhabit the stances, mannerisms, and angsts of Italian Americans, Irish Americans, Jewish Americans, and African Americans demonstrated a unique Spanglish ability to "try on" various personalities at an accelerated pace, absorbing and discarding as he went along.

> So I'm having some green beer, and since everybody's Irish
> on St. Patrick's Day, I figured I'll try out my gift and river-
> dance over to her, and I talk to her in the thickest Irish
> accent I can manage.
>
> "Toy, hello lassie, how's the Emerald Isle? You ever
> fuck a leprechaun? Erin go bragh and begorrah. Why are
> you looking at me like that? Is my shillelagh hanging out?
> Are my shonanigans banging about out?"
>
> She took a long draw on her cigarette and said, "You
> don't look Irish to me."
>
> "Oh, but I am, black Irish."
>
> JOHN LEGUIZAMO, *Freak*

It's clear that many would attribute Leguizamo's journey into
multiethnicity a classic example of the New York immigrant experience. What's more, the ability to mimic different ethnic groups has
been a staple of American comedy since the reign of the Borscht
Belt. But Leguizamo goes beyond stand-up's practiced caricatures;
he gives off the distinct impression that he has *lived* the chameleon
life. While I've been in his presence, he has reacted to things with
the Jewish declamatory shtick, reminisced about his youth in Jackson Heights with a proto-hip-hop clarity, lusted after white chicks
with a Northeastern liberal arts degree fascination.

Chameleon is an extremely important motif in the phenomenon of
La Farándula del Norte. Starting from the ancient days of José Ferrer's *Cyrano* and Paul Muni's performance as the mestizo revolutionary Benito Juárez, the centrifugal pull of the undefined
chameleon has been at the center of the intersection between Anglos in drag as Latinos and Latinos completely flattening their identity into comic clown (see also Leguizamo's role in *Spawn*).
Witness Puerto Rican–born Benicio Del Toro's breakout film role
in *The Usual Suspects*. While most people remember that movie
for Kevin Spacey's Academy Award–winning performance, Del

Toro's role was so subtle and enigmatic that he was almost unnoticeable. He had so thoroughly inhabited the character that his own presence was completely submerged—it was some kind of twisted Peter Lorre in the body of Marlon Brando's bastard son.

I met Benicio while he was on promotional tour for Terry Gilliam's adaptation of *Fear and Loathing in Las Vegas*. He had that kind of combination of awkwardness and grace that made him simultaneously nervous and relaxed at the fabulous 57-57 Restaurant. He was an unapologetic rebel, Paris café–style, twirling an unlit cigarette, unfazed by a waiter who'd just come over to tell him he couldn't smoke. For *Fear and Loathing*, Del Toro had to play the part of the deranged Oscar Acosta, a man who matched Hunter Thompson drug for drug, and in fact claimed he had invented gonzo journalism, something that turned into a legal battle through which he obtained book contracts from Thompson's Straight Arrow publishing house. For the role Del Toro had gained forty-eight pounds in nine weeks, by eating "chairs, tables, buildings, and bridges. But what really tipped the balance was doughnuts."

Del Toro was a Spanglish Puerto Rican in the mold of ex-Menudo stars Ricky Martin and Robi Rosa. He was born and raised in Santurce, a suburb of San Juan that he insisted likes to think of itself as the Manhattan of the Caribbean. The strapping Del Toro is the son of a country lawyer who shipped him off to boarding school in Pennsylvania when he got into teenage trouble. A self-described basketball freak, he jumped at the chance to come to the States because he desperately wanted to see the Rolling Stones in person. He stayed, going to UCSD, where he split his time between painting and acting class, studying with Chicano theatre guru Dr. Jorge Huerta.

But even though he visits his Puerto Rican home now and then, he feels a little caught between two worlds. The fact that Oscar "Zeta" Acosta, the Dr. Gonzo character in the film, was a Chicano activist lawyer who had a similarly ambivalent identity made Del Toro unusually qualified for the part. Acosta's writing in *Autobiography of a Brown Buffalo* made a big impact on Del Toro, perhaps because of its quality of self-invention and stubbornness.

Maybe it was California, or being drawn to rock and roll, or something about his family, but Del Toro has a strong sympathy for the counterculture and the idealism of the '60s. When we've talked he likes to bring up books like Eduardo Galeano's *Open Veins of Latin America*, which details the economic exploitation of Latin countries by imperialist North America. Apart from the actor's craft, which demands taking a character and making it your own, Benicio Del Toro fuses rock and roll California and the cynicism of colonized Nuyo-Santurce into a powerful new worldview that informs his sneering, detached characters.

With his Oscar-winning performance in Steven Soderbergh's *Traffic*, Del Toro broke through to the mainstream with the most significant Spanglish performance in American film. He became the first actor to win an award for performing a major part of his role in Spanish in an English-speaking film. Although he is from Puerto Rico, he mastered a regional Mexican accent, and then spoke in English with the same accent. His role was also prototypically Spanglish in that his character was at the very nexus of the intersection between the North and South; he was the Greek chorus and the voice of sanity negotiating between two worlds that had gone insane.

When Jennifer Lopez got into trouble by standing by her man, Sean "Puffy" Combs, just before the new millennium celebration in December of 1999, a lot of the reaction from the Latin community was predictably negative. Lopez, who has morphed from the standard dark-haired Bronx Puerto Rican "Fly Girl" into the honey-brown, coiffed, green-eyed pseudo-Anglo that tempted George Clooney in Steven Soderbergh's underrated *Out of Sight*, was perceived as violating her good mainstream fortune. What is Jennifer doing with that man? Mamis and mommies were buzzing from the Bronx to Staten Island.

The mainstream Latin community was shocked at how the Maybelline girl who defined Latina better than the magazine of the same name was throwing it all away hanging out with a hip-hop outlaw like Puff Daddy. What most of these naysayers didn't realize is that despite Jennifer's amazingly polished English- and Spanish-speaking personas, at heart she was a Bronx-bred homegirl who was more at home with r&b divas than anything else.

I got to spend an hour in the green room at MTV studios alone with Jennifer and she is a classic Spanglish twentysomething, ready to be whatever the situation calls for at any given moment. I was writing the piece for the *L.A. Times* Sunday Calendar, but I could tell her with all honesty that I spent some time growing up in the same neighborhood she was from, Castle Hill. There was little about our conversation that left the sphere of the professional entertainment media interview—it was one of my most impersonal encounters with the stars of *La Farándula del Norte*. Still, she had one of the most intense, in control personalities I've ever met. She also managed to convey the essence of her Bronx character.

When she described the video from "Feelin' So Good" from her debut album, *On the 6* (appropriately named after the subway line we shared in our respective childhoods), she painted a picture of the East Bronx–girl mindset—street, but not desperate; unpretentious, and a little naïve. "The video was like when I was living in the Bronx, young girl, just outta high school, with her friends, you don't have a care in the world, that day you wake up and everything's going right. It's sunny outside, your mother made you what you wanted for breakfast, you go outside and find a twenty-dollar bill on the floor, the train is on time. Then that night you're going out with your friends, you've been looking forward to it all week, you get out of work early, that outfit you wanted was on sale, that top you want, all that stuff. That's what the song is about, enjoying the little things, because those are the important things. There's nothing more important than your happiness. You can have all the money in the world, all the materialistic things, all the diamonds, all the ice, everything, everyone can know you, and you can be the most miserable person in the world."

Jennifer now has all the diamonds, all the ice, and she's freeing herself from the relatively tight grip her family had on her. Her involvement with Puff Daddy represents her feeling of freedom to go with a man that delighted her Bronx girl fantasies. The prince of hip-hop may have a sleazy side, but any Bronx girl knows her hero is destined to be flawed—he has to show heart through being hard, and surviving a world of guns. No way he would survive the Bronx without heart. Besides, hiphop aesthetic preaches that the gangsta way is the grim reality of political rebellion for the young male of color from the inner city.

Still, the most compelling evidence for Jennifer's loyalty to Puffy is his central position in the development of contemporary mainstream hiphop, a story that many Latinos are not aware of. Combs was the producer behind the meteoric careers of Mary J. Blige, who was instrumental in bridging r&b and women's tastes with hiphop, and Biggie Smalls, a.k.a. Notorious B.I.G., who was widely acknowledged as New York hiphop's poet laureate. Combs had a major hand in creating the ultimate symbol of new jack, woman-oriented hip-hop soul and the rapper with the best heart-credibility in the business. Puffy and Jennifer are so alike—city kids with large ambitions who have reached the top of their game. The bulk of the reaction against their relationship is evidence of a veiled racism among New York Latinos, and Lopez's loyalty to him, apart from a demonstration of a sincere sexual and emotional attraction, owes to her Spanglish creativity in inventing a Bronx girl hiphop persona. It's no accident that she broke into show business as a "Fly Girl" dancer for one of the '90s most successful black-oriented TV shows, *In Living Color*.

Still the most obvious manifestation of Lopez's Spanglish sensibility is the way she chose to put together *On the 6*. Despite the fact that the Latin pop explosion she had prepared her album to burst out of was primarily focused on conventional pop and tropical Latin beats, Lopez chose to create a hybrid fusion she called "Latin soul." "I knew I had to combine many elements in a way that is unique and different," Lopez told me. "And I think it still needs to evolve. Right now I would define it as pop music with influences of Latin and r&b music, urban."

Lopez grew up in the Bronx during the early stages of hip-hop and urban contemporary pop. At any time, her CD player could be stocked with singers like Diana Ross, Madonna, and Luther Vandross, as well as rappers like Nas. By adding just the right touch of Latin rhythms to this r&b mix, utilizing the talents of Roney, Combs, and Gloria Estefan's husband and producer, Emilio, *On the 6*'s Latin soul sound can potentially receive airplay on several different radio formats. Regardless of its quality, which many reviewers felt was mediocre, *On the 6* is one of the first Spanglish records ever made that hybridizes late '90s' styles, going beyond Latin-influenced fusions like salsa and *bugaloo*, and creating an American-influenced Spanglish style that gives predominance to African-American "urban" aesthetics.

But Lopez is first and foremost an actress, the signifier of the big ass that is safer for white consumption than an African-American butt; the quasi–Native American/Mexican with the crooked nose that sucks in Sean Penn in Oliver Stone's *U-Turn*; the possessor of Selena's soul. Jennifer Lopez is such a good actress that her authenticity is seamless, airtight, almost to the point of not being there anymore, of dissolving into a next scene that never fades up.

As I write this, there are still no major Latino film stars besides Lopez, unless you want to count Jimmy Smits, who for a few years was a major television icon. Although Smits is a pleasant enough presence, and goes out of his way to identify with Latinos, he doesn't really have that major Hollywood impact. Including half-Cuban Cameron Diaz is a little bit of a stretch, especially since she has yet to play roles that make reference to this, and she rarely approaches the public with any significant display of her Latino identity. Directors like Gregory Nava (*Mi Familia, Selena*), and Miguel Arteta (*Star Maps*) have contributed to the Latino film canon but have yet to make a truly significant film. Because of the enormous cost of producing films and the rigid, formulaic approach that seems to be the only way to get a film made, the Latino *farán-*

dula is destined to remain dispersed and fragmented until an extraordinarily talented filmmaker comes along.

For a moment, with *El Mariachi*, it looked like Robert Rodriguez would be it, and he's gone on to ultra-violent sci-fi, and most recently, sophisticated children's film with *Spy Kids* in 2001 (significantly, this film has a largely Latino cast). It must be admitted that when, in 2000, two films about Latinos in boxing premiered, the one directed by Latinos *(Price of Glory)* was vastly inferior to the one directed by an "Anglo" *(Girlfight)*. But as long as Hollywood demands strong racial types that can be played up by actors who aren't Latino, such as Jeffrey Wright's Dominican drug dealer in *Shaft*, the Spanglish star will remain obscured by his or her multiple possibilities.

Toward the end of 2000, Hollywood was increasingly looking toward Spanglish and Latin America for subject matter, with mostly disappointing results. Movies like *Proof of Life* and *Blow* maintain Colombia's horrific image as a kidnap-crazy, druglord-wracked country. Even though there is truth to the nightmares still going on in that South American country, these movies are dotted with cartoon roles for the locals and the heroic victimization for North Americans, ignoring the fact that it is Colombians who are the biggest losers. *The Mexican* revives the sleepy-eyed but dangerous, dark bandit types that *Treasure of Sierra Madre* made famous. We are still waiting for a breakthrough, perhaps by someone like Spaniard Penelope Cruz, who does a little bit of spitfire reviving herself in *Blow*, to stay the fate of the Spanglish chameleon—to fade into the background of the multimillion-dollar sets and celluloid dreams that cloud southern California and Manhattan.

Clearly, the evolution of the Spanglish face in American cinema from Al Pacino's rabid, bug-eyed Tony Montana to Jennifer Lopez's cool, chameleonlike Karen Sisco is a welcome development. To see Montana on the screen, as a Cuban American, for a Latino is a kind of unsettling experience in which you recognize yourself, but it's not you at all. It's like a bad dream when a version of yourself is acting in the dream, but you are quite clear that it isn't you. The you is so externalized as to produce an uncertainty of who you are. But Lopez, who is at once African American, a New Yorker, possibly Italian, or vaguely Latina, most of all a princess, is much closer to what we are. She allows the Spanglish subject to exist on a comfortable continuum of possibilities, from the schoolgirl that voyeuristically sees her on a computer screen during the video of "If You Had My Love," to an insurance salesman that sees his daughter, or lover. When she appears with Ja Rule, singing "I'm Real," for which she was criticized as an outsider uttering the word "nigger," you know that she is, in fact, real.

5.

LA MÚSICA:

The Essence of Spanglish

Oye como va
Mi ritmo?
Bueno pa' gozar
Mulata
    —TITO PUENTE

It's that song that you hear when the basic notion of whatever Latin music is pops into your head. The rhythmic keyboard pattern played on piano by Puente's band, electric organ by Santana's, puts a swagger in your step: "Dat-dat, dat DAT, dat-dat, dat-DAT." You feel the swing inside you. The music of Spanglish culture is the unrestrained yet perfectly plotted expression of the Spanglish body. It is the easiest way to identify yourself as Spanglish, because those chords, because those codes, because those clave rhythms are a rite of passage.

With the death of Tito Puente in June of 2000, an extremely significant historical path for Latin music was revealed for everyone to see. While it was something that was not in the front of everyone's consciousness, it was a kind of shared subliminal knowledge about Spanglish pop history. The year 1999 had seen the rise of Latin pop in the mainstream American consciousness through the unexpected success of Ricky Martin, Jennifer Lopez, and Marc Anthony. As the year drew to a close, most people were schooling themselves in Latin music, convincing themselves they had known about it all along, had been paying attention from "La Bamba" through "Bang Bang," and on to Santana. In fact, it was the stunning ascension of Santana, whose career had been dead in the water, to the top of the pop pile that seemed to convince everyone, especially doubters, of the validity of the matinee idol excesses of Martin, Lopez, or Enrique Iglesias.

With the sudden reemergence of Santana, the historical link between him and Tito Puente through the song "Oye Como Va" was revisited, albeit with little understanding of its significance as a parable of miscegenation. Like many Cuban-derived mambos, "Oye Como Va" contained lyrics that made reference to the miscegenation between Spanish-identified creoles and African or indigenous women. "How's my rhythm going?" the song's narrator asks. "It's good enough to have fun with, *mulata*," he responds. The key word in that verse is "*mulata*," the object of the narrator's desire. In many Afro-Cuban songs, the singer expresses a sentimental fondness for the sexual excitement he derives from either a purer African woman or a "mulata," a woman of mixed-race who retains African physical characteristics.

The preponderance of sexual activity between colonizing Spaniards and African and indigenous women in Latin America accounts for the most significant differences between Anglo-American and Latin-American culture. While much of this sexual contact resulted from rape, there were many consensual unions, eventually leading to a broadly based mestizo/mulatto population that contained the seeds of Spanglish culture in North America. When Tito Puente or Carlos Santana sing "Oye Como Va" they are retelling the story, which is the literalization of the music they are playing.

You can hear that basic Afro-Cuban swing most clearly in the way the piano sets a rhythmic pace that is a signal to the hips to begin to sway. The percussion established by congas and timbales propel movement of the lower body in a particular motion, and then, and only then, do the horns, strings, or reeds embellish the whole proposition with a warm, semi-erotic melody. Afro-Cuban music is dance music, designed for a legion of proficient dancers who absorb this artful form of body expression from generations of tradition. The Latin dance tradition is one of the most central to the evolution of Spanglish culture in the U.S.

One of the most obvious place to see the evidence of Spanglish is on the dance floor. Latin dance is a visually elegant syncretism of elements from Europe (the French contredanse), America (big band jazz), and Africa (rumba). The creative site of the dance is one that has no racial or class hierarchy, and a great deal of social meaning. Fittingly, it is a performance of movement that is as kinetically stimulating and complex as anything you'll see in the postmodern world. The sleek dark clothes whipping in all directions as the feet move in chaotic precision. The lead steps back and the follower spins ecstatically. The beat is almost always syncopated and threatening to jump out of itself. Bodies press together tightly despite whatever standing relationship preexisted. The starting place is never the same as the destination. When the final notes drop off the edge of the drummer's cymbal, the dancer is filled with the dizzying rush of having undergone a quick, highly pleasurable metamorphosis.

The centrality of ballroom dancing to U.S. culture in the '40s and '50s provided a crucial entry point for Spanglish culture at a time when immigration from Latin America was becoming increasingly significant. Latin music arrived in America as the soundtrack for the new dance that would amuse people who were hungering for life after the fox-trot or the lindy. Long before Americans began flocking to Mexican restaurants to eat tacos and nachos, they were trying their hand at the latest "exotic" dance from South of the Border: the cha-cha, the rumba, or the mambo.

Although the first rumblings of Afro-Cuban music were heard in North America in movie soundtracks of the '30s—old stars like gangster icon George Raft danced rumbas in the postsilent era—the impact of Latin music was first felt strongly in the early '50s, when the mambo began filtering up from Mexico. Ironically, the mambo was developed in Mexico City by a Cuban musician named Damaso Pérez Prado, who began to mix North American swing and bebop influences with traditional Cuban swing.

Unsurprisingly, Pérez Prado's music hasn't survived the scrutiny of Latin music purists very well; he has been attacked by several for his music's lack of authenticity and its simplicity, in addition to its pandering to American uncouthness. It's the kind of Latin music that one might remember apes playing in the old Ernie Kovacs skit; Prado's beats flow in a kind of jerky, awkward meter, and his pauses are exaggerated and often punctuated by a kind of frat house–inspired grunt. Prado was an eccentric who admired Stravinsky; his music was a kind of flat disarticulation of a music that was beyond most Americans.

Prado's mambo was a deconstruction and reduction of traditional Afro-Cuban music. It stripped away much of its formal structure and left it an improvisational shell of itself. This allowed elements like an expanded horn section to play sardonic melodies, as well as leaving spaces for Pérez Prado's demented yelps. By 1955, Pérez Prado had scored the first Number 1 charting hit in Latin music's history in the U.S. with an album called *Cherry Pink, Apple Blossom White*. During this period he also recorded "Mambo No. 5," which recently became a top ten hit for Lou Bega, a Sicilian of African descent. Pérez Prado's dominance in the U.S., alongside Cubans Desi Arnaz and Xavier Cugat, were examples of Spanglish's growing pains.

But there was another, more profound force working behind

the scenes of American music history that would create the most significant entry of Spanglish into this country's popular music tradition. It was personified by Mario Bauzá, an intensely proud Cuban of African descent who came to New York in the '30s. Bauzá was a classically trained member of the Havana Philharmonic who realized on an earlier tour of the U.S. that two strands of musical tradition had come to the New World from the Yoruban culture of West Africa. One was the basis of Afro-Cuban music, and the other had ended up in New Orleans and greatly affected the development of jazz and blues.

When Bauzá came to the U.S., he began playing with American bandleaders like Chick Webb—he did a fairly well known clarinet solo on a recording of "Stompin' at the Savoy." But he began to change the jazz world when he, and his fellow Cuban expatriate, the percussionist Chano Pozo, began to teach Dizzy Gillespie's band Afro-Cuban techniques, including composing melodic lines for brass instruments from Yoruban ritual drum patterns.

According to the late musicologist Robert Palmer, Bauzá's influence was primarily responsible for the development of most of the transitions American music has gone through since World War II—from swing to modern jazz; rhythm and blues to rock and roll; rhythm and blues to funk. Dizzy Gillespie described going out on the town with Bauzá in the late '30s to hear Cuban bands. Gillespie heard the bassists playing short, broken-up patterns, which he adapted for his famous song, "A Night in Tunisia," one of the first jazz songs with a strong Latin feel. Gillespie insisted that those same bass patterns provided the basis for modern-day funk music.

Rumba patterns from Cuba have since been credited as the rhythmic basis for tunes by early rock and roll artists like Fats Domino, Lloyd Price, and Little Richard, and according to the composer of one of the acknowledged all-time classics of rock and roll, "Louie Louie," an obscure Cuban cha-cha record was that song's main inspiration. The lack of currency of this theory undoubtedly stems from the fragility of the American ego to accept outside influences in the development of its popular music. It was enough for Americans to stubbornly admit, and finally embrace, the contributions, or actually, the dominance of African Americans in the development of U.S. popular music, and it feeds the primacy of the White Negro argument to view things this way.

Even if North Americans were willing to accept that the Afro-Cuban influence was significant, it might still be viewed as a historical accident caused by immigration and the penetration of a "foreign" culture. But the influence of Afro-Cuban music is an organic one, most likely caused by a nineteenth-century historical event. The first declaration of independence from Europe following the one in North America occurred in Haiti, and as a result, many Spanish sugar entrepreneurs moved with their slaves to two different destinations: New Orleans and western Cuba.

So Bauzá's rapport with Gillespie was merely the rejoining of two urban African (American) men that reunited two lost musical tribes separated by the diaspora. But perhaps the most significant element of what Bauzá brought to America was a renewed emphasis of the clave rhythm, a five-beat pulse that most Americans recognize as "the Bo Diddley beat." If that's not a clear enough reference, try The Grateful Dead's "Not Fade Away." At any rate, the clave beat turns out to be not entirely of African origin. The rhythm has been traced back to the Gypsys of southern Spain, who may have picked it up from the Moors emigrating from northern Africa, or somewhere along the way in their travels from northern India.

While there was a significant penetration of Afro-Cuban music into the West Coast jazz style, most notably through Cuban expatriate Mongo Santamaria and his partnership with arranger/bandleader Cal Tjader, the main Spanglish fusion that was going on in California had to do with r&b and rock and roll. David Reyes and Tom Waldman's book *Land of a Thousand Dances* tells of the preponderance of doo wop and soul groups in Southern California that were racially mixed and often dominated by Chicano musicians.

Mexican Americans have always been huge supporters of r&b music, and to this day, '50s oldies are still worshipped by the lowrider types in a way that exceeds the interest of any other group, including African Americans. There were many groups—most notably Cannibal and the Headhunters, who made a successful version of "Land of a Thousand Dances"—that played venues like El Monte Legion Stadium and established an audience that would become crucial to the development of California's rock audience. This audience development may be the Chicanos' most important legacy in that state's music history. While discussions of Ritchie Valens dominate the history of this era, it's not as well known that Valens's successful years on Tom Keane's Del-Fi label created the financial capital for that label's later success with surf music.

While Afro-Cuban music had a clear influence on the development of rock and roll, the Mexican American influence on "Louie Louie," a song that is often cited as containing the essence of rock's primal energy, is again one of the key moments in the genre's history. The most famous version of the song was done by a Seattle group called the Kingsmen, but the original is credited to Richard Berry, a graduate of Jefferson High School in South Central L.A. in the early '50s. Berry was a doo wop–turned-rocker who was becoming heavily influenced by Afro-Cuban music when he wrote "Louie Louie." He said in published interviews that the song was derived from Rene Touzet's "Loco Cha Cha," and his original plan for recording it included using Afro-Cuban percussion such as timbales and congas, but the producer turned him down. The five-note vamp that runs through the song is played on an electric organ, resembling the son clave, 1-2-3, 1-2, and the song progresses through tumbao figures that are strongly reminiscent of Afro-Cuban music.

Berry's band, an early rock band, was ethnically mixed, including blacks, Latinos, and Filipinos. In fact, the late avant-garde rocker Frank Zappa began his career in several such bands, and was said to have stolen money from his father to buy a ticket to a Ritchie Valens show in El Monte Legion Stadium. Posted in the liner notes of Zappa's first album, *Freak Out*, which appeared in 1964 and is widely acknowledged as the first avant-garde rock record, is the following slogan: "The present-day Pachuco refuses to die."

The rock–Mexican American crossover occurred in an era when Chicanos became the first audience to assimilate black and white tastes simultaneously, before blacks and whites themselves actually did. Their love for soul reflected a level of assimilation that Puerto Ricans and Cubans in New York wouldn't attain until the '60s, and their interest in rock probably evolved from the traditional mariachi and *norteño* music they listened to at home, which sometimes featured electric guitars. The Spanglish cultural fusion that was going on with Mexican Americans in California and the Southwest would create the longest-running rock scene dominated by Latinos in the U.S., producing several Chicano bands and strongly influencing the development of punk rock in Los Angeles in the late '70s.

Afro-Cuban music thrived in New York, and to a lesser extent, in Los Angeles, through the '50s and '60s, then retreated into the status of an extremely popular ethnic music in the '70s and '80s, only to reemerge in the '90s as a bona fide "American" music. In clubs like the Palladium, Roseland, and the Copacabana, there were continuous revues in which musicians like Cuban expatriates Chico O'Farrill and Bauzá's brother-in-law Machito played to a wild mix of ethnic audiences. In the '50s, a sharp competition emerged between Puerto Rican bandleaders Tito Puente and Tito Rodríguez, with Puente winning out in the end, as

Rodríguez went to Miami and his homeland to become a pop-ballad singer.

Born and raised in East Harlem, Puente brought a special street edge that could be qualified as Nuyorican. As a percussionist, he brought the timbales to a position of great prominence, nurturing its high-pitched, sharp striking sound as the punctuation of Spanglish street slang. Puente emerged from an East Harlem that was brimming with cultural exchange; fellow New York native Joe Cuba (Gilberto Miguel Calderón), who would create the first Latin/r&b fusion music in the '60s, *bugaloo*, would play with Cuban expatriates Patato Valdez and another fellow Cuban, Changuito, who eventually returned to the island to play with what some call Fidel Castro's house band, Los Van Van, and future West Coast percussionist Willie Bobo.

The creator of the first million-selling Latin music hit, Joe Cuba pioneered *bugaloo*, an r&b/salsa hybrid that uses occasional English lyrics and had a crossover success. One of the first-generation New York Puerto Rican musicians, Cuba grew up in East Harlem and learned to play music with peers like Patato Valdez, Changuito, and jazz percussionist Willie Bobo. Cuba began his career in the '50s by taking over leadership in the Joe Panama Quintet, renaming it the Joe Cuba Sextet. Members of the old Panama crew had been experimenting with the use of English lyrics, and the Cuba edition continued this tendency, expanding their audience by playing Jewish and Italian dances. The Sextet's first big success was a hit single, "El Pito (I'll Never Go Back to Georgia)", but they'll be forever remembered for "Bang! Bang!" one of the most significant top forty Latin hits since Ritchie Valens's "La Bamba." It was a moment when the feeling of Latin music fused with an African-American sensibility—the chorus was simply "Cornbread, hog maw, and chitlins."

The New York scene was known for its featuring of the popular dance form mambo, but it became the breeding ground for wide-ranging developments in Latin jazz, and ultimately the controversially named "salsa." Salsa, of course, is one of those quintessential words that express the idea of Spanglish; it literally means "sauce," which includes whatever ingredients are handy at the time. As a result of the Cuban revolution, New York musicians lost touch with developments in Cuba, and a specifically Nuyorican and Nuyo-Cuban culture began to emerge. Musicians like percussionist Ray Barretto and trombonist Willie Colón, whose experiences were primarily forged by a new urban identity, began to make music that reflected the reality of the shock of immigration. Many of these musicians were signed to Fania, a label owned by an Italian American entrepreneur named Jerry Masucci.

The Fania label became the Motown of salsa music by monopolizing most of the emerging talent: Fania All Stars shows of the '70s were the most dazzling displays of a music that was reaching maturity at the same time that the Young Lords and the FALN were inciting militant insurrection in the streets. At the center of the Fania movement was Willie Colón, who, like Puente, moved his instrument to the front and center of the stage. Colón's band always had the most impressive salsa singer, or *sonero,* beginning with Hector Lavoe. Lavoe had emigrated to New York from Puerto Rico in the early '60s, bringing with him the styles of island singers like Bobby Capó and Ismael Rivera. Colón was one of the first to experiment with rhythms from Panama, Colombia, and Brazil to produce several innovative dance floor hits.

The teaming up of Colón and Lavoe was electric. It was a fusion of traditionalism and modernity—one presaged by the great Puerto Rican musician Rafael Cortijo in his modernization of the folkloric beat, the *bomba.* Lavoe brought the soul of a forgotten rural point of view and Colón the cutting edge of the street intellectual, looking to make his music American and international. During this period Cuban expatriates Johnny Pacheco, an influential songwriter, and Celia Cruz, who would become the genre's most celebrated female vocalist, would also galvanize the New

York public that was beginning to become conscious of itself as a Spanglish culture.

The Golden Age of Salsa climaxed after Hector Lavoe, troubled by health and drug problems, had to leave Colón's band. In 1975, Lavoe's spot was taken by Panamanian *sonero* Rubén Blades. Blades, who went on to become a major solo star and has even put together an impressive Hollywood film career, was a fascinating figure in that he "passed" for a Nuyorican even though he was from a relatively middle-class family in Panama and did graduate studies in law at Harvard. He had a passion for the great *soneros* of Puerto Rico, and Panama has a similar colonial relationship with the U.S. But Blades got deep into the city's heartbeat, starting out as a stock boy with Fania Records and prowling New York clubs like the Corso, the Village Gate, and Casino 14 like any Nuyorican.

His collaboration with Colón yielded some of the classic recordings of the period, most notably *Siembra*, which became a staple for a generation of socially conscious Spanglish New Yorkers. Blades and Colón had become the Lennon and McCartney of salsa, an unprecedented team that produced groundbreaking songs. *Siembra* included "Pedro Navaja," a kind of barrio reworking of *Threepenny Opera's* "Mack the Knife," and "Plástico," a song that warned against the evils of the materialist Caliban culture of the North. "Pedro Navaja" became the "Stairway to Heaven" of salsa, the most requested song of the genre, because it reveled in street storytelling and ultimately climaxed with a roll call of nations that called for Spanglish unity. The chanting of Latin American country names has become a fixture in salsa concerts to this day.

In the early '80s, Blades and Colón went their separate ways, with Blades becoming highly successful and crossing over as a "world music" performer and acting in over fifteen films alongside the likes of Jack Nicholson and Harrison Ford. In Cuban Leon Ichaso's film, *Crossover Dreams*, he played a character of a less successful singer. *Crossover Dreams* is perhaps the most significant

159

Spanglish film of the '80s because it portrays the pain of assimilation and the no-turning-back to hyphenated hopes stage of New York salsa culture. Ichaso is a Spanglish bohemian, a Nuyo-Cubano Miami transplant from Washington Heights; a kind of hippie nephew to the protagonist of Hijuelos's *Mambo Kings*, he has taken on the task of documenting the cultural milieu of the Fania era. Although it was a very effective, poignant film, it was a little ironic because it represented the paranoia Blades may have felt in leaving his tight-knit salsa community behind. In 1996, he made an unsuccessful run for president of Panama and has always remained politically active.

For part of the '90s, Colón was bitter about the breakup and seemed to try to match Blades move for move. He acted in TV ads and Mexican soap operas and even ran for state senator in the Bronx. When I first interviewed him in a back room of the Fania offices he jokingly drew a gun and pointed it at me when I asked about Rubén Blades. But as the decade drew to a close, the two reunited to record a nostalgia CD, called a truce, and continued their roles as keepers of the tradition.

As the '70s ended, Spanglish culture was thoroughly invading the American musics of the postwar and post–civil rights era, rock and roll, and hip-hop. There had always been a Latin sound in rock and roll, from the Beatles' ballads to their covering of the Isleys' "Twist and Shout," to Love's "Back Again" (which was covered by the late Selena's husband Chris Perez in a 1999 album), to the Doors' "Break on Through to the Other Side," a weird overlapping of bossa nova and clave rhythm. In fact, one of the purest Latin rock stylings ever was done by the blind Puerto Rican singer Jose Feliciano when he covered the Doors' "Light My Fire." (Ironically, Feliciano was the first musician, well before Jimi Hendrix, who performed rock-inflected version of "The Star Spangled Banner," a very '60s phenomenon.)

Rock history is dotted with a list of participants and folklore that cry out in Spanglish epithets. Obvious examples are the Spanish-descended Jerry Garcia and The Grateful Dead's use of clave on "Not Fade Away" (a song by Buddy Holly, who died in a plane crash with Ritchie Valens); Stevie Wonder's "Don't You Worry 'Bout a Thing," in which he actually engages in Spanglish, rattling off several cool slang words, including "chevere" which was the Spanglish equivalent of "groovy"; and Steely Dan's "The Royal Scam," which sang the praises of the noble underdog role of Nuyoricans in Manhattan.

But there were other, less obvious manifestations of Spanglish in rock history. Redbone, who had a '70s pop-rock hit, "Come and Get Your Love," often appeared in Native-American garb, but were really Chicanos. "?" and the Mysterians, another Chicano group, this time from Detroit, had a huge hit with "96 Tears," another primitive rock song that many critics have identified as seminal to the punk aesthetic. The original lead singer of Black Flag, which became one of Los Angeles's major contributions to hard-core punk, was Ron Reyes, a rare L.A. Puerto Rican. The invention of the scissors-cut holes in T-shirts, a London and New York punk staple, was attributed to a Puerto Rican tailor named Frenchy who accompanied the New York Dolls on a European tour. "Blitzkrieg Bop," one of the Ramones' signature tunes, is a dead ringer for Ritchie Valens's "Come On Let's Go." Even the "artistic director" of the Ramones, the man who designed their famous pseudo-military logo was Chihuahua, Mexico-born Arturo Vega. The lead guitarist of Roxy Music, one of London's seminal post-glam, modern rock bands, was Phil Manzanera, of Colombian descent, who was raised English.

But the most important Latin rocker was Santana, who is still the only musician to successfully combine Afro-Cuban rhythms with rock instrumentation. He was a key icon for the Spanglish flock that was drawn to the counterculture, and his performances were among the best of the classic rock bands. Although Santana is a spectacular instrumentalist, he's not a great songwriter, and didn't have that narrative voice that made a significant impact in an era of singer/songwriters wielding electric guitars. While Santana did bring "Oye Como Va" to the hippie hordes, perhaps his biggest influence was on kids growing up in Latin America who would begin to play an entirely new Spanglish hybrid of rock music. Santana was a transnational migrant himself; he wandered from the border-town circus of Tijuana to Oakland, California. Living in a town with a large African-American community was a major influence on his adoption of Afro-Cuban rhythm (unusual for a Mexican American) as his musical base. When he hooked up with Bill Graham's countercultural machine in neighboring San Francisco, Santana successfully hybridized New York salsa and California acid rock, and solidified his place as an immortal in pop music history.

Santana was one of the few rock groups that built a bridge between Spanglish culture and the post–White Negro countercul-ture. But after he disappeared into the relative obscurity of the jazz fusion world of the '70s, Latin rock also disappeared. Growing up Puerto Rican in New York, the capital of salsa, or Miami, the home of tropical pop, often entails a ban on listening to rock music. But in the early '90s, Latin America began to internalize the rock music that was coming in from the North, rework it to reflect its own reality, and make a music that was every bit as exciting as someone like Hendrix or the seminal punk rockers, the Clash. Led by Chicanos and recent Mexican immigrants to the West Coast, Spanglish Americans were ready to rock again. The first waves were from places like Argentina, which began to make its own rock music when it stopped listening to the British after the Falk-lands War, and from Spain.

Metal/punk groups like Heroes del Silencio and La Ultima Fila, from Spain, and Charly Garcia and Soda Stereo, from Argentina, made a small splash in New York and Los Angeles, but the phenomenon of rock *en español* didn't start making a loud noise until the Mexican bands arrived: Groups like Maldita Vecindad y los del Quinto Patio, manipulated images of punk pachucos and became iconographic representations of urban, lower-class, indigenous solidarity. In a spectacle as astonishing as the early days of hip-hop, swarms of brown-skinned slamdancers could be seen in an L.A. mosh pit, writhing to various forms of art-rock, ska, psychedelic, alternative, gothic, metal, punk, and power pop.

The phenomenon of rock music in Mexico has extremely important implications for Latin rock across the Americas, and, more significantly, the way American pop culture impacts Third World nations around the world. As summarized in his book *Refried Elvis: The Rise of the Mexican Counterculture*, Eric Zolov asserts that rock music in Mexico acted as a kind of antidote to the contradictions of the national culture created in the wake of the 1910 Mexican Revolution. The Revolution, which used Vasconcelos's Cosmic Race myth to unify disparate groups in various sectors of the country under one "revolutionary family," was exposed by an interloping rock popular culture that placed a premium on intergenerational conflict. The ruling party's corruption was shockingly symbolized in its role of assassin in 1968 when it ordered Mexico City police to fire into a crowd of student protestors in an effort to rid the city of messy protests on the eve of the Olympic Games that summer. That incident made rock music, at first just an exuberant challenge to the patriarchal morality of the ruling government, into a major symbol of defiance against corruption and the PRI's dictatorial status, something that came to a head when it was finally voted out of office just as Mexican rock, which had been illegal for most of the '70s and '80s, was flourishing.

In 1992, I made a pilgrimage to Mexico City and trekked to the Teotihuacán pyramids for my first time-traveling experience. Built over seven hundred years ago, the pyramids were the center of a pre-Columbian city that in its day was the largest city in the Western Hemisphere, bigger than many European cities. It was the kind of place that every Casteñada-addled hippie who ever went on too long in a college dorm pot party was always trying to explain. The sky was a mixture of grays, reds, and neon blue, sometimes congealing into a kind of lavender. Clouds were rolling in from the west, and bolts of lightning flashed in patterns that suggested a kind of symbolic communication.

The legends about the ritual human sacrifice at Teotihuacán made me susceptible to imagining traveling back in time and almost feeling the pain and suffering, cries and moans of the victims in the plaza below. I imagined myself seeding the clouds that hovered over the Avenida de los Muertos (Street of the Dead) and felt myself seeping into the soil. I wondered what the hell was going on, but it isn't every day someone offers you an out-of-body experience. I left with the smell of the damp earth permeating me, making me feel like I did when I spent time at my grandfather's house in Puerto Rico.

The Teotihuacán experience had penetrated me so that I made a shrine on my bulletin board with photos of the pyramids. Then I got a couple of CDs in the mail by a Mexican rock group called Caifanes, a major seller in their country with a large following in Los Angeles. At first it seemed Caifanes had a derivative Cure-ish, U2-ish sound but somehow there was a palpable sincerity to frontman Saul Hernández's feline yowls, and an eerie continuity of darkness in his lyrics.

Somewhere around the third listen to *El Diablito*, their second album, something clicked when I unconsciously translated these lyrics to "Antes de que Nos Olviden" (Before You Forget Us): "We'll ascend into the heavens/And come down with the rain." It was almost the same image suggested by my friend at the pyramids. I remembered imagining being transformed into raindrops and falling from the pregnant clouds. Despite the spacey experience I had with it, the song had a deeply political content. "That song is about the student protesters who were killed in Mexico City in 1968 by the national police, about how their souls watch over us," Hernández would tell me a few days before Caifanes' first appearance in New York in 1993. The massacre took place because the growing student movement in Mexico was perceived by government authorities as tarnishing the capital city's image, something they didn't want to happen on the verge of the 1968 Olympic Games to be held there. In the U.S., student movements were repressed systematically, and the '60s counterculture was absorbed into the language and reality of multinational capitalism. In Mexico, it was simply forced underground. Now, twenty-five years later, amid NAFTA and the Zapatistas, it was all coming back.

But while it is easy to diminish the importance of rock *en español* by referring to its seeming "copying" of North American and European rock styles, what impressed me about Caifanes and other groups is the way they are understood as products of a syncretism that is central to Mexican culture. It's a kind of syncretism that is parallel to the creation of Afro-Cuban Santería, in which Yoruban deities are worshipped in the guise of Catholic saints. It's the same kind of syncretism that in turn allows the mestizo-dominant Mexican mainstream to unite behind the Virgin of Guadalupe as a kind of historical cultural leader.

On my second trip to Mexico City, I went to Chapultepec Park to see a free concert by La Castañeda. The show was one of a series commemorating the October 2 anniversary of the '68 student massacre. La Castañeda is a concept band, one of a new generation that formed in art schools, their consciousness raised by the events of the mid-'80s. Their name is derived from the main asylum in Mexico City during the reign of dictator Porfirio Díaz. Some kept in its walls were lunatics, others just enemies of Díaz. Affiliated with a group of performing artists under the rubric of Garra Productions, La Castañeda creates a catharsis by suggesting the escape of "lunatics" from the asylum.

Salvador of La Castañeda takes the stage with a gaggle of performers, insects on stilts, green-skinned women wearing papier-mâché sculptures of bashed-up TV sets on their heads, others wearing oversize Ubu-Roi style masks. Barking out the lyrics of "Contra Las Profecías" in his oddly affecting husky voice, Salvador counsels, "The apocalypse shouldn't penetrate you/The world is ending and we have to/Go against the prophecies!" Then he takes a long stick and proceeds to smash it against an oil drum, placed strategically at center stage, in time to the music.

The crowd, which had been engaged in a mad-mosh singalong up to this point, appeared to fly upward on to the stage, until there were about forty kids swarming around the band. I remember what a member of Maldita Vecindad told me about Mexican slamming: "It's a loving, festive act. We joke that slamdancing comes from weddings when after the groom is spun around by his extremities and they catch him. It's a communion of bodies, individuality is broken, and it becomes a collective feast." The heaving, pogoing mass of brown-skinned kids, the bright red and yellow flags of the sponsoring student league swirl together and suggest a vaguely Situationist vibe—is this what London looked like in '77?

Mexico, like much of Latin America, has historically looked to Europe for cultural models; it is not unusual for children of middle- to upper-class Mexicans to spend a year in Paris studying. The educational system values the plastic arts much more than the U.S. does, and this sort of art appreciation seems to combine with deep-seated indigenous traditions of ritual and ceremony. Afterward, when I asked Salvador why there's so much performance art going on in Mexican rock, he explained, "It's part of the genetic syncretism of Mexican culture. It's a deep-rooted tendency, a sentiment of ritual and ceremony, a possibility of integrating different forms of expression in one context." The syncretism they refer to, the constant acknowledgment of the debt Mexican culture has to its indigenous people, owes to the legacy of José Vasconcelos, who after writing *La raza cósmica*, became the man in charge of Mexico's entire educational system, as well as institutionalizing the Mexican muralist tradition.

The habit of simultaneously processing different cultures in Latin America anticipated postmodern pastiche and recycling to the point where it could be affirmed that Latin American culture . . . was in some ways postmodern before the First World, a pre-postmodernity so to speak."

—CELESTE OLALQUIAGA, *Megalopolis*

When the Mexican band Café Tacuba released their 1993 album, *Re,* the quintessential style of Latin alternative materialized. While Tacuba's first album was mostly ballads and hyperactive ska/*norteño, Re* is a smorgasbord that synthesizes Afro-Cuban, traditional Mexican, hardcore punk, classic rock, soul, disco, and even Trio Los Panchos. The most telling song on the album is "El Borrego," featuring noisy, almost Nine Inch Nails distorto-riff backing a hardcore rant about the conformity of nonconformity—a Mexican teen proclaims several contradictory political and cultural loyalties ("I am an anarchist/I'm a neonazi/I'm a skinhead/I'm an environmentalist/I'm a capitalist/I'm a pacifist"). But the kicker of this song is a simple declaration at the end: "At shows, the slam is the thing/But at home I kick the tropical." This stunningly contradictory announcement sums up the essence of Spanglish culture that is now slowly beginning to take hold of U.S. Latino youth. The "bohemian," "hipster," post–White Negro culture that is necessary for initiation into Anglo America is merely a possibility for a Spanglish kid, who is permanently grounded in his own hybrid culture, his own hybrid music, which was created more than half a century ago to reconcile racial differences.

By 1995, a night in a downtown New York club could look like this: A Venezuelan light-skinned rude boy wearing a shimmering maroon sports jacket, festooned with a sneering jester logo, flanked by an Afro-Venezuelan in dashiki and full-blown Hendrix 'do on guitar, and a Chinese-Venezuelan bass player, bobbing her head to her plucked beats, while a Dominican drummer cymbal-and-snares the odd soca-ska punctuations with a manic grin splitting his face. The vocalist draws his megaphone to his lips and shouts "Jump! Jump!" as his band, King Chango, lurches into its signature tune, "Latin Ska." The crowd—an unlikely conflagration of Azteco-long-locked metalheads, Dominican pseudo-B-boys, and langorous blond Argentine babes swathed in oversize blue-and-white-striped soccer shirts—obeys without hesitation.

> *Hybridity is dynamic, mobile, less an achieved synthesis of prescribed formulas than an unstable constellation of discourses.*
>
> —ROBERT STAMM AND ELLA SHOHAT,
> *Unthinking Eurocentrism*

"I used to love Kiss, I used to hate *cumbia* and *vallenato* (Colombian traditional music)," says Andrew Blanco, Venezuelan national and lead vocalist for King Chango, the first Latin alternative band signed by David Byrne's Luaka Bop records. "But now I'm into everything—ska, reggae, perico ripiao (Dominican genres) merengue, *bachata*, salsa. My mom is from Brazil, you know, and so I like samba, too." Blanco was part of a scene in New York that is about how the variety of race eventually makes race meaningless. In between sets on the dance floor, metalkids and flannelkids bop to Caifanes, then the DJ shifts gears with "El Trago," a hip-hop/ house club stomp by Two in a Room, which features bilingual rapping, and some B-boys flow to the fore. The next week another Venezuelan group, Los Amigos Invisibles, which plays acid jazz laced with tropical and Funkadelic, will take the stage. The fragmentation that has divided America's radio stations and lifestyles into a myriad "urban contemporary modern rock (no rap or soft rock)" variations is not in effect in the Latin alternative world.

One encouraging aspect of the expanding hybridity of Latin alternative is its recent expansion into hip-hop (although some might say it's hip-hop taking over Latin alternative). A mini-boom of rock-rap fusion began in Monterrey, Mexico, by El Gran Silencio, a folk–hip-hop group that had long practiced break dancing and graffiti art, and Control Machete, influenced by L.A.-based Cuban rappers Cypress Hill, who have recently released an album of their gangsta rap in Spanish. Machete actually share a producer with Cypress Hill and have appropriated the defiance of the African American stance, transposing it to the Mexican point of view. One of their most famous lines, "We're human beings but they call us Mexicans," is a reaction to the anti-immigration fervor that took hold in Texas and California in the '90s.

In New York, however, Puerto Ricans had been involved in hiphop from the beginning, in an almost parallel fashion to the way Chicanos had been involved in the inception of rock and roll. It's usually dropped by "Boricuas," an island coinage borrowed from the Taino name for Puerto Rico, which through the streets has become the affectionate code name for Nuyorican nationals. Representing Boricuas in hiphop has often been restricted to a few casual asides, like the Beatnuts' Psycho Les calling himself the bilingual Mandingo or Cru shouting out to "all my Boricuas in the Marqueta." Frankie Cutlass, in his single "Boriquas on the Set," made a lasting impression by just repeating "Black People! Puerto Rico!" over a murky break-beat.

But there is a bonafide Latino canon of hiphop that is often recited by scholars and Spanglish folks who have the need to isolate their influence: Legendary figures like Charlie Chase of the Cold Crush Crew and break-dancers Crazy Leggs and Wiggles, who formed the Rock Steady Crew, participated in the crucial Afrikaa Bambaata gatherings in the Bronx that were said to have birthed hiphop in the late '70s. Latin music has been sampled since the early days of hip-hop, from that Tito Puente riff on "I'm Still Number One" by Boogie Down Productions, to the early days of Sugar Hill, where the studio bands would have timbale and conga players, and there was even a timbale break on Kurtis Blow's "The Breaks."

New York Latino youth is largely drawn to a self-named "urban" culture, which is basically a Latino spin on the codes, slang, clothing and lifestyle of African-American youth, and actually has its own magazine, *Urban Latino*. Strong identification with hip-hop coincides with a new wave of activism surrounding issues like police brutality, college tuition hikes, and Puerto Rico's pseudo-colonial status. Los Angeles's Mexican-dominated youth subcultures do feature an "urban" hip-hop element, but it tends to appropriate African American defiance separately, paralleling the reality of the street gangs that define themselves along stricter racial lines. Hip-hop acts like Kid Frost, Lighter Shade of Brown, ALT, and Latin Alliance appeared in California as large selling acts before Nuyorican acts like Fat Joe, Big Pun, and the Beatnuts made their presence felt. But Nuyorican hip-hop has been much more integrated with mainstream hip-hop, and in the late '90s, acts like Puff Daddy, Lil' Kim, and the Fugees' Wyclef Jean have actively included Spanglish lyrics in their songs.

The hip-hop–Latin crossover has always been strong in New York's dance clubs, creating a hybrid in the '80s and '90s called Latin freestyle. At first dominated by female acts like TKA, Expose, and Lisa Lisa and Cult Jam, Latin freestyle featured high-pitched vocals over intensely percolating rhythms that recalled complex Afro-Cuban patterns. An argument can be made that Madonna herself was a proto-Latin freestyle star, having emerged during a period of that genre's gestation, and having employed Latin freestyle's preeminent producer, Nuyorican Jellybean Benitez, on her first two albums. Two of her early singles, "Everybody" and "Lucky Star," were indistinguishable from Latin freestyle.

Coming out of the waning stages of the Latin freestyle era were two Latin house singers, La India, and Marc Anthony, whose decision to return to their Latin roots changed the course of Latin pop history. They had been working with producer Little Louie Vega, who also had a history of hanging around Bambaata in the bad old days, when Vega, who got involved with Tito Puente, got them gigs at the Palladium club, where Latin house was sandwiched around live salsa acts. It wasn't long before India and Anthony were recording salsa in Spanish, adding to their audience by leading a trend that some sociologists call "reverse assimilation." A revival of the Young Lords was spurred by a PBS documentary produced by ex-Lord Iris Morales, and suddenly young college kids, having heard the soundtrack to the Spanglish revolution, wanted to hear salsa again.

Marc Anthony is the ultimate product of Nuyorican-style Spanglish, having been born and raised in East Harlem, a bilingual skinny street kid with a dream. He played the young Salvador Agron in Paul Simon's ill-fated Broadway production *The Capeman*, and he cites Rubén Blades, who played the older Agron, as his hero and mentor. Marc Anthony is a layered construction of conflicting opposites. Like Sinatra, whom he is often compared to, he's a brilliant singer and a mediocre actor; he has an angelic side and a nasty street side. He'll tell you he's worn an *escapulario*, or saint emblem, around his neck for most of his adult life because his mother gave it to him, and then he'll turn around and cuss spectacularly at his bass player for asking him what time it is. He's a bit of a con artist, denying rumors of affairs with Jennifer Lopez, playing the humble man of the public role, when he's bursting with an understandably huge ego about his talent, his stardom, and his sexual prowess.

> *I get up every morning, I get headaches, just like anybody else, I have stomach aches, I get nervous, I get scared. I argue with my girlfriend, I'm alive. When success came along, I was already my own man. I had my own opinion about things. I didn't become a success. Why change? I'm still in a hurry, just like anybody else. I don't float, I don't do magical things. I believe in the art and I close my eyes and I sing, and whatever comes out comes out and I thank God every day.*
>
> —MARC ANTHONY, 1999 INTERVIEW

He's fierce about giving himself the proper credit. When I bring up the influence of producer Sergio George, the man behind new-jack salsa hybrid Dark Latin Groove and often credited with infusing tropical music with a vitality not seen since the Fania days, Anthony is quick to maintain he was the dominant force in their collaboration. But what's most important about Anthony is that, when he's onstage, at least, his sincerity and shyness and surprise about his enormous abilities are authentic. When Anthony fills Roseland, or Radio City Music Hall, or Madison Square Garden, it's the ultimate ceremonial ritual of the Church of the Spanglish Nation. His Spanish-language salsa tunes are the unquestioned last words on life and love in the ruthless big city; his English-language pop tunes, although derivative and lacking in lyrical spark, are moodily brilliant turns around the still-cold world of New York's demimonde, or just simple statements of devotion to a child from a relationship that didn't work out. His performances are filled with the wildly shifting suffering and joy of New York's struggling Spanglish working- and middle-classes. They are well-attended by urban celebrities like John Leguizamo and Rosie Perez, rap artists like Fat Joe and the late Big Pun.

Marc Anthony is the matinee idol for the new Nuyorican nationalism, one that he helped to create by returning to his salsa roots. He is at the epicenter of the flag-waving raucousness that occurs at the National Puerto Rican Day Parade on Fifth Avenue every summer, and the nascent Spanglish presence in hip-hop. With rappers like Puff Daddy, Busta Rhymes, Black Rob, and Lil' Kim dropping Spanish into their rhymes, the Boricua vibe is no longer in the background, and hip-hop expands its urban Latino component.

If Marc Anthony is Spanglish youth's dark prince, then Selena is its patron saint. Emerging from the border culture of south Texas, a Spanglish formulation if there ever was one, Selena's martyrdom may be directly related to the forces she unleashed with her attempt to mount the ultimate Latin pop crossover. A native of

Corpus Christi (literally: the body of Christ), Selena Quintanilla-Pérez became one of the most celebrated figures in the history of Tejano music only to be murdered just as she was about to break that genre into the mainstream of American pop. Tejano is a bouncy, *cumbia*-flavored (Colombian-Mexican) music that is more favorable to dancing than other forms of regional Mexican music, possibly because the role of Africans and African Americans was more pronounced in the Texas gulf region than in Mexico or California's interior.

As the story goes in Gregory Nava's sentimental but effective biopic, Selena and her siblings formed a Tejano group as children at the urgings of their father, Abraham Quintanilla, a frustrated Mexican-American rock and roller. In evocative Spanglish fashion, the movie has several scenes that demonstrate Mexican American involvement in rock and roll, and the double rejection Quintanilla's father faced from both a Tejano-phobic Anglo and skeptically traditional Mexican-American audience. They are sequences almost directly drawn from Villareal's *Pocho*, filled with a simultaneous sense of humiliating pain and the giddy quest for freedom.

Selena was forced by her father to learn Spanish and sing Tejano music (which, even though it had traditional roots, was constantly evolving into a contemporary Spanglish form) to avoid his suffering. The band cut their chops playing at local restaurants, clubs, and outdoor festivals, sticking to the Spanish-language ethnic style even though they were predominantly English-speaking. As she reached her early twenties, Selena began recording albums, two of which, *Entre a Mi Mundo* and *Amor Prohibido* went gold, while a third, *Live*, reached platinum status. Not content to merely reproduce the rollicking, two-step *cumbia* sound of contemporaries like La Mafia, Selena began to experiment with dance-club influences on songs like "Techno Cumbia." ("Techno Cumbia" may have been an indirect influence on a fin de siècle collective of DJs from borderland Tijuana called Nortec. Nortec's claim to fame is its incorporation of *norteño* and *banda* rhythms from northern

Mexico into the kind of trance music that keeps people up all night at Ibiza raves.)

Having grown up listening to American pop and having a great affinity for singers like Donna Summer, Selena began to inflect her work with a different accent, as shown in her reworking of the Pretenders' "Back in the Chain Gang" (Fotos y Recuerdos), on *Amor Prohibido*. Conversely, she had begun to work on her Spanish and was beginning to master the language in press conferences in Mexico just before her death.

She became a symbol for a generation of Mexican Americans, and possibly, northern Mexicans, who were yearning for pride in their identity. Selena's goddess-like appearance had strong indigenous, and possibly African, characteristics. During a time when Spanish-language television shows featured an absolute majority of European-featured images, Selena was a "brown" media star.

Although the details surrounding her life before she was killed are shrouded in mystery, the cold facts are that she was gunned down by the president of her fan club in March of 1995. The rumors that swirled around her like vultures included speculation that she was having an affair with a plastic surgeon in Costa Rica and that she was killed by a jealous lover. Undoubtedly there was a danger surrounding Selena that had to do with her sexuality: As the movie shows explicitly, her father was engaged in an extremely protective mode about her, grudgingly allowing her to perform in scanty halter tops, and finally, marry her bandmate boyfriend, guitarist Chris Perez.

But despite the considerable power she unleashed through her sexuality, Selena may have been martyred because she had invoked a powerful storm around her by attempting to be both traditional and contemporary at the same time. Just before her death she had been putting together an album intended to be her breakthrough effort. Released in the summer following her death, *Dreaming of You* was a delightful, eclectic work featuring r&b, disco, flamenco, and even a collaboration with David Byrne. In 1996, *Selena*, a film based on her life was released, starring Jennifer Lopez—who iron-ically would accomplish Selena's crossover dream years later—in the title role. In my interview with Lopez, she told me that the Selena role was one of her main inspirations to pursue a recording career she had dreamed of earlier. Using a strategy parallel to Selena's by including a traditional salsa duet with Marc Anthony and an Emilio Estefan Latin-disco song on an album dominated by r&b/pop influences, Lopez literally stepped into Selena's ghost and revived it. It was the first Spanglish reincarnation, and it happened with the full backing of the multinational media machine.

6.

CALIFORNIA DREAMIN'

Was Jim Morrison infected by a Spanglish virus when he gyrated, spitting out the hotly howled chorus of "Break on Through to the Other Side," a piece of *bugaloo* blasphemy that conflated sex and the border? Was James Dean really in love with a pseudo-Spanglish juvie as portrayed by the granddaddy of Latin street kids, Italiano-en-brownface Sal Mineo? Does the Grateful Dead resonate in the California self-image because its "Day of the Dead" iconography reflected the "hot" urbanism of Mexican Americans both in Jerry Garcia's home state of Texas and his adopted one of California?

The 2000 Census tells a story about the inevitability of Spanglish in California—non-Hispanic whites have been supplanted by Latinos as the majority. Although California's becoming majority Latino is a stunning new development, it may be that the Anglo domination of California between 1848 and now was the aberration. California has the scent, the feel, the touch of Spanglish, in the red-roofed mission churches of San Juan Bautista that Alfred Hitchcock admired, the quiet echo of norteño music that serenades the agricultural workers in the rolling plains of the San Joaquin Valley, the marriage of desert

expanse, ranchero reality, and flirtatious palm trees that give it a tropical tint. Southern California is a thousand-legged spider of roadways
that stretch from Oxnard to San Diego, a mass of intersecting massive
concrete highways that suck in all the bad energy of Aztlan. When you
roll down the sacred Chicano promenade of Whittier Boulevard to
the east, or flit along the new Latino bohemia barrios of downtown
San Jose, and when you speed up Route 5 trying to outrun the sunset
over Chula Vista, less than twenty miles from the border, you are
becoming intimate with the Spanglish slant of California.

California is so resonant with the motion of Spanglish culture
that the very land itself is unstable. Landing in Los Angeles International Airport just a few days after a major earthquake is like
touching down in the middle of an ocean storm. Days after the
earth has stopped trembling, creating fissures all along Hollywood
Boulevard into the northern edge of the barrio at Western Avenue,
your very sense of stability is still challenged. Memories of Mexico
City, ten years earlier, and the emergence of Super Barrio, a costumed hero that would take the place of failed government efforts,
loom larger than the sound of anti-immigration propositions and
the end of bilingual education.

It doesn't matter if sacred barrios were razed at Chavez Ravine
to make Dodgers Stadium possible, because Fernando Valenzuela
rocked the house for the home team and made Mexican Americans
distinctly visible on the Southern California landscape. The urban
vitality of what sociologist-historian Mike Davis calls a "shared con-
viction between Iberian and Meso-American civilization that civilized sociality is constituted on the intercourse of plaza y mercado"
transforms the old corridors from downtown to Firestone Boulevard in Downey, from the North Valley to the South Valley, from
Pasadena to Pomona.

California is the incubator of the transnational suburb, where
whole communities from Mexico are lifted up and transplanted
into Orange County, like a luxury liner lifted from its berth and
placed down in another sea. It is a place where hardworking immigrants place themselves into voluntary servitude for months as gar-

deners and busboys and domestic servants and return to Mexico with enough money to buy houses with Direct TV satellite dishes. A village in the state of Oaxaca reenacts its yearly soccer game in a suburb of Long Beach. It is a place where the gang society that was established through years of largely unjust imprisonment in places like Folsom and Chico State reigns supreme over barrios.

Yet middle-class Chicanos thrive to the extent that they sometimes forget Spanish and intermarry at a high rate with Anglo-Americans. They become "not overtly Mexican American media figures" like David Navarro, the spectacular guitarist of Jane's Addiction and Red Hot Chili Peppers. In Southern California, Mexican Americans and Asians live across from each other in posh suburbs and work across from each other in South Central fruit and vegetable markets. But the mythology of East L.A., and Cheech Marin, and the tragic death of journalist Ruben Salazar at the hands of an overzealous policeman, as well as the omnipresent Edward James Olmos, who helped make *Miami Vice* and *Blade Runner* part of American entertainment folklore, are far from being erased from that city's cultural landscape. Along the streets of Venice prowl the ghosts of Orson Welles and Marlene Dietrich, acting out their absurd ballet in *Touch of Evil*, playing off a bronze colored Charlton Heston.

The California burrito comes with a whole-wheat tortilla and brown rice. The most populous state in the union is at once the ultimate home of the TV Land suburbia that made the myth of middle-American culture and the seed for the most explosive expansion of immigrant influence in the U.S. Right now, 43 percent of the Latino population is under eighteen. The light is shifting now, as white flight has dragged millions of Anglo Americans to Arizona, Nevada, Oregon, Washington, and Idaho. A lot of scores have to be settled in California, some political ones over the coalition that elected Tom Bradley and the one that elected Richard Riordan. The echoes of the Watsonville women farmworkers and the magic Mission District of San Francisco and the *chilaquiles* of a diner in East Los are brown and proud.

> *I'd often planned on going West to see the country, always*
> *vaguely planning and never taking off.*
> — JACK KEROUAC

As a rambunctious nineteen-year-old, I was drawn west to California like all good Americans, in search of the freedom that the road brings. Inspired by the book *Fear and Loathing in Las Vegas*, I drove from New York to Los Angeles in four days. While ostensibly not looking for more than the adventure and peril of navigating our nation's interstate highway system, I was drawn to Hunter Thompson's hallucinatory refusal to accept the direction the country was heading in. While he understood that the '60s were over in 1970, when the events in that book took place, I was stubbornly deluded about America's descent into sitcom and disco escapism.

In California I expected to find a kind of dreamed-of liberation, but what I found was a sleepy decadence and a subliminal sense of Spanglish space. Immediately upon seeing the Spanish-style red-roofed houses as I descended from the San Bernadino mountains on I-10, I felt a sense of home that I had never felt anywhere else in the fifty states. The street names all seemed to refer to Latino-ness; the endless sun made me imagine a southern Spanish valley I'd never seen. As I rode shotgun with my Anglo driving partner, an old friend from the north Bronx, I had unwittingly taken the role of Oscar Acosta, a.k.a. Hunter Thomspon's three hundred-pound "Samoan" attorney, a.k.a. the Brown Buffalo.

I had no idea at the time that "Zeta," as Acosta called himself, was one of a kind, a Chicano lawyer living in Los Angeles who was directly involved in several political actions during the period leading up to Ruben Salazar's murder by the police. As a civil rights lawyer he represented members of the Brown Berets and the poet Corky Gonzales. He ran for sheriff of Los Angeles County as a representative of the radical party La Raza Unida. Still, he was ostracized by much of the Chicano community because of his excessive, decadent, drug-consuming behavior, often living in fleabag motels. His story, documented in *Autobiography of a Brown Buffalo* and

Revolt of the Cockroach People, reads like a cross between a brown William Borroughs, the writings of a '60s radical, and the sardonic desperation of a Kafka or Gogol.

Hunter Thompson met Acosta in Aspen, Colorado, a place where he would later run for sheriff, perhaps inspired by Zeta. They were introduced by Bill Kennedy, who was once an editor for the *San Juan Star*, for which Thompson wrote in the early '60s. (Thompson's ravings about his Puerto Rico days, at times dripping with gringo paranoia, are on display in a novel called *Rum Diaries*.) Acosta provided Thompson with an indispensable wealth of information about the growing revolutionary fervor in East Los Angeles for an article Thompson wanted to write for *Rolling Stone* magazine, "Strange Rumblings in Aztlan." It was after that episode that Thompson came up with the idea of writing an article about going to a narcotics officers' convention in Las Vegas, which became the basis for his famous book.

I turn up the radio full blast . . . It's "Sgt. Peppers' Lonely Hearts Club Band." The boys have finally got themselves a winner. But I can't distinguish the words from the noise of the horns, the skidding brakes, the jangled nerves and my gas-laden belly. Is it a language problem, I ask myself. Or a hearing problem? And how can anyone possibly understand even if he does hear?

"It's all bullshit," I console myself. "They intentionally make nonsense to sound like poetry so that no one will be able to put them down."

My shrink says, "And is it the same when you hear a new song in Spanish?"

"Fuck, I haven't heard a song in Spanish since I was a kid."

"Oh? You don't like Mexican music?" he stabs it to me.

But I don't have time for that racial crap now. In ten years of therapy the only thing the fucker has wanted to gossip about has been my mother and my ancestry. "Sex and race. It's one and the same hangup."

     —OSCAR "ZETA" ACOSTA,
     Autobiography of a Brown Buffalo

After *Fear and Loathing* appeared, Acosta was outraged, feeling that Thompson had stolen most of his material from his drug-addled ravings. He was so angry, and perhaps had enough of a point, that when he sued Thompson for co-author credit, the author and his publishing company settled by offering Acosta a two-book deal, which he used to write *Autobiography of a Brown Buffalo* and *The Revolt of the Cockroach People*. When you examine these works, it's clear that Acosta lived at a fever-pitch, high-anxiety pace, continually fueled by drugs and raving paranoias that seem to stem from feelings of sexual inadequacy, and more important for Spanglish purposes, pain and confusion over his Mexican identity. He was a *pocho* with a classic story: He grew up in El Paso, Texas, the son of a Mexican immigrant who, like many of his generation, joined the armed forces so he could establish a legitimate claim to citizenship. Acosta grew up American, schooled in mostly white institutions, had his flings with Anglo women, until he reached that point of not fitting in, which was probably exacerbated by his considerable girth and strongly Aztecan looks.

When you read Acosta's work, you can feel the real intensity and rage of what Thompson claimed to invent—gonzo journalism. The word *"gonzo"* itself even has a Hispanic tinge to it, echoing the "loco" imported from the Old West. Thompson's writings in Puerto Rico, years before he met Acosta, had none of the intensity of Acosta's. Even Benicio Del Toro's reading of Acosta in the uneven Terry Gilliam movie *Fear and Loathing in Las Vegas* possessed most of the charge in the film. The bathtub scene where he tries to commit suicide by plunging a radio into the water as the Jefferson Airplane's "White Rabbit" climaxes; the frustrated sexuality he projects onto a waitress in a sleazy café; the horrible transformation into a satanic serpent during one of the extreme drug sequences—they are all the pure "id" of the gonzo writer on display. Thompson's role seems merely to observe, rein them in, and recontextualize them into his own maudlin reverie about the end of the counterculture. He did this literally, as is shown in the movie, by recording every single moment they shared together—the movie, and the book's narrative, seem to collapse when they're apart.

Vibing on Thompson's experience may have been an unconscious connection I was making with Acosta's *pocho* alienation, with his growing anger about his own people's political oppression and his inability to really connect with them. Acosta, who disappeared mysteriously in Mexico in 1974, was increasingly trying to make up for this by spending more and more time in his native land, learning more Spanish, and dreaming of a separate Chicano homeland along the lines of the Plan de Aztlan bunch. Although his legacy is darkness and destruction, his memory may yet point toward a Spanglish utopia.

Could it be found in California? Maybe it was the Carlos Casteñeda books that I casually absorbed during that time, lusting after psilocybin mushrooms that I could never quite find, or the funky feeling of eternal hippie culture that permeated the place. How could I explain that I found the raggy dress that still insisted on hints of Native American jewelry, the natural food restaurants and stores, the incessant Grateful Dead music, comforting?

> We bounced over the railroad tracks in Fresno and hit the wild streets of Fresno Mextown . . . groups of Mex chicks swaggered around in slacks; mambo blasted from jukeboxes; the lights were festooned around like Halloween. We went into a Mexican restaurant and had tacos and mashed pinto beans rolled in tortillas; it was delicious. I whipped out my last shining five-dollar bill which stood between us and the New Jersey Shore and paid for Terry and me. Now I had four bucks. Terry and I looked at each other.
> "Where are we going to sleep tonight, baby?"
> "I don't know."
>
> —JACK KERUOAC, *On the Road*

In California (and in Colorado, for that matter), Mexicans fulfilled the muse needs of hipster Kerouac the same way blacks did when he was in Chicago. In the Midwest or New York, the free-wheeling subculture of Miles and Bird, blowing their trumpets and saxes, drowning out the pain of not fitting into the American dream like a bottle of cheap cabernet, was the White Negro cure for alienation. Once he got west of the Rockies however, Kerouac and the hipster world appropriated the ethos of places like Colorado and California. The intermingling of white bohemia with California Mexicans has been discussed in previous chapters—Ritchie Valens's pivotal role in the birth of rock and roll, and his plane-crash death with Buddy Holly, a friend who happened to be married to a Puerto Rican woman; Oscar "Zeta" Acota's pivotal role in the creation of gonzo journalism; Grateful Dead as the house band for the Merry Pranksters, a group of dropouts that included Jack Kerouac's Dean Moriarty from *On the Road*.

It follows, then, that much of the outward paraphernalia and life-philosophies of the '60s counterculture was a direct outgrowth of Mexican-infused California, just as Thoreau's *Walden* was inspired by contact with Native Americans. The fixation with going back to the land, with using mind-expanding drugs, even the wearing of fringed leather vests, are all inspired by a reverence for the indigenous American. At the same time that these tastes were being shaped, Chicanos were immersed in an identity consciousness raising that focused on the revival and predominance of indigenous roots, as spelled out by El Plan de Aztlan. Despite the fact that Chicanos have faced, and continue to face, a stubborn, not so subtle discrimination, California is still Mexican territory.

Actually, it's not really Mexican, because even when it was part of Mexico, California was still a remote outpost, one that was not connected to the motherland in a very tight way. Californios, as they call the people of mixed-race, Catholic priests, Spanish-lineage families, and indigenous people who inhabited California for two centuries before the Americans arrived, were a stubbornly independent lot. But with the staggering immigration of the last fifty years, with successive waves of Mexicans, Salvadorans, and other Latino groups invading Southern California, it's safe to refer to Los Angeles, as many Mexicans do, as the second-biggest city in Mexico.

In many ways, Los Angeles is a quintessential Spanglish city because it's all about motion. Its disturbing interstate-highway lattice defines daily life and migration, intertwined like the irrigation channels that surrounded the island-city of Tenochtitlán, the city Cortés conquered for Spain. Cruising Whittier Boulevard in East L.A. is a sedated fantasy of summer afternoons in deep Queens. The lazy, palm-lined streets remind me of the suburbs of San Juan that my aunts live in. And there's the unerring, headlong plunge toward the coast on the Santa Monica Freeway—it almost has the same feel as a leisurely walk all the way down the Ramblas, past the newspaper stands and birds for sale in Barcelona or barreling toward Valparaiso, Chile, on a three-hour drive from Santiago, to kiss the coastline at all costs.

The patterns of settlement in Los Angeles continue along highway lines, unlike rivers in much of the rest of the country. Formidable middle-class Latino and Asian communities spring up along Route 60 in the San Gabriel Valley, along Route 5 to the San Fernando Valley, where the southern stretches, near the epicenter of the Northridge earthquake, are magnets for Mexican Americans and new immigrants. The Latino suburbs of Montebello and Southgate straddle the Firestone Boulevard aircraft industry corridor adjacent to heartland hometowns like Downey. The bridge that arches across the barren Los Angeles River into East Los Angeles was once the path that an isolated community followed; now it is the entrance into the heart of Spanglish Los Angeles.

Los Angeles suffered through two major traumas in the early '90s— the Rodney King riot and the Northridge earthquake—that seemed to catapult it forward into its current phase of economic boom and uncertain race dynamics. The riots were a combined reliving of Watts and the Ruben Salazar moratorium, where blacks and Latinos rioted simultaneously, but not necessarily alongside each other. One of the more underacknowledged facts about the riot was that there were more Latinos arrested than blacks, and that much of that rioting occurred in recent-immigrant (often Salvadoran) areas like Pico-Union, and not the Chicano bastion of East Los Angeles.

While the riots expressed the outrage of an angry, underemployed people, redrew racial lines, and had a hand in the explosion of anti-immigrant sentiment, the earthquake was a short, sharp wound, a lingering paper cut that humbled everyone. One of its extraordinary effects was to heighten awareness of the divide between white, privileged Los Angeles, the expanding nature of Latino Los Angeles, and the slow contraction of black Los Angeles. The earthquake severed the Santa Monica Freeway, perhaps the area's most traveled intracity highway, at La Brea Avenue, the point widely acknowledged to be the dividing line between the increasingly Latino areas of Hollywood, Silver Lake, and Downtown, and the affluent, 310 area code addresses of West Hollywood, Beverly Hills, and Santa Monica. The sight of the cracks on Hollywood Boulevard near Vermont Avenue being gingerly walked around by a core population of Latinos was another reminder of Hollywood's turnover. It was as if the movement of the earth itself was a necessary and appropriate announcement that Los Angeles would became a majority Latino city officially in 1999.

The riot and the earthquake revealed the evolving L.A. landscape of continuing immigration and new formations of Spanglish spheres of influence, from the emerging Salvadoran influence to the slow birth of hiphop-era identification of certain sectors with African-American cultural forms. It's taken for granted that Los Angeles is a Chicano city, and there is no question that the dominant Spanglish culture there is Mexican American–derived, but there are so many on the periphery. Sen Dog and B Real, the two rappers that make up the core of the first hybrid hip-hop group, Cypress Hill, are among those on the margins of Chicano L.A.

They are Cuban Americans, part of a small exile community that escaped to the West Coast rather than remain in Florida or push northward to New York.

Cypress Hill's self-titled debut album gained quite a bit of attention for their high-pitched, squealing style of rapping (often compared to the Beastie Boys) and their stubborn insistence on praising the virtues of marijuana on several songs. Sen Dog's childhood home, where he grew up with his father, Senen Reyes, a casual jazz musician, is in Southgate, a mixed-ethnicity town next to the largely white Downey, not too far from South Central. B Real, the auteur behind the aforementioned nasal voice technique, was more open about himself. Because of his Cuban perspective, he had experienced confusion about whether to identify with Mexican Americans or blacks, and had been a member of gangs of both ethnicities. He had a strong anti-Castro bent—he claimed his mother was an escaped member of Alpha 66, a paramilitary group intent on removing Fidel Castro from power. He was calm and bitter about his gang-banging days, revealing that he'd been shot, but that the escalation of retaliation between violent youth was clearly a fact of life, and an actual principle, a comforting axiom of human nature, the classic gangsta pose.

Their upbringing on the edges of the Chicano-dominated gang structure and their at times uncomfortable interaction with the majority, as well as the highly combustible hybrid energy they brought from Cuba, was instrumental in their forays into combining rock music with rap, using skull iconography in the same way the Grateful Dead did. As part of the new wave of Latino immigrants slowly displacing the Anglo majority of the Southgate-Downey area, Sen Dog and B Real engaged in recombinant Spanglish activity. Cubans raised in California, they reinvented themselves as hybrids of the black and Mexican gang style, while also carrying some of the Anglo rock influence in their performance. When they perform before a howling crowd of devotees, singing "Stoned Is the Way of the Walk," they are conflating South Central and Woodstock. Cypress Hill is not just a hiphop band, but a quintessential California Spanglish band.

The Valley of Valdez

There's something about the physical geography of California that heightens awareness of any latent indigenous urges. The same immensely wide, arid valleys that are found in Mexico open up before you in many corners of California. In the San Joaquin Valley just south of San Francisco, side-stepping the major arteries that bring you into the Silicon Alley area around San Jose, you can turn off and head toward San Juan Bautista, the town United Farm Workers activist-playwright Luis Valdez lives in. Although much of Valdez's notoriety stems from his theater troupe, Teatro Campesino, which incorporated Mexican forms such as tent theater (*teatro carpa*) in a grassroots labor movement that once united Cesar Chavez and Robert Kennedy, Valdez tries to keep a hand on the pulse of the future. Valdez had a calendar on the wall that depicted an image of an indigenous Californian, or Mexican (Valdez has done years of research into his family's connection to the Yaqui tribe) seated at a computer terminal, typing away like he was born to word-process. This was the future of California, he said, an indigenous person who had conquered technology.

When Valdez got into his concept of indigenous cultures, he began to float into a new world of being. Perhaps in a more researched way than his Aztlan-oriented contemporaries, he considered himself a descendant of Yaqui Indians and was intent on reconciling his roots with his Spanish and English-speaking cultural overlay. The same man who was heavily involved in the UFW Movement, once a target of COINTELPRO investigations, having chosen a strategic location from his house because he could see everyone who was coming, was also very interested in grounding himself in the concept of zero:

> *It turns out that the Mayan conception of zero isn't like this two-dimensional ring, it's a sphere. It's a full emptiness and an*

empty fullness. It's the most basic state of life there is, you know,
a sphere of potentiality. So out of this comes a spark, a spark of
life. It doesn't just happen automatically, the conditions have to
be ripe for this to happen. But what this spark does, is that it's
very much like a sperm, it ignites the whole thing. The human
being evolves in the same way, you have the mother's egg, then
the sperm comes into it and boom, it becomes two. So our human
form is really spherical, or egg-shaped. It's not just the image of
two arms and legs, it is these things in motion. The very space
that we articulate with our bodies is a sphere. Everything is a
sphere. The joints all circulate. And your head is one and your
eyes are one. And when you walk, you're really rolling.

— LUIS VALDEZ, INTERVIEW

For Valdez, so connected to the history of migrant workers that he had to leave town as a child with his migrant family just as he was cast in his first theater role, ground zero is always in motion. First discovered on local San Jose television while doing a puppet show with English- and Spanish-speaking characters, Valdez understands the dynamic of opposing forces that spin in a spherical unity. His move to invent Chicano theater in an alliance with Cesar Chavez involved staging plays for farm workers on flatbed trucks. The stage itself, although containing metaphoric elements of the proscenium, literally rolled into the communities it was intended for. In his year 2000 play, *The Mummified Deer,* Valdez takes elements of sensationalistic Latin American tabloid journalism and the close-to-the-border miscegenation between Europeans and Yaqui tribes.

When you roll away from Valdez's San Juan Bautista headquarters and point your vehicle in the direction of Los Angeles, you find yourself on Route 5 and the San Joaquin Valley, a potentially windy, dusty, and boring drive. But after about an hour, all the radio stations seem to disappear save for one coming out of Fresno, a festive barrage of Spanglish advertisement and the insistent big beat of *norteño* music. Los Tigres del Norte and their tales of border angst, the conflict between generations over language and customs, take you on a straight shot to Bakersfield, doing ninety with the sixteen-wheelers, flashing through the starless night with a cloak of protection from the dancing ghosts of migrant workers all along the roadsides.

CHICANO CHIC AND POCHO RECONSTRUCTION

Access to state college public education, the counterculture, and the slow assimilation of Chicanos into the early stages of postmodern America allowed for the growth of a new irony, a new detachment in Spanglish creativity. A child of the '50s, Harry Gamboa Jr. grew up in a working-class Mexican-American home in East Los Angeles. As a student at East Los's infamous Garfield High, Gamboa was active in student government and as an organizer of various student-initiated reforms, most significantly the 1968 "East L.A. Blowouts"—a series of protests against the inferior conditions of the public schools in neighborhoods that were majority nonwhite.

At Garfield High, Gamboa met Gronk (Glugio Nicondra), Patssi Valdez, and Willie Herrón to form the avant-Chicano art collective Asco. Translated from the Spanish as "nausea," Asco represents the nausea of dislocation for the Chicano artist in colonized surroundings, and perhaps of the expectations of being Chicano. From a generation that emerged just after the Chicano political renaissance, Asco was decidedly nonpolitical, at least in the conventional sense. Asco was intent on revealing the absurdity of urban life through a kind of alienated Chicano youth perspective. Asco members published an influential magazine, *Con Safos*, which operated outside the orbit of Jose Montoya's Royal Chicano Air Force, as well as more conventional Chicano groups like Teatro Campesino.

While *asco* (nausea) obviously references Sartre and existentialism, it also predated the song with the same name on the seminal L.A. punk band X's debut album, and Gronk's obsession with the decline of Western Civilization through L.A. eyes anticipated

Penelope Spheeris's documentary about the punk scene. Asco's production of a "No Movie," made without the use of film, came before New York punk's no wave movement. Asco was decidedly against artwork that included *rasquache** images like the Virgin of Guadalupe or any number of corn goddesses. "I can only do what I'm about, and I'm an urban Chicano living in a city," Gronk said in an interview. "I can't impose upon my work other things. I can be influenced by a war that's taking place, that's killing off people. I can look at the world and say, 'Yeah, yuk, it's disgusting at times as well. And being tear-gassed in your own country.'" Gamboa, whose more recent work like "N/either H/ere N/or T/here," is still concerned with his tumultuous identity search, employing the slashes that are popular among academics taking gender into the equation.

In the early '90s some of the remnants of Asco began a new scene at the Troy Café, a Chicano poet hangout run by Sean Carrillo and Bebe Hansen. The Troy was a home for performers like Marisela Norte, Diane Gamboa, and the East Los art mob. It was also the home to Bebe's son Beck Hansen, who I met in the early '90s, having just emerged from behind the Troy's counter, mop in hand. Beck Hansen, whose father has been credited with the first "happening" in hipster history, has become emblematic of an avant-garde Anglo with a strong Spanglish influence. Beck's albums, which are praised heavily by the rock press, are complex pastiches of several different styles of rock and r&b music, very much like Café Tacuba, a Mexico City group that is now compared to Beck. In fact, it wasn't until a year after Café Tacuba's mixed-genre masterpiece, *Re*, appeared on the market that Geffen Records publicity people were trumpeting Beck's new album, *Odelay*, as an innovative, hybrid album.

---

*Defined by critic Tomás Ibarra Frausto, *rasquachismo* is the do-it-yourself-ism that characterizes working-class Mexican and Mexican-American aesthetics as "a sensibility that is not elevated and serious, but playful and elemental. It finds delight and refinement in what many consider banal and projects an alternative aesthetic—a sort of good taste of bad taste."

Beck's stepfather, Sean Carrillo, had been part of an L.A. performance art scene with a long tradition of mixed-identity exploration. One of these pioneers is El Vez, a.k.a. Robert Lopez, original member of L.A. proto-punk group the Zeros, who is now one of the world's most successful Elvis Presley imitators. If Elvis was a singular phenomenon in rock history because he was a Southern white man preferring the gait, inflection, and soul juice of a black man, then El Vez is just another Latino guy who rolled out of bed in the morning with a panoply of light and dark cultural influences simmering in his genetic code. El Vez explores the problem of being mestizo on the verge of a multicultural millennium by mixing, mixing, and mixing again. He'll take the tune to "It's Now or Never," overlay that with some semiserious lyrics about gang-banging tragedy in East Los, and end it with an uplifting coda to the tune of Rod Stewart's "Maggie May." "Stop the violence, become educated/All celebrity voices are impersonated," he implores, creating a Mexicali Mobius strip out of a simple *Mad* magazine parody.

While El Vez does a terrific Elvis, his show is much broader than that: It completely slays the everyman rock and roll heart by quick-cutting though a huge swath of rock history just like the hiphop DJ for New York's Ghetto Original break-dance troupe races through "Numbers," "Planet Rock," and "White Lines." "En el Barrio," a homage to "In the Ghetto" (which in a way was an instant parody, appearing at the height of the '60s' War on Poverty) somehow manages to fuse elements of Traffic's "Dear Mr. Fantasy" and the Beatles' "I've Got a Feeling." Vez's intimate knowledge of the great riffs involves the crowd in such a profound manner that it's primed to absorb his subversive, if simplistic, Chicano advocacy propaganda.

At one point he pays homage to Bowie and T-Rex, announcing that the Revolution would be a "Glitter Rock Revolution." These pyrotechnics show his roots in a community of L.A. Latino art intelligentsia—his whole El Vez act was birthed at an opening of a folk-art gallery he ran in the late '80s. When El Vez explains the concept of *pochismo* ("I don't speak Spanish, but I'm hardcore") he shares the basic philosophy behind L.A. graphic artist/comedian Lalo Lopez's *Pocho* magazine.

I first met Lopez backstage at a theater festival in San Antonio when he was part of a comedy performance troupe called Chicano Secret Service. The group did sketch comedy that satirized the overseriousness of militant Chicano nationalist groups, trying to break from the Valdez tradition. Lopez's *Pocho* magazine is a kind of a Generation Equis bible, fusing older photonovela and UFW agitprop cartoon styles with an irreverent take on issues from then-governor Pete Wilson's rabid anti-immigrant campaigns to the corruption in the PRI, Mexico's ruling party. He took the name *pocho* because it was an epithet he'd heard growing up—it was a kind of badge of difference, and even though it was pejorative, there was kind of a liberation from traditional Mexican culture. The word *"pocho"* literally means "faded," or even pale, indicating that from a Mexican point of view, Chicanos are pale imitations of true Mexicans.

Even though Chicano Secret Service was serviceably witty with most of its material, Lopez's true genius seemed to lie in his cartoons, which he does on a weekly basis for the *L.A. Weekly*. One of my favorites, released around the celebration of Che Guevara's seventy-fifth birthday, depicted Che in his famous Cuban revolutionary poster gaze, wearing his trademark beret, only this time his headgear had a Nike swoosh logo on it. The cartoon seemed to capture at once the changes in the Cuban economy and the commercialization of the counterculture among Latinos in the U.S. But there was one guerrilla theater action that Lopez did which was one of the most bizarre, and largely unnoticed, pieces of Spanglish agitprop ever performed.

On September 16, 1994, Mexican Independence Day, I received a mysterious press release from *Pocho* headquarters. "The National Pochismo Institute, a Southern California think tank, joined the Pete Wilson reelection campaign in announcing the creation of Hispanics for Wilson," read the fax. The purported chairman of the group supporting anti-immigrant governor Wilson was "landscaper and personal groomer Jonathan Tapadonez," who was quoted as saying, "Illegal immigrants are living the good life by hogging all the low-paying jobs that Americans have the God-given right to refuse."

The release called for the "creation of Self Deportation Centers which will encourage all Hispanics to return to their countries of origin." The message was reacted to angrily by many sectors of the Chicano activist community, and it also landed Lopez, who was posing as Daniel D. Portado, a guest appearance on *Sevcec*, a nationwide Spanish-language TV talk show.

Lopez and partner Steven Zul's appearance on *Sevcec* was one of the great comic hoaxes in the history of television. They managed to enrage a legitimate anti-Wilson organizer, having fun with the piousness of Chicanismo, while at the same time making Latinos who supported Wilson (a sizable number actually voted for Proposition 187) look like buffoons. Since the message was also posted on the Internet, it was an early use of that medium for subversive purposes. But the Daniel D. Portado incident exposed so many different levels of contradiction while at the same time producing a concrete result. By posing as a Republican Hispanic, Lopez was at once playing the role of "assimilated" *pocho,* which was superimposed on his ambivalent *pocho* self, one that strongly supported pro-Latino politics, but was antsy about its traditional trappings. (The hoax has repercussions that were felt recently, when it was discovered that in her book *Guess Who's Coming to Dinner Now? Multicultural Conservatism in America*, Professor Angela Dillard naïvely referred to Daniel Portado's "Hispanics Against Liberal Takeover" as a legitimate example of Hispanic conservatism.) As in the carnival, Lopez had to put on the mask of *pocho* so he could take off his mask, his fear of criticizing respected left Latino leaders. Like El Vez says, "I don't speak Spanish, but I'm hardcore."

Still Lopez, and many reformed "assimilated" Latinos, have

plunged heavily back into the mother tongue, caressing it, coaxing it, possessing it again like a lost lover. *Pochismo* is now a wide-open space of possibility for California Chicanos like Norte, or Harry Gamboa's sister Diane, or self-described *Chicana falsa*, Michelle Serros. It is a dynamic site for hybridity, for fearless use of Spanglish and recombination with Anglo-American culture. Mexican kitsch has become the subject of the bohemian avant-garde, perhaps most obviously in rock music, which has a number of intersections with fetishized Latino symbols. Beck's first hit record, "I'm a Loser" had a Spanish phrase, *"Soy un perdedor,"* at the center of its refrain. In the late '80s, Perry Farrell, the creator of the Lollapalooza alternative music festival and one-time leader of the hard-rock band Jane's Addiction, put out an album called *Ritual de lo Habitual*, which featured cover art filled with Mexican kitsch iconography. Farrell, whose group's lead guitarist, Dave Navarro, is an L.A. Gen X Chicano, soon invited groups like Maldita Vecindad and Café Tacuba to play at his festival.

Los Angeles has become the capital of rock en Español, or Latin rock, or Latin alternative, as various factions have named it. It is the only city in the U.S. where Latin alternative shows are consistently attended by a "mainstream" audience, and it has produced several of its own bands. On any given night you can go to House of Blues on Sunset Boulevard and see a local band like noise-pop quartet Pastilla, whose members consist of Mexican kids who were recently relocated to Pomona by their parents, or Mexico City rap-rockers Molotov. In southern California (and increasingly, the Bay Area), it's not unusual to see a triple bill with Venezuelan funk parodists Los Amigos Invisibles, Monterrey, Mexico, art-noise fabulists Plastilina Mosh, and London Indian fusionists Cornershop.

But one of the most archetypal Spanglish bands in all of the country resides in Los Angeles, and are just as likely to play The Conga Room (a salsa palace co-owned by Jennifer Lopez and Jimmy Smits) as the House of Blues or even the Viper Room. They are called Ozomatli. When I saw them in the Conga Room, a full house joined their frenzied samba procession to the stage, engaging in their nightly carnival. While their roots lay partly in political activism, it can be said that Ozomatli makes a political statement just by being a multiracial band that fuses funk, merengue, *cumbia, ranchera*, and hiphop. The sight of a barrio-raised Jewish bassist dancing in circles with Chicano *salseros*, a Japanese American tabla player, and an African-American MC serves notice that L.A. is healing its post–Rodney King riot wounds quite nicely.

The strength of Ozomatli's experiment is their seamless mingling of the salsa and hiphop worlds, which even though technically separate, are increasingly merging. Ozomatli are coining an Esperanto of Spanglish music. They have direct lineage to the California school of political bands like Rage Against the Machine (which features Zack de la Rocha, a half-Chicano lead singer, and Tom Morello, a half-black, half-Italian guitarist), they've opened for the Cure, and they play in Latin alternative circles as well. Ozomatli does for Los Angeles what the Nuyorican Poets Café did for New York: It offers a Spanglish cultural construction, salsa music (parallel to the Café's bilingual poetry), as a jumping-off point for a new North American experiment in multiculturalism. Their music is a place where inter-Latino differences (salsa vs. *cumbia* vs. Mexican regional) fuse with African American exigencies (hiphop, funk), while presenting a lineup that includes whites and Asians.

Coming from San Francisco, where they once teamed with Marga Gomez, a half–Puerto Rican, half-Cuban comedian from New York, and poet Jose Antonio Burciaga, Culture Clash has survived through the years to stake a legitimate claim to being the dominant figures of California's Spanglish theater movement. Made up of one Chicano, Richard Montoya, son of Jose, the founder of the Royal Chicano Air Force, and two Salvadoran Americans, Ric Salinas and Herbert Siguenza, Culture Clash combines politics, comedy, and identity search to produce some of the most vital narratives of the Spanglish experience today.

Playing with icons like Che Guevara and Julio Iglesias, Culture Clash skewers holy figures of Latino consciousness by presenting them in an MTV context. Lampooning post-Bamba Chicano reality with a dark sarcasm that belies the myth of the complacent Latino, Clash employs a Marxism much like that of the '60s California-based comedy group Firesign Theater: they're equally indebted to both Karl and Groucho. They trade in a rich swirl of ideas examining the dilemma of mixed-race identity, the quirky differences between individual Latino groups, and the dislocation political activists felt as the swinging '60s crash-landed in the Reagan '80s.

Founded in 1984 at the tail end of the *teatro movimiento* era, Culture Clash performed the heroic feat of not letting left and anti-assimilationist politics die in their attempt to get away from the stodginess and one-dimensional mournful tone of that sort of work. In early skits like "The Return of Che," Chuy (Montoya), is a bug-eyed burned-out radical hooked on football, pining for the bygone era of Chicano activism. His friend Juan Santero (Salinas) is on a Caribbean-identity trip, obsessed with Afro-Cuban Santería one week and Rastafarianism the next. In "Stand and Deliver Pizza," Jaime Escalante (Siguenza) mediates a dispute between a brown-and-proud, hiphop-influenced *cholo,* and an "Axel Rose, 7–11 Slurpee drinking, MTV whiteboy wannabe" Chicano. Salinas, the best dancer of the three, also does a skit that harps on the skilled mambo dancing identity of East Coast Latinos as something out-side most Chicanos' experience.

Over the last several years Culture Clash has fought wars with the Hollywood establishment, producing one short-lived regular television show on Fox that came in the wake of the success of black/white spoof *In Living Color.* But for the most part their efforts have been put on eternal hold, their projects canceled. This is most likely because they refuse to compromise on the complexity of Latino identity, which is anathema to the narrow marketing imperatives of commercial entertainment. The ferocious humor of their politics struck home for me once when backstage at a Latino comedy revue at New York's Village Gate, they became enraged

197

when iceberg lettuce, a product still boycotted by the UFW, was served for the performers. Montoya grabbed all the lettuce and furiously poured it directly into trash containers, stomping up and down on them for emphasis.

In the last few years Culture Clash has sharpened its interest in "other" Latino cultures by writing and performing a series of plays about Miami, San Diego, and finally New York. The Miami play was most effective when it pointed out the long-held resentment by the black community of the Cuban community, something that started when the Cuban-American mayor of Miami denounced the visiting Nelson Mandela as a terrorist. The San Diego play took on the border attitudes of Mexican Americans, recent Mexican arrivals, and of course the Anglo and border patrol types, and exploded what is probably the most tension-filled anti-immigrant area in the U.S.

More recently, Culture Clash has been working with Jesús Treviño, who filmed the Chicano Youth Liberation Conference in Denver where the plan of Aztlan was first presented. The director, who co-executive produces the Latino-themed television show *Resurrection Boulevard*, is collaborating with Culture Clash on *In Search of Aztlan*, an hourlong docu-comedy.

In early 2001, Los Angeles had a mayoral election that in many ways is a preview of its future. Former California Assembly speaker Antonio Villaraigosa came extremely close to becoming the first Latino mayor of Los Angeles since the nineteenth century. He is a third-generation Chicano who has risen to power by making a series of varied political alliances, as well as playing at a kind of centrist politics that embraces both liberal and conservative stances. Villaraigosa built his reputation as a state senator in Sacramento by not necessarily supporting every "Hispanic" issue and deigning to make alliances with other ethnic groups. He built a coalition of white liberals, Hispanics, and unions, finally breaking the Republican control that Riordan represented. But the fact that most of the black vote went to James Hahn, his opponent, seems to indicate that Los Angeles hasn't solved its black-Latino conflict, which goes back to the days when Tom Bradley used a Jewish-black coalition and left Mexican Americans on the outside looking in.

Villaraigosa failed to win black support despite the fact that he helped form Los Angeles's black-Latino Roundtable in the '80s, and has been active in the fight against police brutality, an issue that resounds loudly in the city of Rodney King. But there may have been other factors at work that denied him the support of blacks—ironically, the increasingly powerful union movement of Los Angeles janitors, a phenomenon that radicalizes recent immigrants, protects jobs that were once held by blacks. The center of African-American geographical power, South Central, has been increasingly colonized by Salvadorans and recent Mexican immigrants. There seems to be a ready-made socio-political tension between blacks and Latinos in L.A.

Conversely, Bronx Nuyorican Fernando Ferrer's mayoral bid in 2001 seemed to fail because he constructed a successful black-Latino coalition—he got astoundingly few white votes. Both Ferrer and Villaraigosa were victimized in the end by negative campaigning. Villaraigosa was wounded by an ad that connected him with a drug dealer, Ferrer with subliminal implications that he was a surrogate for activist Al Sharpton.

The way that the various Spanglish tribes comingle, as well as how they make alliances with blacks and Asians, will determine a lot about the possibilities of a Spanglish future. As we wrestle with the possibilities and incongruities of a monolithic Latino consciousness, we bump up against each other's sensibilities and find enormous differences. The main fault line in this exploration is between East and West; but there are considerable outposts of difference to the South and in the Midwest.

7.

EAST COAST–WEST COAST:

The Imagined and Real Properties
of an Intracontinental Latino Cultural
and Political Divide

I wanna dress like a Chicano because
Plaid flannels feel right to me
I wanna dress like a Chicano because
I like the sound of the word cholo
I wanna dress like a Chicano because
I'm bored with conventional, male-female cross-dressing
I wanna dress like a Chicano because
I got a little low riding, Cisco Kid was a friend of mine
Vibe in me
I wanna dress like a Chicano because
Some of my best friends are Chicano
I wanna dress like a Chicano because

Puerto Ricans are living on the border, too
And I got a Nuyorican passport to a Magic Mountain
Where roller coaster rides are free
I wanna dress like a Chicano because
I got all the razas in the world inside of me
                                              —ED MORALES

Tupac versus Biggie; Suge versus Puffy; the names that epitomize what is known as gangsta rap came to symbolize a split in the hiphop community that was at the same time very real but also imaginary. The East Coast–West Coast split garnered much publicity because of rumors surrounding the violent deaths of two rappers, and the real violence carried out by their respective managers. While this apparent conflict has been correctly downplayed as relatively insignificant in the larger picture of how African Americans get along culturally and politically in the U.S., it did reflect the struggle over political and cultural capital between the East Coast and West Coast. In the mainstream world, this split is evident in the rivalry over cultural capital between New York, the publishing capital, and Los Angeles, the film capital, and also an emerging "dot-com" rivalry between the Bay Area's Silicon Valley and an upstart high-tech business community located in Manhattan's Flatiron District.

The idea of a contiguous, monolithic Latin identity in America while we are just beginning to find ourselves as a people is blatantly absurd. Rather, as marketers strive to find the key elements about Latinos so that they can catch and keep our attention, they reveal an East Coast–West Coast split between Latinos that is equally obscure to the mainstream. The divide is roughly defined by the two dominant Latino groups in the U.S.: Puerto Ricans on the East Coast and Mexicans on the West Coast. While Cubans, Dominicans, and, increasingly, South American and Mexican immigrants are significant players in the East, and Central Americans are more important in the West, the highly defined "Spanglish" cultures of

New York Puerto Ricans and L.A. Chicanos are the groups this chapter will focus on to make the East Coast–West Coast distinction. In fact, it can be argued that outside groups on either coast assimilate into the Nuyorican and Chicano model to a large extent: L.A. native Benjamin Bratt, of Peruvian background, is often assumed to be Chicano; and John Leguizamo, the comic actor of Colombian ancestry, has claimed a partial Puerto Rican ancestry and is in many ways a classic Nuyorican.

The essence of the East Coast–West Coast split can be attributed to the legendary difference between the coasts' principal cities, New York and Los Angeles. New York has been settled by a variety of Hispanic cultures from all over Latin America, particularly those with a Caribbean port. The unsettled political status of Cuba and Puerto Rico and the necessity to create a Spanglish identity in New York, the city of the melting pot, as well as the greater diversity of racial types among the Caribbeans, nurtured a multi-Latino identity formation. But in Los Angeles, a city with sharply defined and segregated communities that afford little interaction in places like subways and crowded downtown streets, there was a Mexican American hegemony and a premium placed on Chicano identity, to the exclusion of other existing groups. Even more telling is the fact that a majority of Latinos in New York engage in interethnic marriage with other Latino groups, whereas, according to Mike Davis's *Magical Urbanism*, in California less than 15 percent of Mexican Americans marry outside their Mexican group.

While there are pronounced differences in speaking accents, dress, food, and mannerisms between Nuyoricans and Chicanos, there are haunting similarities. The importance of extended family, the vestiges of Roman Catholicism, the soft, sad brown eyes and light brown skin that constitutes the vast middle ground of Latino phenotypes carry significant weight. But for practical purposes, East is East and West is West and rarely do the twain meet. The essence of Nuyorican/Chicano cultures is not interacting on a significant level because we are separated by large tracts of land, and there are important differences in our respective ethos. There are several fundamental distinctions between the East Coast (Nuyorican-dominated) and West Coast (Chicano-dominated) Latino. The first is the striking difference between Puerto Rican, or Caribbean culture, which features a strong African component, and Mexican culture, which features a strong indigenous component. Another is the fact that the East Coast presence was established by a relatively more recent wave of migration of Puerto Ricans as opposed to the Chicanos, many of whose roots go back to the days when California was part of Mexico, and who have a longer period of assimilation into North American culture. In many Latino-dominated cities in California and Texas there are different neighborhoods that reflect different levels of Chicano assimilation. In San Antonio, the West Side houses more recent immigrants and is a kind of Mexican American "movement" museum, whereas the South Side is more Americanized and allows for a multifaceted playing around with lifestyles—salsa, Tejano, techno, punk rock.

Another key difference between the coasts is each region's approach to immigration: California is a place where difference is smoothed out in an attempt to create a "generic" American. The nonregional accent that is standard on broadcast journalism had California as its milieu. On the West Coast, even some Mexican Americans support the idea that some form of immigration control is necessary. In New York, on the other hand, ethnic difference is celebrated to both positive and negative effect. The New York speaking accent is described as an amalgam of European ethnic groups like Irish, Italian, and Jewish, and African American (despite the existence of a "black English," which strives further and further to be separate as a key aspect to identity). Former New York mayor Rudolph Giuliani, a social conservative whose policies have resulted in the criminalization of Latino men, was a staunch supporter of immigrants' rights. If the Anglo attitude toward Mexican Americans is conditioned primarily by an anti-immigrant prejudice, in New York, the attitude toward Puerto Ricans is more parallel to the racism reserved for African Americans, because of many factors. First, Puerto Ricans are technically not immigrants because they are born American citizens; second, the political movements of the '60s and the close proximity to African Americans in city neighborhoods have prompted many Puerto Ricans to "assimilate" as blacks.

Most Southern California Chicanos have grown up in, and are comfortable in, a suburban milieu. While Latino presence in the suburbs of New York is increasing, Nuyorican-ness is defined by an urban sensibility. These differences are today perhaps most emphasized in taste in popular music. As the '60s gave way to the '70s, rock and roll slowly evolved from a genre that mixed black r&b with white country blues, which cultivated fans of all races, to a mostly white genre that was played by and for a white audience. As the '70s wore on, the salsa world exploded and the hiphop world was being born, and the exigencies of segregation in New York created a situation in which most Nuyoricans identified with African-American tastes, and therefore balked at "white" rock music. On the island, Puerto Rico's colonial relationship with the U.S. allowed the development of a core of elite students from the privileged classes who studied in English schools; they became the majority of rock fans on the island, while the masses identified with the Afro-Cuban rhythms of salsa. Much of Latin America's left, whose music was the *nueva canción* of Argentina's Mercedes Sosa and Cuba's Silvio Rodriguez, rejected rock music. That antirock strand joined with Puerto Rico's race- and class-charged rejection of rock; to be a fan of rock and roll was a doubly traitorous thing for Puerto Ricans.

In Mexico, and increasingly in Southern California, rock and roll is being embraced by a Latino culture to express its political alienation that paralleled '60s-style rock but still possessed a unique voice. But the predilection for rock in Mexican and Mexican-American culture, which contrasts with the loyalty to Afro-Cuban salsa among Caribbean cultures, is a major split between the East and West Coast right now. As alluded to in *Refried Elvis*, rock represents a North American modernity, a space where Latin American youth can create some breathing room between themselves and the traditional family-oriented male-dominated culture. But just as Mexico has an uncertain method for including Africans in their national culture, the way rock has evolved provokes a hostility from Caribbean Latin cultures that are heavily invested in the African interest.

The African influence, or lack thereof, had already created a divide between East and West Coast in the world of "traditional" Latin music, where little overlap exists between fans of traditional Mexican music like *rancheras, corridos, norteño*, and Tejano (which are primarily derived from Spanish folk and German polka influences), and the Afro-Caribbean sounds of salsa and merengue that dominate the East Coast. This opposition is rooted in the regionalization of Latin American cultures. In the future, the beat that might bring both coasts together is the *cumbia*, a rhythm that is a strong favorite of Mexicans but was begun by Colombians, a group attaining increasing importance and influence on the East Coast.

One of the main reasons Latinos have had a difficult time promoting a united political agenda is the East Coast–West Coast split in political alliances. While African Americans have the NAACP, Latinos have the National Council of La Raza, which despite its attempts to act as an umbrella group, is predominantly a Mexican American power base. Mexican Americans constitute about 60 percent of the entire Latino population in the country, and their presence has been established the longest, so it follows that their political power is the most massive. The Mexican-American agenda can run the gamut from left-wing to conservative, but it functions more as an *American* political group, with little or no ties to the mother country. This is further reinforced by the remarks of Mexican president Vicente Fox's foreign minister Jorge Castañeda, who has said that Mexico should pursue a foreign policy that conformed to the interest of Mexico and not Chicanos. One of the striking aspects of the votes to control illegal immigration in California is that while the Chicano left was strongly against the proposed legislation, there was a sizable Mexican-American middle ground that actually voted for it. In 1996, a solidly Latino congressional district in El Paso County, Texas, elected Silvestre Reyes, a former official of the U.S. Border Patrol and a planner behind Operation Hold the Line, the INS strategy to prevent illegal immigration along the Southwest border.

Most people don't realize that during L.A.'s Rodney King riots of 1991 more Latinos were arrested than African Americans. But even if you were cognizant of that fact, it doesn't reveal that most of the Latinos arrested were from the heavily Salvadoran Pico-Union district, and not the Mexican-American stronghold of East L.A. A year later, while several constituencies grappled over the federal monies allotted for reconstruction, there was political jockeying that pitted East L.A. Mexican Americans against African-American groups. This flare-up came to a head that fall when Mexican American political groups threw their support behind Mayor Riordan in his reelection campaign over an African-American candidate.

As *Zoot Suit* establishes, the Mexican-American experience in Los Angeles is very much akin to the African-American experience in major urban areas in America. But this experience is more of a direct claim to oppression or "blackness," rather than an attempt to make an alliance with blackness. This probably stems from the fact that at the dawn of the civil rights era, Mexican Americans had their own Supreme Court case, *Peter Hernandez v. Texas*, where it was ruled that Mexicans were "a distinct class" who could claim protection from discrimination. The equal protection under the law amendment of the Constitution was therefore used as separately for Mexicans as it was for blacks and women.

The Mexican-American hip-hop that has been created in L.A. by groups like A Lighter Shade of Brown, Kid Frost, and Proper Dos seems another direct claim to "blackness" in which the Latin experience is separated into a kind of private hip-hop domain. On the other hand, Nuyorican hiphoppers like the Beatnuts, Noreaga, the late Big Pun, and Fat Joe Cartagena make little claim to Latin-ness outside of occasionally giving props to "Boricuas." The Nuyorican component of hiphop tends to become obscured by or swallowed up by the hegemonic black experience. In her book *Changing Race*, Clara E. Rodriguez interviews the late Fat Joe Cartagena, who identifies himself as "a Puerto Rican of African descent."

With the exception of New Jersey's and Florida's Cuban-American representatives, most East Coast Latino politicians are Nuyoricans who follow an agenda that is essentially a reflection of the African-American agenda. The growing nationalism in Puerto Rico has done much to spur Nuyorican loyalty and deep connection to political issues in Puerto Rico. Congressman José Serrano has been one of the staunchest opponents of the Navy's bombing practice held for the last thirty years on Vieques, a small island just off the eastern coast of Puerto Rico. Congresswoman Nydia Velázquez was formerly a key figure in that island's Commonwealth Party, and is also an Navy-out-of-Vieques activist, and Congressman Luis Gutiérrez of Chicago occasionally flirts with open calls for independence for the island. The left bent of Nuyorican-dominated East Coast Spanglish politics coincides with issues specific to the Puerto Rican community: Vieques and the independence movement, police brutality against Latino youth, and decline in population, and therefore political clout—they are activist politics. This is happening just as Mexican Americans are gaining greater success through institutional channels and beginning to produce politicians who don't restrict themselves to a Latino-oriented agenda.

To be fair, there are exceptions to the tendencies I have pointed out above on both sides. The 2000 election in Mexico of opposition party candidate Vicente Fox was in part accomplished by unprecedented campaigning by Fox (as well as his opponents) in U.S. cities. Their barnstorming tours were brought about because of a new Mexican policy to encourage voting by ex-Mexican nationals now living in the U.S. Of course Fox, from the conservative PAN party, benefited most from this because most recent arrivals were disaffected from the almost-dictatorial seventy-two-year reign of the PRI party. This policy can be contrasted with Puerto Rico's refusal to allow mainland Puerto Ricans to vote in the island's status plebiscite for fear that emigrated islanders would vote heavily for statehood. And just as California and Texas have elected conservative and neoconservative Latinos to office, New York City has the political presence of Herman Badillo, a Giuliani appointee as chancellor of the city university system, and the '90s tenure of Antonio Pagan, a pro–real estate city councilman.

The East Coast–West Coast split manifests itself in an ironic way through television and movie casting. The trend over the last ten years has been for the film industry, when it produces stories about Latinos, to focus on Mexican-American stories (*La Bamba, Selena, Lone Star, Mi Familia*). The excellent Showtime series *Resurrection Boulevard* is also Chicano-focused. But while the stories are about the West, most of the actors used to fill the roles are from the East Coast: Esai Morales, who plays Ritchie Valens's brother in *La Bamba*, is Nuyorican; Jimmy Smits and Jennifer Lopez, Nuyoricans, dominate *Mi Familia*; Elizabeth Peña and Miriam Colón, a Cuban American and Nuyorican respectively, play Tejanos in *Lone Star*; and most famously, Ms. Lopez, over the protests of Mexican Americans, appeared as Tejana music star Selena. Perhaps the best explanation for this is the larger number of theater opportunities for actors living in New York, while the most influential Latino film producers (Moctuzema Esparza, Ed Olmos, Gregory Nava) are Mexican Americans based on the West Coast.

THE SWEET *SCIENCIA*

With the recent focus on boxing by the advertising-media world in an attempt to delineate a contiguous identity between East and West Coast Latinos, it would seem valid to focus on a particular boxing match to get a feel for the intracontinental divide. A unique metaphorical manifestation of the East Coast–West Coast conflict was the 1999 boxing match between the Puerto Rican resident Felix "Tito" Trinidad and the Mexican American Oscar de la Hoya.

Trinidad, who is light years behind de la Hoya in terms of glitz and recognition, is the kind of quiet, unassuming country boy that Puerto Ricans, who have their own longtime love affair with the underdog role, love to love. The San Juan Spanish-language daily *El Nuevo Dia* characterized Trinidad as a "healthy, humble guy who always has time for his fans and his community." Trinidad had to overcome early doubts from the public about his not fighting in the Barcelona Olympics by winning steadily in spite of the criticism, and avoiding the falls from grace over drug abuse that ruined the careers of previous Puerto Rican heroes like Edwin "Chapo" Rosario, who died of an overdose in 1997; Wilfredo Gomez, arrested in 1994 on charges of domestic violence and cocaine possession; and Esteban DeJesus, who had public struggles with drugs and AIDS.

Most importantly, however, even though Trinidad is an island boy, he has substantial support in New York. This sort of cross-migratory appeal is another of the distinguishing characteristics of Nuyoricans that make for a crucial difference with their Chicano counterparts. The facility of traveling back and forth between New York and San Juan, both in low airfare cost and the lack of need for a passport or visa, make Nuyoricans and Puerto Ricans much more tightly linked than Chicanos and Mexicans.

Meanwhile, on the West Coast, Oscar de la Hoya is a one-man financial empire. He has recorded a pop album with EMI records and made close to $40 million in 1999, making him among the highest paid athletes in the world. His pop-idol looks rival Ricky Martin's, he's impeccably bilingual, and plays up his Mexican roots by wearing nouveau-Zorro outfits into the ring. In 1996, de la Hoya slayed a significant dragon by defeating Julio César Chavez from Mexico, in a fight that seemed to finally define the Chicano boxing fan as separate from the Mexican boxing fan. But his incredible crossover success has brought him criticism.

His road to success from East L.A. to Bel Air makes him a target for some, and an object of admiration for others in the Mexican-American community. He fits into the mold of a '90s Gen X Chicano, albeit with a strong hardworking striver ethic, but has been known to dally with the occasional *Bay Watch* babe. Many Chicanos question his commitment to the barrio despite the fact that he runs a boxing clinic there that features social programs in education. He still faced the problem of leftover Julio César Chavez fans, more Mexican immigrants who felt de la Hoya was too assimilated, and in defense dragged mariachi bands into the ring with him to prove his national identification with Mexico. I happened to travel to Mexico City the week before the fight, and in several impromptu interviews with hotel attendants, cabdrivers and other locals, I found a profound lack of interest in de la Hoya's fortunes.

The so-called Fight of the Decade was a natural rivalry between the stoic, purposeful Trinidad, and the existential, artistic de la Hoya. Fiery Boricua versus Chill Chicano. The entrance of both fighters into the ring that fateful night would be a spectacle that said much about the distribution of nationalism in the battle of the Coasts. While de la Hoya had scored some points with his two-flag, American-Mexican mixed-message entrance in previous fights, this night the dynamic symbolism belonged to Felix Trinidad.

As is his wont, de la Hoya was masterful in inhabiting the green and red imagery that so many regional Mexican musicians do—all that was missing was the Virgen de Guadalupe. But his almost yuppie demeanor—which was so evident in postfight interviews in which he explained his defeat by alluding to the judges' inability to appreciate his technical skills, when they so clearly had voted against his lack of passion—muted his nationalist ploy.

Trinidad, on the other hand, was a powerful signifier of both Nuyorican and Puerto Rican nationalism, one that had less to do with the island's political status than its dynamic transnational culture. The fight took place in the middle of a fierce political battle that was going on between the island and the U.S. Navy over the bombing of Vieques. Tito Trinidad appeared in the ring with a sign demanding an end to the bombing of Vieques. In addition, he appeared in a *pava*, a *campesino* hat co-opted as a symbol of the status-quo Commonwealth party (PDP), and boxing trunks with the logo of Westernbank, an institution the pro-corporate state-hood party has done its best to accommodate. But perhaps most importantly, Trinidad invited rappers Big Pun and Fat Joe to do a musical invocation to his effort, a clear manifestation of the boxer's willingness to include Nuyoricans in his nationalistic spectacle. The celebration of his victory was almost as big in New York as it was on the island.

All of this is not to deny that there are tensions between Puerto Ricans and Nuyoricans—in fact, the term, according to Nuyorican Poets Café founder Miguel Algarín, was coined by islanders as a way of distancing themselves from what they considered to be infe-rior versions of Puerto Rican-ness. Nuyoricans speak too much En-glish, have forgotten the great cultural heroes of the island, and except for the left and during occasional issues like Vieques, are uninvolved in its politics.

This rejection by the mother country is a similar dynamic to the one that happens between Mexicans and Mexican Americans. But the gulf is wider there because of the fact that California and Texas were different regions once part of Mexico with their own indige-nous and European ancestors. Puerto Ricans can only be nostalgic about their Taino roots—the indigenous inhabitants of the island have disappeared save for vestiges in our genetic information and things like food and hammocks. There is also a leftover feeling among Mexicans that many among their Mexican-American breth-ren betrayed the mother country by leaving in the middle of the 1910 revolution. Much time and space haunts the tenuous ties between Chicanos and Chilangos (a nickname for inhabitants of Mexico City). "At present, the only thing that unites those who left Mexico and those who stayed is our inability to understand and accept our inevitable differences," said Guillermo Gómez-Peña in his essay, "Danger Zone: Cultural Relations Between Chicanos and

Mexicans at the End of the Century." Still, the extreme left of the Chicano movement, the true believers in returning to a separatist, secessionist territory that might resemble Aztlan, believes in rejecting the European influence, in relearning the ancient language of Nahautl, while Puerto Ricans, who trumpet their identification with Africans, rarely reject their Spanish roots.

SPANGLISH COUNTRY MOUSE, SPANGLISH CITY MOUSE

The Intracontinental Spanglish divide can be compared to ancient rivalry between town and country, in this case more like the separation between the coast and the plains, one that exists in most Latin American countries. The Caribbean, a dynamic contiguous culture spread over several islands, as in Antonio Benitez-Rojo's "repeating island" paradigm, informed the rhythms of my thinking. The *s*'s are dropped at the end of the word, the vowels become more sensual, the speech more staccato. The Caribbean psyche is impatient with the humidity, sweaty and aggressive. It is informed by the vitality of the coast, the bustle of commerce in coastal port towns, the daring of escaped slaves reinventing themselves as Latin Americans.

California and Mexico present an arid expanse of calm, of airy guitar chords slipping along on desert winds. There are always lurking spirits and psychedelic herbs, drinks, teas, funguses to turn the world on its head. In California I found an easy willingness to make a newly accented English mainstream, a lack of guilt about becoming Americanized, and among many, a reverence for the mother country and its myths.

Mother. Is that the big difference between Nuyoricans and Mexican Americans? I was always impressed when during Mexican rock concerts, young bare-chested men at the height of testosterone-fueled adolescence would fanatically wave a portrait of La Virgen de Guadalupe as a symbol of nationalism. Isn't *la virgen* what womanist author Ana Castillo would call the universal symbol of matriarchy? While most Mexican women would staunchly assert the indelible presence of sexism in their men, there is an undeniable air of matriarchy expressed by Chicano culture. In a performance done by Lalo Lopez's old theater group, Chicano Secret Service, there was a skit about women making tortillas—and it was played for laughs!

In Culture Clash's 1999 play about Nuyoricans, *Nuyorican Stories*, they focused on the overwhelmingly male character of certain Nuyorican institutions like the Nuyorican Poets Café and the Young Lords. There was an excellent caricature of Miguel Algarín and his bawdy personality and Pedro Pietri and his spaced-out demeanor. According to the version of the play that I saw, in the words of the Algarín character, radical politics died in the '70s and sexual curiosity took its place. There may be a truth to that idea that is considerably more universal than the perspective of U.S. Latinos, but in the way that it gives the imperative to the male point of view, it seems to capture the masculine-driven nature of Nuyorican that is at least visible to outsiders as such.

Interestingly, most of the important literary work around sexual identity and Chicanos has been done by women like Gloria Anzaldua, who reinvigorates *La Raza cosmica* as a pansexual project; Ana Castillo, who re-creates Aztlan fantasies as a woman-empowering mythology; Cherrie Moraga, who finds a way to riff on matriarchal inevitability through the structural impetus of UFW agitprop theater. The Chicana feminists rehabilitated the figure of La Malinche, who was denounced by Luis Valdez in his 1971 play *The Conquest of Mexico* because "not only did she turn her back on her own people, she joined the white men and became assimilated."

In much of this chapter I have alluded to the idea of blackness as a component of Latin identity and that a major difference between Nuyorican and Chicano, or East Coast and West Coast, is the relative amount of blackness each group feels is a part of its identity. It must also be recognized that there is no shortage of racism in the Puerto Rican community. While Puerto Rico on the whole is a mulatto/mestizo island, that majority possesses a skin-color privilege that puts darker, African Puerto Ricans in a position of disadvantage. Still, the migration of Puerto Ricans to New York seems to liberate black Puerto Ricans, giving them freedom to identify with African Americans, and in a way overturn the vestiges of colonial racism that exists in most of Latin America.

Thankfully, societies and cultures evolve quickly in the information age, and things change dramatically. In Los Angeles, a music group like Ozomatli, which has strong political concerns, represents a partnership between Mexican-American music and African-American hip-hop (as well as featuring a Jewish bass player and a Japanese percussionist). The Conga Room, whose co-owners include Jimmy Smits and Jennifer Lopez, is one of Ozomatli's favorite places to play, and the club is a major player in the proliferation of salsa and merengue on the West Coast. The mainstream East L.A. mindset is very much in tune with hip-hop and salsa—radio stations in Los Angeles like The Beat 100.3 focus on Latinos and hip-hop, and salsa clubs open up by the minute in West Side areas like Universal City.

A Mexican graduate student in performance art studies, Guadalupe Garcia has been living in New York for the past several years and has been engaging in research about Mexico's African past. It was Garcia's involvement with a Santería sect in Manhattan that provided much of the material for an article I did on Santería in 1996. The musical group Café Tacuba, from the northern suburbs of Mexico City, has also given nods to the African influence in Mexico in several of its songs. Undoubtedly cities like Chicago, which is the largest city in the U.S. to have a significant Puerto Rican and Mexican population, will point the way toward the resolution of East Coast–West Coast opposition. And as CNN correspondent (and Chicago Chicana) Maria Hinojosa likes to say, Mexicans from Puebla are making a major impact on my hometown New York, including a dominant influence on El Barrio in

Manhattan and Sunset Park in Brooklyn, two very significant Puerto Rican neighborhoods.

COLOMBIAN GOLD

When examining the split between Nuyoricans and Chicanos, between Puerto Rico and Mexico, the possibilities of Colombian culture are invigorating. During a recent trip to Colombia, I found that it appeared to have everything that I admired and cherished in both Puerto Rican and Mexican culture. To be Colombian is to simultaneously celebrate European, African, and indigenous culture. In my travels I found the fast-talking Andalusian modern-Spanish slang that peppered Caribbean speech and the rock and roll, straight-black-haired, spacey indigenous mysticism that holds sway over Mexico. It was a place where salsa and rock were played with great proficiency and blackness seemed as important as the legacy of the Chibcha, the indigenous people who forged a thriving civilization along the Rio Magdalena. Relatives of the Chibcha may have migrated up the river to the coast and across the Caribbean to become the Tainos of Puerto Rico.

They dance the *cumbia*, a Mexican favorite, in Colombia; it's a dance that began along the coastal areas of that country and evolved as settlers, slaves, and indigenous people propelled by their Spanish conquerors, made their way into the interior of the country. The *cumbia* is a unique rhythm in Latin America because it combines indigenous and African influences. Colombian composer Jose Barros's *cumbia* "La Piragua" tells the story of a sixteenth-century Spanish declaration that standardized boat and canoe personnel used to transport goods from the interior, via the Rio Magdalena, to coastal Cartagena. There would be six indigenous rowers and six Africans. This division of labor began centuries of interactions between indigenous people and Africans that yielded the *cumbia* and the *vallenato*, among others. The unique hybrid of musical traditions was not found in the Caribbean islands, where the indigenous populations had died out from disease or genocide.

When I was in Colombia I was privy to the good-natured ravings of a group of pseudo-Marxist musicologists who believed in the *cumbia*'s transcendence over the accepted framework of "Latin" music. They felt the *cumbia* was different from the Cuban clave-based musics because the African element, like Brazil's samba, may have derived more from the Congo-based cultures than the Yoruban-based cultures. They relished in making the point that the *cumbia* has a shamanic element because it stresses the upbeat. The musical influence of Colombia in present-day Latin music is becoming increasingly important. Latin rock groups like Aterciopelados and Bloque were among the first to include Afro-Latin percussion in the "alternative" genre, freeing it from its progressive-rock trappings. And the revolution in Latin pop was strongly affected by Colombian producer Kike Santander, who had a major role in the success of Emilio Estefan stars like Thalia, as well as his wife, Gloria.

The East Coast–West Coast conflict just scratches the surface of intra-Latino rivalries that probably won't shake out into pan-Latino harmony for another century. Within the New York area, conservative Cubans, based in New Jersey, live almost completely physically and spiritually apart from the rest of the area's Latinos. A rapidly growing immigrant community from the Dominican Republic, based largely in Washington Heights, Manhattan, which the Cubans abandoned in the '70s, has outworked Puerto Ricans, taking over the *bodega* (grocery store) business from them, creating a new rivalry. South Americans like Colombians, Peruvians, Argentines, and Venezuelans cluster in Queens in areas that share space with Asian and South Asian immigrants, but these areas don't have significant black populations. In Washington, D.C., Salvadorans are establishing growing presences, living, in Puerto Rican–like fashion, in close quarters with African Americans. In Los Angeles, Salvadorans are displacing blacks in South Central and even challenging the dominance of Chicano gangs. Salvadorans have become the dominant Latino group in South Central, but are establishing Puerto Rican–like ties with African Americans in that majority black city. In Miami, newer immigrants from Central and

South America are challenging the dominance of the Cuban community, much of which has moved out of the inner city and into the white suburbs. And Mexicans are increasingly moving into towns all over the U.S., from the heartland to New York City.

All of these groups have differences that are based on the subtle variations between Latin American countries, which are all tied to historical events that affected the balance of Spanish, African, and indigenous contributions to their respective gene pools. But the one thing that I seem to find constant about Latino schisms is that the more we believe ourselves to be different, the more we are revealed to be the same. As much as Cubans and Puerto Ricans have developed a rivalry and have become each other's political opposite vis-à-vis the U.S., we are virtually the same people, two wings of the same bird, as a famous song states. When I traveled to Colombia, locals were surprised that I knew what a *sancocho* (meat or fish stew) was, when it was a staple in Puerto Rico. No sooner did I assume that the typical Colombian form of greeting, *"Que hubo"* was a national trait, than I read of its being used between Mexican American gang members in Luis Rodriguez's *Always Running*. The moment I assumed Argentina had excised its African influence is the moment I found out that the tango has its roots in African dance.

Demographic wisdom seems to indicate that California is the window we can look into to see the future of America. While the U.S. is projected by the Census Bureau to become majority nonwhite by the year 2059, this has already happened in California. The fastest-growing minority groups, Latinos and Asians, are increasing in number exceptionally quickly in California. The fastest-growing rate of intermarriage among minority groups is occurring among Latinos and Asians in California. What's more, the relative conservatism of nouveau middle-class Latinos and traditional, socially conservative new immigrants have made Latinos in California more susceptible to the political pitches of Republicans and conservatives.

But while the new presidency of Vicente Fox Quesada may bring a new resonance between Mexican and recent Mexican-American immigrant attitudes, a new generation of Chicanos may rebel against their parents and rally to the defense of the Zapatistas in Chiapas, just as middle-class professional Nuyoricans are rallying around the cause of the new Puerto Rican nationalism.

TEJANOVILLE

In some ways Texas is the most Spanglish region in the United States, given its bizarre history of landgrabbing and final dislocation from a crumbling Mexico. Tejanos are fiercely distinct from California Mexicans, and their presence is much more historically important than that of the Californios, those who lived in California when it was part of Mexico. Within Texas there is a distinction between Houston Mexicans, who have become part of an American urban sprawl equation, now joined by a sizable Guatemalan immigration, and South Texans, who live more dispersed in smaller cities and towns, and who have a more organic tie to the history of Aztlan, Mexico, and the Lone Star State.

Although San Antonio sits some two hundred miles from the border of Mexico in southwest Texas, it is in many ways a spiritual center of Aztlan. Once you get past the weird energy surrounding the Alamo, you can relax and enjoy the mariachi guys at the cheesy Market Square restaurants. But the contrast between the Riverwalk, where tourists slurp down cactus margaritas at trendy sidewalk cafés, and the city's West Side, bordered by a huge network of railroad tracks, is jolting, a textbook example of what happened to American cities in the '80s—downtown gentrification at the expense of minority neighborhoods. Along Guadalupe Street, rows of ramshackle wooden houses lean forward in seeming melancholy, the kind arising from a deep and long-standing poverty.

But the South Side, which borders the King William district that is home to Sandra Cisneros, is making noise as a Tejano arts stronghold. The typical array of trendy restaurants, cozy kitsch boutiques, and coffee shops line South Alamo Street. San Antonio is a place where Tejanos have succeeded economically and politically, at least on the surface. Famous for two of the country's most visible Latino politicians, former mayor Henry Cisneros and one-time firebrand Congressman Henry Gonzalez (who once introduced a bill in the House to impeach President George Bush over Desert Storm), San Antonio is a place where brownness is present at all levels of society. Recently, traffic between Austin, Chicago, and San Antonio has created a kind of Tejano Spanglish intelligentsia. Filmmaker Jim Mendiola made a classic Spanglish short film, *Pretty Vacant*, in which a young San Antonio Tejana explains her identification with punk rock. The town's most famous artistic resident is Sandra Cisneros, whose insistence on painting her house a garish yellow-red raised sustained vehement protest from homeowners in her neighborhood. Cisneros's choice to use the bright colors of Mexican tradition illuminated the incipient cultural bias among San Antonio residents who believe that her choice in home decoration would decrease property values in her neighborhood.

In his brilliant memoir, John Phillip Santos captures the multi-leveled drama of the border region by telling the story of his family, one of the first Mexican families to own their own home in San Antonio. Mining the memories of his family, some given freely, some painfully extracted, Santos pieces together the "double betrayal of Mexico" that his relatives represent. His mother's side of the family was abandoned by Mexico when Texas was left to the Anglos; his father's side chose to abandon northern Mexico for San Antonio in the 1910s, when the Mexican Revolution turned their home region into a chaotic battleground.

Both branches tightly held on to their traditions, but as Santos grew up, he felt the Mexican in them fade. Santos's tale describes the slow erosion of his family's Mexican memory, even as he longs to plunge deeper into it. He contemplates the Aztec concept of Inframundo, a place containing both heaven and hell, and when it invades his Manhattan apartment, he meets the ghost of his uncle

Raul. Returning to San Antonio from New York, he elicits unlikely sagas from various relatives: One branch of his family claimed a distant relation to the King of Spain; his great-grandfather, Teofilo, was once kidnapped and raised by Kikapu Indians in northern Mexico. His story illuminates the propensity for movement that is at the root of Spanglish—the nomadic urge that propelled the original Mexicans to move from the Chaco Canyon in Arizona, the center of Aztlan, to Tenochtitlán, the capital of Mexico City. From the movement and the mix of cultures, Santos observes classic Spanglish ambivalence: "For generations among the Santos, there had been an undeniable dichotomy within the clan. There were those among us whose destiny it was to carry what seemed an indelible sadness not of their own making, while there were others who carried a reservoir of ceaseless laughter." In the end, for Santos, his family's ultimate truth was that even though they were the most established Mexican-American family of San Antonio, "there were no more places of origin, just the setting out, just the going forth into new territory, new time."

In some parts of the states that exist within Aztlan, there is a sense of timelessness, an idea that these areas remain archaic reminders of Mexico in the nineteenth century, and in New Mexico's case, where cults of self-flagellating Catholics still exist, sixteenth-century Spain. In Laredo, Texas, a booming border town of 200,000 residents—95 percent of whom are Latino—Washington's Birthday is an intensely observed holiday. It consists of a sixteen-day ritual with events ranging from a parade and a jalapeño-eating contest to a colonial ball and a strait laced U.S.–Mexico bridge ceremony.

The parade features floats populated by Martha Washington Society debutantes, wearing handmade colonial velvet and satin gowns that can cost up to $25,000. Although the society's founders were mostly Anglo women, today's members and debutantes are mostly wealthy Latinas. Laredo's privileged classes have practiced intermarriage as part of the *"mejorar la raza"* rule, which has the affect of compelling Anglo newcomers to assimilate into a bicultural, bilingual society. Laredo's George Washington celebration was founded in 1898 by the Society of Red Men, a fraternal order made up largely of Anglo immigrants from the north. By setting up this patriotic festival, the Red Men sought to bring an American-style holiday to a largely Mexican community. But the Washington celebration, which started as a method of acculturation, quickly evolved into something that reflected the unique bicultural blend of the border region. In a syncretic way that recalls the Carnaval celebrations of Latin America, as well as New Orleans's Mardi Gras, George Washington becomes the "saint" worshipped as an afterthought by a community intent on preserving its Mexican-ness.

Still, many of these border traditions can be seen as cultural negotiations between Anglo and Hispanic forces to smooth over the historical contradiction of Texas's incorporation into the U.S. Incorporating Mexican-ness into American tradition, and vice versa, has the effect of reinforcing the border's dividing power. The strange way Laredo Mexicans remain Mexican is by becoming American—and the "American" way they feel Mexican is probably the reason for Laredo Mexican American's politically expressed desire for tighter border controls, and their disdain for the kitschy, *rasquache* Spanglish renaissance of San Antonio.

The East Coast–West Coast Intracontinental Divide is still about Mexican American consolidation and the primacy of brownness on one side, and the utopian Bolivarianism of the other, but the political necessity of rapprochement is paramount for the Spanglish world in the twenty-first century. The Mexican Americans and Puerto Ricans seem to be in a state of peaceful coexistence in Chicago, the largest city in the U.S. with a somewhat balanced population split between the two groups. Mexican Americans, who began arriving in 1910, number about 60 percent of the Latino population, while Puerto Ricans are at about 23 percent. It's a place where you can go into a bar and find a Mexican White Sox fan drinking with a Puerto Rican Cub fan, best of friends. With the exception of Cleveland, with its large Puerto Rican community, the Midwest in general is still very much dominated by Mexican Americans. Chicago is a place where Chicanos and Nuyorican are strongly identified, where a Puerto Rican U.S. Representative, Luis Gutiérrez, successfully appeals to both camps to keep his House seat. (Still, Gutiérrez acted more like his Chicano counterparts from Los Angeles, delivering a pan-Latino voter alliance to help reelect Mayor Daley over an African American candidate.)

Chicago also has the multilayered neighborhoods that reflect different stages in Mexican immigration, and an explosion of new immigrants from Central and South America. It is most fascinating in the way that it contains the seeds of both East Coast and West Coast Spanglish culture. It's no accident that Luis Valdez staged the twentieth-anniversary revival of *Zoot Suit* in the city.

Latinos in the U.S. are sharply divided, but what we have in common is ultimately more important. The continual evolution of Spanglish reality will incur more and more recombinations of Latino culture, until we begin to recognize ourselves in the mirror of hybridization. Perhaps we won't become a harmonious social and political force until we become more like say, Colombians, who find a way to embrace both their indigenous and African heritage. Until we find that balance we won't be able to speak in one voice.

8.

I AM CUBA

The Cuban folk singer (or *nueva trovador,* as he is known in the parlance of Latin American popular music) Pablo Milanes wrote a song called "Son de Cuba a Puerto Rico" a lyric that comes up repeatedly when Puerto Ricans and Cubans talk positively about each other. *Cuba y Puerto Rico son dos alas del mismo ave* (Cuba and Puerto Rico are the two wings of the same bird). In that way it can be said that we are opposite, that is, left and right wings, and in another way it can be said that we are identical wings. Both assumptions, though contradictory, are of course true, since the saying is descriptive of the two islands' simultaneous rivalry and deep amity.

Milanes, being an ideological exemplar of Cuba's socialist revolution, invoked the phrase as a way to call Puerto Rico to its ultimate destiny, to join Cuba on the socialist road to freedom, where rivalries created by capitalist competition and imperialist divide-and-conquer strategies would dissolve. It's a song best made into a music video depicting a utopian vision of schoolchildren dancing and the dove of peace that landed on Fidel Castro's shoulder at the start of

the revolution flying into a shared sunset. It is a vision, a kind of hallucinatory fantasy that I find no problem indulging in—I have
always seen Cuba as the wealthier older cousin to Puerto Rico.
Cuba is the birthplace of José Martí, one of the great anti-colonial
thinkers of the late nineteenth century. It is the island that dared to
stand up to the U.S. after the Spanish-American War ceded it as war
booty, and finally the nation that engaged in a political experiment
that would throw off the American influence so resoundingly that it
was made unwelcome in the community of nations.

But another part of me feels that Cuba is suffocating itself with
paranoia, that Milanes's invitation to Puerto Rico to share its socialist destiny is a condescending gesture from a much more privileged
child of Spanish colonialism. There's a part of me that feels I could
never live under the watchful eyes of the Committees for the
Defense of the Revolution; that I couldn't entirely reject large
parts of human history for merely being part of a bourgeois ideology; that I could never be happy under a government that has insti-
tuted a virtual apartheid of its own people, restricting them from
tourist areas, even if it feels it is protecting them from contamination by consumer fetishism. It's the part of me that can't help but
reject father figures, and Cuba, more than any other place in the
West, is ruled by the ultimate aging patriarch.

Still I can't help but be in awe of Cuba's stubborn sense of rebellion. The socialist revolution was Latin America's great "fuck you"
to Yankee domination, a defiance Puerto Ricans can only dream of.
For all the hemming and hawing about gringo this and gringo that
emanating from John Huston's Mexican bandits in *The Treasure of
Sierra Madre*, to the Venezuelan egg-bashing of Richard Nixon
during his visit in the early '70s, to the outcries of leftists in countries like Guatemala, El Salvador, Chile, and Argentina who were
squashed by the subterranean outfits trained by the CIA, only
Cuba was able to extend its middle finger with any efficacy. Cuba,
so close to the U.S. in geographic and cultural terms, has thrown a

forty-three-year wrench into the project of American hemispheric continuity, and for good reason.

> *It is necessary for us to remain nationalist until we are able to achieve a true internationalism, that is, as soon as the dangers of the many imperialisms that attempt to subjugate, not to civilize, disappear.*
> —JOSÉ VASCONCELOS, *The Cosmic Race*

On the Malecón, the waterfront boulevard that is the quintessential proscenium stage for Havana's bizarre anti-imperialist sentiment, one can feel all its contradictions flapping in the warm breeze. German and Italian tourists stroll by, seeking picture-postcard views to remember a romantic vacation by, as afternoon-shift prostitutes wave at the trickling stream of cars that pass for rush-hour traffic. As you approach the back side of El Hotel Nacional, the most luxurious hotel in Havana, once owned by Miami-based gangster Meyer Lansky, you reach the large public square where the rallies favoring the return of Elián Gonzalez were held. A youth rally is under way, but a young woman in military dress approaches you and tells you no photographs are permitted. You look up, and surrounding the plaza, and increasingly numerous along the Malecón as you approach Centro Habana, is a series of billboards with slogans.

En cada barrio—revolución	In every neighborhood—revolution
La vida no es negociable	Life is not negotiable
Lo nuestro es lo neustro	What's ours is ours
Lo que mas vale son las ideas	What are most valuable are ideas
Aquí no tenemos amos	We don't have masters here

The idea of these slogans peering down at me in lieu of the incessant advertising you're subjected to in the "free world" is kind of a fantasy for me. I want to imagine every neighborhood promoting its own social change, in pursuit of several new ideas at once, unburdened by a corporate master. And how badly do I wish I owned something that was really mine, or at least knew that the wealth from its creation was shared by someone close to me. "What's ours is ours" is the most provocative, most controversial of all these slogans. Yes, the Cubans own the fruit of their labors—the restoration of Old Havana by schoolchildren, for instance. But as they have more contact with the outside world through tourists, media images, remittances from relatives, and limited travel, they want more.

Cuba's extreme nationalism, predicated still on the wishful-thinking Marxist prediction that once socialism is achieved, the state will "wither away," has accomplished a great purpose at an equally great cost. The ideally classless society of Cuba no longer exists—there are those with dollars and those without dollars. The U.S. dollar has become the official currency of exchange in Cuba, but only an elite of party members has substantial access to them. The rest must struggle over limited opportunities to get dollars, usually in jobs like taxi driving and hotel service jobs, where dollars are received in tips. There is a limit to capital accumulation, and most people are afraid to exceed them by a hundred dollars a month or so.

In turn, the nation of Cuba exists in two formulas, in two abstractions, in two moments in today's world: one as the island-nation that constitutes its essential identity, and another in an almost opposite site, Miami–Dade County in Florida. The exile community in Miami functions in parallel fashion to, although in vastly dissimilar ways from, the Puerto Rican community in New York. It is a site for intensification of Cuban nationalism, just as New York is for Puerto Rican nationalism, but it is also a place where Cubans engage in the task of completely forgetting about their homeland, a phenomenon that is the inverse of what happens in New York.

The reason for these differences is, of course, politics: It is the same reason why Cuban Americans hold the highest standard of living of Latinos in the U.S. and Puerto Ricans the lowest. While Puerto Ricans came here in great numbers in the '50s to alleviate a crisis in unemployment that accompanied the island's industrialization, Cubans came here to escape the very socioeconomic system that was public enemy number one on America's hit list. Puerto Ricans were used up in temporary work, stigmatized, demonized, and, as Steely Dan said in their song "The Royal Scam," "hounded down to the bottom of a bad town." Cubans were supported by a slew of government programs providing grants and easy loans for educational, small business, and institution-building needs. Cuban exile groups have created a Latino fantasy world in South Florida— a thoroughly middle-class, Spanish-speaking, tropical attitude–laden theme park that has become the capital of Latin American show business, also known as *La Farándula*.

Though I have traveled to Cuba only once, I have been to Miami several times. I know the island through the lens of Tomás Gutiérrez Alea's camera, through the sweetly rustic *son montuno*, through the enormous hands of jazz pianist Chucho Valdés. *I Am Cuba*, an agitprop work made by Soviet filmmaker Mikhail Kalatozov is the kind of surreal vision of Cuba that captures the hot tropical underbelly of the country of Sin as it fuses ideologically with an unreal vision of a workers' paradise. I know Cuba through its theater, and actors willing to discuss the details of agronomy and nineteenth-century German philosophy.

I have sat in the grand garden of the Hotel Nacional, sipping exquisite *mojitos* (rum and sugar cane concoctions), and impressing the trio singers with my challenging ballad requests. I have bargained with booksellers at the Plaza de Armas over old Alejo Carpentier books, rubbed shoulders with queasy throngs in Hemingway's favorite haunt, La Floridita, been lectured about the secrets of *palo monte*, a voodoo-like variation of Santería, in the Casa Africa museum in Vieja Habana. I have gawked at the photos of Fidel's occupying army in the bizarre Hotel Havana Libre, which seems to have copied its design from Jean-Luc Godard's *Alphaville*. I have sat down to a dinner of lobster tails filled with the intrigue of an illegal after-hours club—ushered furtively into a basement room at an underground *paladar*, or privately owned restaurant, because it was over the limit of twelve paying customers at once. And I have watched as Cuban police continuously intervened at beaches at Varadero to make sure they were free of Cuban nationals.

Cuba exists in a reality that is so removed from the post–Cold War era that it is in an unreal place, a dream space. Still that dream contains a reality perhaps more real than ours; it is a place where the hierarchy between European tourists and local residents is explicit, where the precious necessities of medical health and mental literacy are granted as a given instead of a possibility. Everyone knows about Hemingway, and you can hear Eminem playing on radios in kitchen windows; it is the one place in Latin America that is both most like the U.S. and most unlike the U.S. at the same time.

> *I saw a lot of Buster Keaton movies, the Marx Brothers, those were movies that I liked. I have a cousin and we had a routine where we sold newspapers, and then went into the movies and saw tap dancing movies. Fred Astaire, Ginger Rogers, Shirley Temple, and Bill Robinson. He was Fred Astaire's teacher. We would watch that, me and my cousin. We made up an English in our style. I'd say get me that glass, in English. We all grew up watching Hollywood. We'd say, hey, whatta you?*
> —IBRAHIM FERRER, VOCALIST OF THE
> BUENA VISTA SOCIAL CLUB

The irony of the U.S.'s still-unflagging refusal to treat Cuba like a full-fledged entity in the family of nations is the fact that

Cubans are probably the most North American–like of all Latin American nations (including U.S. possession Puerto Rico). With its famous ninety-mile proximity to Florida and equally infamous period of Mafia/showbiz penetration, Havana has been an extension of North American glitz since the turn of the nineteenth century. In almost every interview I've conducted with musicians still living in revolutionary Cuba, the importance of American influence comes up.

"There was always communication with American music," Chucho Valdés told me in an interview. "We heard Coltrane music from the '60s and Bill Evans, and McCoy Tyner, and Herbie Hancock. There can be political differences between countries, but I'm not aware of any musician from whatever planet or whatever system who wouldn't say that Ellington was a genius. Those values are above everything. Ellington is a genius for the whole world, and if Ellington were born on Mars, and Mars and the Earth were not getting along, Ellington would still be a genius. Because that's art, that's not politics."

Between 1910 and 1956, there were eighty-three songs written in English about Cuba, including eight different tunes called "Havana." There was "My Cuban Dream," "Down in Old Havana Town," "Sidewalks in Cuba," "Yankee in Havana," "A Weekend in Havana," and "The Cuban in Me," to name a few. Americans flocked to Cuba as part of a process that marked their throwing off of Victorianism. Through the social dancing of the '30s to the '50s, Americans were beginning to emphasize physical contact in their dancing, and the onslaught of the Cuban rumba in the '30s brought an even more intimate edge to the dancing. (As explained in Louis A. Pérez Jr.'s *On Becoming Cuban*, the rumba was actually a misnomer. The music that Americans danced to was really the more civilized Cuban *"son,"* and the actual rumba is a ritual dance of overt sexual foreplay associated with Afro-Cuban Santería.)

A weekend in Havana became synonymous with overthrowing the deep Protestant fears of decadence, of opening up the American character to "corrupting" influences at the same time that the mass migration from Europe was maturing into its second and third generations. It was no coincidence that organized crime began to set up shop in the various hotels of Havana and was heavily involved in entertainment revues and prostitution. The Cuban Revolution of 1959 was probably the biggest single reason for the development of Las Vegas, since Havana, a major staging area for the Miami mob, was lost to the revolutionary will of the people.

Novelists like Ernest Hemingway ("Cuba is great for fishing and fucking") and Graham Greene began to immortalize Cuba for its liberating possibilities. From the '30s to the '50s, an era when sexuality was greatly repressed in North America, Cuba became the place where it could be had easily and without recrimination. Even Greene, who pedestals dubiously virtuous European women in his novels, joins in the leering about Cuban women in *Our Man in Havana*: " brown eyes, dark hair, Spanish and high yellow, beautiful buttocks lean against the bars, waiting for any life to come along."

The Cuban revolution reacted against the island's reputation as a giant brothel, but almost as a result of some inherent destiny, it has returned to its '50s character, opening itself to legions of European tourists. Street and more subtle forms of prostitution are once again one of Cuba's primary calling cards, despite occasional crackdowns by the state apparatus. The tropical demeanor of Cuba inevitably tends toward sex, just as it does in the other island nations of the Caribbean.

But there's so much more to Cuba and its post–Cold War drama. There is a vast nation of people who live on various levels of

delusion and self-invention, pride and identities that are not determined by the ever-encroaching multinational consumerist norm. It
is a place where the African aspect of hybrid Latin culture has been
allowed to flourish. Despite Afro-Cubans' relative lack of representation in the high level of governments, they are dominant in
music, athletics and religion. About 60 percent of Cuba's population is black, a fact that is largely owing to the vast abandonment of
the island by its mostly white elite.

The opening images of Tomás Guitiérrez Alea's *Memories of
Underdevelopment*, set in 1961, the time just after the Revolution,
tell this story clearly. At a nighttime dance, a vibrant crowd of
dancers is boogieing away to one of Cuba's ubiquitous funk orchestras—the crowd is almost entirely black. The next scene is at the
Havana Airport in the morning, as a stream of Cubans is leaving the
island for Miami and other points north. The people in line are
almost entirely white. Since it is the only Latin American country to
stand up to and toss out American interests, Cuba's white elite, virtually in its entirety, was lifted up out of the country and trans-
ported into the U.S., mainly South Florida.

Still there is ambivalence about racism in Cuba. While there are
many more black doctors per capita in Cuba than in the U.S., there
are few in positions of political power. And while Castro allots time
and expense to address inequality, virtually no pro-black organizations or institutions are allowed. Fidel Castro has installed a kind of
despotic paternalism in which all forms of consumerism manifested
by the people are strictly controlled. Certain reading materials and
products are forbidden, and foreign travels are limited to three
weeks. What the Cuban Revolution fears most is contamination of
its people. The ruling party looks down on the people through
Committees for the Defense of the Revolution, intent on preventing their exposure to forbidden fruit.

And in a sense, who can blame the Cuban ruling party for its
intense attempt to control human nature? The consumer world is a
constant call to corruption for the citizens of the world. As Eduardo
Galeano says in his book, *The Upside Down World* (2000), the

manic consumer messages constantly received in the globalized world are an incitement to crime to those who cannot afford the items that the advertising apparatus insists one must have. The world of corporate logos has robbed us of our identity, because we can't feel like we're alive unless our clothes somehow bear them, and our resources are directed to their purchase. For the Cuban, who has been sheltered from this world for forty-three years now, exposure to consumerism would induce a kind of shock not unlike that of a diabetic who misses his shot of insulin. Just the mere existence of a consumer society corrupts absolutely, and the entire architecture of the Cuban revolution is destroyed in mere moments.

So the flaw of the Cuban revolution is revealed as the flaw of all those protective fathers who wish to shelter their children from the world's inevitable corruption. The world is not perfect, and therefore an inhospitable place for revolution, and the very staging of this kind of inflexible revolution is at least in part antithetical to basic human nature. This is precisely the point made by celebrated anti-Castro Cuban novelist and noted homosexual Reinaldo Arenas, who transforms the oppressive apparatus of the ruling party into a carnival of repressed sexual desire. Still, there is nobility here, if only because, having escaped the daily clamor of consumerism and the increasingly decadent turn brought on by multinational corporatism, the Cuban people have retained the sense of humanity, that romantic "realness" that we in the developed world are rapidly losing.

Fidel Castro understood the importance of developing a strong loyalty among Afro-Cubans and mulattos. Since the opening days of the revolution, when he made an appearance in the main square of Havana, and a white dove landed on his shoulder, Castro has cultivated the community. For the dove that coincidentally nestled on the great leader as he spoke carried with it a powerful spiritual message to the Cuban people. The revolution had been blessed by

Santería, the highly influential syncretic religion that carries Yoruban pantheistic beliefs under a cloak of Catholic saints. The dove was a symbol of Changó, the most revered god of the Yoruba pantheon, and Castro had metaphorically become the country's *babalawo*, its head priest.

If there has ever been a part of me that has wondered how the Cuban revolution has survived the death of communism, I have to explain it with the strength of Yoruban religion. Not only has the power of the Soviet Union to shelter and provide for its soviet republics been completely smashed, but even the power of socialist ideology, of a class-based critique of capitalism, has been brought to its knees. Even Castro has given in and made the dollar a legal currency in Cuba, putting the island on the same currency as Puerto Rico, if not its mortal enemy, the Yankee nation. What most people can't see is that Cuba is *protected*.

The oversimplistic notion that communist countries produce a society without religion is belied by Cuba. Only about 15 percent of Cuba's population of eleven million is athiest, with the number of regular Catholic churchgoers estimated at between 150,000 and 500,000, with an almost equal number devoted to Protestant religions. Baptized Roman Catholics do not turn their backs on Afro-Cuban beliefs, nor does the church officially find such beliefs inconsistent. Most Cubans can merge the concepts of a particular Catholic saint and a particular diety of Yoruba-inspired Santería, or don't believe such beliefs need to be neatly compartmentalized. In Cuba more than anywhere else in Latin America, the spirituality of Europe and Africa is syncretized.

Years ago I was invited to a function at a Santería "house" in upper Manhattan, an anniversary celebration of a young boy's initiation. The boy, whose *orisha*, or chosen deity, was Changó, was the youngest son of a family that had just recently arrived from Cuba. The rite of passage was not unlike that of a bar mitzvah, but for devotees of the Santería religion, the initiation is recelebrated yearly with an extended family that is composed of members of a "house," or "temple." As I entered the apartment, the typical sights and sounds of a lower-middle-class Latino gathering were immediately apparent. The air was thick with the smell of rice and beans and roasted chicken; the adults were dressed conservatively, the children in jeans and sweatshirts; family members were seated in a long row that started at the entry door and ended in the living room, where merengue music was playing. A proud father was alternately merengueing with his daughter and schmoozing with the guests; the boy whose anniversary was being celebrated was holding court with the other kids in his room off to the side.

Suddenly the music was interrupted and everyone took a seat. A twenty-two-year-old recent raft exile from Cuba lit up a cigar and began reciting a litany of invocations. He is a *babalawo*, a Santería priest, who was a bit of a prodigy; he'd already been involved in two other Yoruban-related religions, and now, in his University of Miami T-shirt, he was presiding over this initiation anniversary celebration. The *babalawo* and a priestess (whose *orisha* is Yemaya, the goddess of the ocean) performed incantations and tossed pieces of coconut to the floor. The coconut pieces' convex or concave shape, read together, amount to a divination of the young boy's future.

The religious leaders decided something was wrong. They ordered the boy to go to his room and change into all-white clothing, which will make him pure. When the boy returned with his mixture of reluctance and repentance, they threw the coconut again and this time they were satisfied with the results. "He's a rebellious kid," one of the devotees told me. "Imagine the pressures of bringing up a kid in this city." I continued to be struck by the similarities with a family gathering in my family; adults cautiously watching children, maybe overprotecting them, in the name of shielding them from inner-city harshness. Even stranger, the duality of Santería meant that the young boy's First Communion portrait hung in the living room—I kept forgetting these people were Catholic, too.

I went to the *padrino*, or godfather of the house, and subtly asked for an interview. I wasn't really interested in his revealing essential truths I'm not worthy of, but he balked. When I tried to question the younger *babalawo*, the *padrino* came over and angrily chased him away. "This is a sacred African religion we're practicing here," he shouted at me, and suddenly everyone in the gathering was looking at us. "This is protection for African culture from the white man, and we have to keep it secret. Someday you'll need this protection!" he scolds me. Even though most of the people here are mixed-blood and many could pass for white, it was clear they had committed themselves to African culture. Like the Cuban revolution, they were protected.

Through this experience, I came to understand the intense syncretizing power that exists in Cuba through Yoruban religion. But this syncretic buzz is something that reaches out and affects the entire society, creating a sense of nationalism based on the active power of hybridity. I remember the insistence of the Mexican rockers on the syncretism that drove their art and society. Besides Vasconcelos's cosmic race mythology, which was already influenced by the socialist utopianism of Europe, Mexico must have been directly influenced by the Cuban revolution. Its Institutional Revolutionary Party, though far from socialist in the Soviet sense, had demonstrated a sympathy toward Cuba unmatched by other Latin American governments. Mexico City had been a hotbed for revolutionary ideology since the '50s when, before spearheading the Cuban revolution, Castro and Che met for the first time. After the revolution, Mexico City was a place of intrigue where KGB spies met Latin American leftists and dodged CIA agents. But now, what is surviving is not socialism, it's the syncretic energy of Yoruba religion, perhaps the most powerful root of the hybridizing energy that is making Spanglish reality so dynamic.

The principle of African religion that allows it to be "inclusive" of what would seem to be a completely oppositional religion like Catholicism is one of the foundation blocks of Spanglish hybridity.

While indigenous mythology seems to predict the eventual arrival and conquering impetus of the "white man," and Mexico syncretism is viscerally attested to by the literal building of Catholic churches on top of indigenous temples, African syncretism adjusts to European mythological structures by incorporating them. Yoruban religion seems to say, "That's your Saint Barbara? Sure, and by the way, she's kind of like Changó, and we're not too uptight to camouflage our most powerful male god (who in some interpretations is bi-gendered) as a woman." It's the same principle that allows Cuba to "include" Soviet-style socialism in its plan of tropical utopian socialism, something that was widely seen as blatantly contradictory to the Cuban national style. It's the same principle by which José Martí, who had few explicit socialist tendencies, could be resuscitated by the government propagandists when a new hero was needed after the disappearance of Soviet aid, and the same principle that reconciles deep spiritual passion with the stunting of organized Christianity.

José Martí, whose statue stands at the southwest corner of Central Park in Manhattan, was a significant visionary of turn-of-the-century Cuba who laid the basis for the revolutionary government's symbolic nod to the necessity of including Africans in the national ideology. In his essay "Nuestra America" (Our America), Martí called out for the need to identify Latin America's "Greece," so that a sense of shared history could be developed by this America's mix of European, indigenous, and African influences. In his essay "Mi Raza" (My Race), he does call for the inclusion of African identity in the modern Cuban sense of self. But perhaps because of his death during an early phase of the war for independence from Spain, his inclusionary goals were lost to a more powerful ideology being developed by Cuban thinkers.

Cuba was so intent on freeing itself from Spain that it was trying to cut the vestiges of its past completely. For labor leader Diego Vicente Tejera, a major obstacle to the forging of a new Cuban republic was an "indolence . . . natural for us. . . . White Cubans descend from Spaniards and Cubans of color from Africa, two races equally lazy." Cuba was so intent on throwing off the four hundred-year Spanish dominance of their island that they were quickly denouncing their roots and looking to America, with whom they were having increasing contact. The heavy influence of consumer culture and materialism and the appeal of maintaining the appearance of European wealth of a city like Havana drew Cubans to emulate Americans, no doubt absorbing some racist tendencies along the way. The process of ultra-Americanization, which appeared to take hold only when Cubans migrated en masse to Miami after the revolution, had been fomenting for almost one hundred years before Castro marched into Havana from his mountain lair.

But perhaps the most dynamic Cuban of the twentieth century wasn't Cuban at all, he was Argentine. His image—once the poster of choice in hip-left college dorms from Boston to Berkeley, forever plastered almost comically all over billboards throughout Cuba, more recently reappearing on Rage Against the Machine T-shirts—is the most riveting of modern-era radical mythology. His straggly long black hair, falling chaotically from his simple black beret with a single gold star, his drawn, intense face, and mostly his withering gaze, inspired the devotion of the masses of Cuba and Latin America in a way no one has since. The most stubbornly independent, enigmatically idealistic of postwar revolutionaries, Ernesto "Che" Guevara carried the promise of Third World liberation on his back until he was martyred, with CIA help, in Bolivia in 1967.

But despite the generally sorry state of the Cuban revolution and the Latin American left, not to mention the loony left of the American '70s (Patty Hearst was code-named "Tania" after Che's East German comrade in his last, fatal Bolivian campaign), Che Guevara lives. He was too right about the raw deal the poor majority was, and still is, getting, and he was too much of a visionary and a leader, and he was too damned sexy.

Che's writings range from naïve poetry to political economy to military manual. What emerges is an amazingly complex man who thrived on contradiction, forever synthesizing and scheming a previously unimaginable form of revolution. Born and raised in Argentina, Che was from a family of aristocratic lineage that had lost its material wealth and lived like aristocrats with little to back it up. Plagued from birth by an asthmatic condition for which he constantly needed medication, Che was at once brilliantly charismatic and something of an outcast, an "attractive oddball difficult to characterize" according to Jon Lee Anderson's 1998 biography. With proto-hippie abandon, he stopped taking baths and was nicknamed "el Chancho" (the pig). Because of the influence of dictator Juan Peron, who was at once an admirable anti-imperialist and a creepy fascist, Che grew into a kind of bohemian rebel with no firm political allegiance.

In Argentina, Che chased women of all social backgrounds and played rugby when he wasn't sick from asthma. As described in the *Motorcycle Diaries*, in the midst of his medical school training he took a daring motorcycle trip through South America, where he first witnessed the spectacle of ditzy American tourists in Peru—key to his developing disdain for the Yankee. In a subsequent trip, he was influenced by Bolivian leftists to check out Guatemala, where he learned the truth about the United Fruit Company, banana republics, and felt firsthand an early CIA counter-revolution.

Then it was on to Mexico City, where he met a swinging circle of Latin American lefties, including his first wife, Peruvian activist Hilda Gadea, and a wild-eyed Havana lawyer called Fidel. Here he received the nickname "Che" from a Cuban comrade. His commitment to revolution crystallized; as "Che" he became everyman, the leader and subject of a new kind of revolution. Just before he took off on the *Granma*, the legendary boat that brought Castro's men to Cuba, Che's letter to his mother symbolized the death of his rootless, bohemian excess: "I believe I can say like a poet whom you don't know: I will only take to my grave/the nightmare of an unfinished song."

During the guerilla warfare in Cuba's Sierra Maestra mountains, Che's dark, disciplinary side began to emerge. He became a decisive voice in the guerilla's debates on whether to execute traitors and deserters. Jon Lee Anderson is quite tough on Guevara, painting a picture of a ruthless squad leader who would kill a man one day and lust after a peasant woman the next. This "cold-blooded willingness to execute" earned him the job of supervising the mass executions of Cuban army war criminals after Castro took power. The unflinching sense of discipline required to keep it together in the jungle led Che to believe that war was "the ideal circumstance in which to acheive a socialist consciousness."

"Revolutions are ugly but necessary," Che said, "and part of that revolutionary process is injustice in the service of future justice." Whether this can be considered a necessary evil or the tragic flaw of Cuba's and Che's form of revolution, it is the central question anyone who is serious about lionizing Guevara must ask himself. Perhaps because he was a threat to Fidel's dominance, Castro sent him on a series of clandestine trips to Asia and Eastern Europe. Che was apparently too radical for the stabilizing process of the revolution, openly expressing disappointment with the Soviet Union for not nuking the U.S. during the Cuban missile crisis. This is a man who believed the revolution to be an unleashing of "the bestial howling of the triumphant proletariat."

As the ultra-austere leader and philosophical brains of the Cuban revolution, Che inspired unflinching devotion because he was so self-sacrificing and tireless. He despised the Soviet Communists because the party elite lived high on the hog while the workers struggled, and he correctly predicted they would return to capitalism. But the pressure was almost too much; like most classic Spanglish types, he admitted, "I live like someone torn in two." He would soon leave Cuba for guerrilla adventures in Africa, and finally, Bolivia, where he imagined he could start a revolution that would spread to four neighboring countries: Peru, Colombia, Brazil, and his native Argentina. There he was finally captured, and his execution was overseen by Iran-Contra CIA operative Felix Rodriguez. Anderson cites Rodriguez as saying "I told him not to shoot Che in the face, but from the neck down."

Transcending the details of his political and social life, Che is an enduring icon of Latin American, and by extension, Spanglish people, because he is such a tangle of contradictions. Having grown up a bourgeois Argentine, he defied the isolationist Buenos Aires stereotype by forging outward and upward, embracing countries with less European pedigree, and more people of color. He lived a postwar American rugged individualist fantasy by going out on the road in his early twenties but the trip merely served as the impetus for him to reject the American way of life. He projected strength and vigorous sexuality when in reality he was asthmatic and had an unremarkable love life. He was a true Cuban revolutionary and he was most certainly not a Cuban. His face—in so many photographic images, smiling—gave Latin American and Spanglish leftists an inviting sense of warmth and nostalgia; but in many ways, Che Guevara was one of the most cruel, dispassionate executioners the socialist world has ever produced.

"The true revolutionary is guided by strong feelings of love," said Che in one of his later diaries. "It is impossible to think of an authentic revolutionary without this quality." To accept the charisma of Che Guevara is to accept the terror of an avenging angel, and this may be too high a price for many people. But his insistence on perseverance and trying to find the best path to a society in which wealth is more equitably distributed is at the backbone of what's left of the Cuban revolution today, and still inspires activists of all stripes. On the bohemian streets of the Bellavista section of Santiago, Chile, there are Che posters and T-shirts everywhere; at every rock en Español concert his image appears somehow, and the smiling visage of Che is an alternate logo for the L.A.–based Rage Against the Machine.

While hard-core leftists could dismiss Miami Cubans as having been justly decapitated from the body of the real Cuban people, they are missing the point. Miami is perhaps the most dynamic and fully Spanglish city in the U.S. as we enter the twenty-first century. In my perhaps dubious conception of myself as a man of the people, I have always subscribed to the theory that if one were to dismiss the majority of people, who actively disfavor socialist reform, then one is talking down to the masses. And if the masses are that stupid, then why are they worth fighting for? For every classic *gusano* in Miami, that is, wannabe Anglo house-and-boat owning, race-baiting descendant of a slave-owning sugar plantation honcho that prowls Collins Avenue on warm spring nights, there are just as many perfectly humble souls who just wanted to get out of Cuba for a variety of basic reasons. The need to live somewhere else, a basic desire of most humans, or the need to express oneself creatively without government approval, or just not being able to make it despite all the wonderful opportunities Castro's socialism offers its loyal citizens. These are the masses of people that make up Miami's exile community.

In some ways, Miami is a dream city for Spanglish people. The weather is eminently tropical, albeit a bit chillier in the winters and insufferably muggier in the summers than most Latin American capitals. The entire city seems to be bilingual, and there is no shortage of noisy salsa music blaring through car windows or storefronts at almost any time of day. It is a middle-class Latino paradise. On my first visit, in 1978, I went to a Miami Beach showing of the *Rocky Horror Picture Show* whose audience was made up almost entirely of well-scrubbed, elaborately costumed Cuban-American adolescents. In subsequent visits I found myself in tony Coral Gables, where entire shopping malls, including health clubs, were populated by seemingly well-off, glowingly suntanned Cuban Americans. It was kind of a freakish feeling, being surrounded by so much Latino conspicuous consumption. I had grown up with images and realities of poor, working-class Latinos living a frugal life, showing up at salsa shows overdressed in clothes they had saved up for a month to buy. Here in Miami, everyone was wearing the same expensive casual wear you'd see in Beverly Hills or Westchester County, New York.

Miami means opulence for Latinos—guided by the fortunes of Emilio and Gloria Estefan, two of the wealthiest people in Dade County. With their group, Miami Sound Machine, the Estefans made a killing in the music business. While it is generally not received as a work of great artistic merit, "Conga" is probably the most significant Spanglish recording since "Oye Como Va," if only because it successfully rhymes "conga" with "longer." "Conga," like MSM's other hits, "The Rhythm Is Going to Get You," and "Doctor Beat," manages to fuse elements of Latin percussion with the electric bass beats of the post-disco era. The Estefans themselves represent a model Miami couple—Emilio is substantially older than Gloria; she has a respectable image that is sensibly sexy but politically earnest. The Estefans made no secret of their hostility against Castro's Cuba during the 1984 Los Angeles Olympics, a '90s visit to exiles being kept in prisons at the U.S.-occupied Guantanamo Bay, and most recently during the Elián González crisis.

Though they primarily speak in English and have made their fortune selling records in the mainstream American market, the Estefans are at the center of a crucial concentration of Spanish-language media. The networks Univision and Telemundo have major headquarters there, and the Cuban-backed management sectors of each company call the shots, often for both networks from Miami (at this moment it is unknown how NBC's purchase of Telemundo will affect this). The main offices of the Spanish-language divisions of major record labels like Sony, Universal, Warner Bros., and BMG-Polygram-EMI are in Miami, dictating marketing strategies for the entire country. Recording artists from Latin America make Miami their main stop for publicity tours, film most of their videos there, and have their testiest meetings with record label management there.

Still, there is a troubling element to the Latin American *farándula*, much of which is overseen by Cuban American executives and investors. There is a long history of repression of free speech that results from pressure groups like the Cuban American National Foundation (CANF), which in 1991 was the subject of a major report by the watchdog organization America's Watch. (In all fairness, America's Watch Report also issued a report that year condemning human rights violations in Cuba, including many chilling incidents of repression against artists.) The report found that the CANF, which is bent on repressing any contact at all with revolutionary Cuba and a staunch supporter of the U.S. embargo of the island, was behind several attempts to coerce Miamians away from buying the *Miami Herald*. The CANF did this because of an editorial that appeared in the paper favoring a dialogue about the possibility of changing U.S. policy toward Havana.

In addition, the report cited several instances in which musicians, either from Cuba, or any musician who had played in revolutionary Cuba just once, were vehemently boycotted and often prevented from playing concerts in the Miami area. (This controversy flared up in 1999 when two Puerto Rican singers, Andy Montañez and Danny Rivera, were not allowed to play at the famous Calle Ocho street festival. The incident stirred up a major ruckus in Puerto Rico, further fueling that island's anti-U.S. and anti-Miami Cuban sentiment. The Cuban exile queen of salsa, Celia Cruz, has not been able to escape this latest flare-up; she has been booed in Puerto Rico and has openly pondered whether she will ever play there again.)

Apart from the boycott of the *Herald*, which involved the smearing of petroleum jelly and human excrement in vending boxes the newspaper owned around the area, there were bomb threats to an art museum that scheduled a show of Cuban artists, and a general tone of intolerance for views that do not coincide with those of the CANF. In 1988, Ramon Cernuda, a Miami-based publisher and collector of Cuban art, became a target of harassment when the Cuban Museum of Arts and Culture organized an exhibit and auction that included works by artists who were still living in Cuba or were sympathetic to the Cuban government. In 1994, I was able to interview Maria Romeu, a music promoter/producer who claimed she lost her job because of the CANF's influence.

Romeu, a single mother living in Miami, walked into her office one spring day and found out that she had lost her job at MTV Latino because of her questionable association with a Cuban pop singer named Carlos Varela. As the result of a bizarre clash of Cuban politics and culture with the international music video giant, Romeu, who convinced the fledgling Spanish-language branch of MTV to air Varela's video, was relegated to the ranks of the unemployed. After putting much pressure on the Miami-based MTV outlet by protesting the video as "propaganda that makes Cuba out to be a problem-free paradise," she was mysteriously fired because she used an MTV Latino fax machine to send out a tourist offer to see Varela in concert in Cuba. While Romeu's use of the fax was an improper use of a company machine to promote her own side business, if not for the repressive atmosphere in Miami she probably would have just been disciplined internally and not fired.

Varela is a singer-songwriter who combines a Bruce Springsteen–like charisma, tropical pop beats, and the earnestness of *nueva canción* (a '70s Latin American protest song tradition). Although he is popular in Cuba and prefers to live there, he has been met with some ambivalence by the Cuban government, belying the CANF claims that he is a Castro stooge. Varela's New York–based manager, Ned Sublette, told me that "while not overtly against the revolution, Varela is critical of certain of its more authoritarian excesses."

Romeu suspected that the CANF, which can influence the advertising decisions of the many corporations with Cuban exiles on their board of directors, got her fired by threatening an advertising boycott against MTV Latino, as well as withholding their crucial influence in getting the channel on to two major cable services in the South Florida area. Romeu, who was nervous about talking to me, felt that there was a growing sentiment among newer arrivals that was breaking away from the CANF mold and willing to have a more balanced view toward relations with Cuba. With recent government policies allowing increased visits by Cuban Americans who have direct family in Cuba, the old ways were clearly eroding. In addition, the Latino population of the Miami area is diversifying, with South and Central Americans moving into urban neighborhoods that upscale Cuban Americans have abandoned.

This new opening up of attitudes was overshadowed in 2000 during the Elián González custody dispute, a remarkable chapter that could mark the end of the hard line CANF era. The saga of Elián became as uncomfortable a spectacle of tabloid journalism as that of Amy Fisher, O. J. Simpson, or Jon Benét Ramsey. The child became a signifier of U.S.–Cuban relations, carrying in his baby-toothed smile the ambivalence about Cuba that I have detailed above. I was drawn to Elián partially because he reminded me of my own photos at his age, and because his Miami relatives seemed to have the kind of working-class lack of polish that seems typical of Puerto Rican migrants.

The Miami relatives held on to Elián with a stubbornness that indicated a desire for more power than Miami society was willing to give them otherwise; they were not the star professional family that Hispanic businessmen like to promote as ideal. They were taken over by the CANF because there's no way they could have afforded high-priced legal representation without their help, but in truth the González family both in Miami and Havana were ambivalent about their own situations. Elián's stepfather, who engineered the fatal raft-crossing attempt, had actually been back and forth between Miami and his hometown in Cuba. For unprivileged Cubans, the choice between South Florida and Cuba is deciding between the lesser of two evils—living in a closed society that afforded medical and educational protections or living in an open society in which they would be relegated to the loser class of the new American economy.

For the most part, I felt simpatico with Latinos who were disgusted by the Miami relatives's intransigence and equated their refusal to hand over Elián with the actions of the right-wing conspiracy that tried to topple then-president Clinton with sex-crime charges. The spectacle of the anti-Castro Cuban community railing about the unfairness of U.S. law would annoy anyone who had witnessed their relentless flag-waving when it came to anti-communism. But the Cuban community, despite its pro-America leanings, has always been a kind of separate political entity, going back to its feeling of betrayal over John Kennedy's failure to back up the CIA in the Bay of Pigs fiasco. Miami has always been an unreal escape valve where the pressurized emotions over the disembowelment of a country were let loose.

Even stranger were the gut feelings of resentment I had when the Janet Reno raid was carried out. Suddenly Cuban Americans had taken their place with all the black and Latino families who had been raided by ruthless policemen and DEA agents looking for drugs. While the Cuban-American community has much blame to claim for the absurd state of affairs of local government, the reaction by the coalition of Anglo and black protestors against them smacked of North American resentment of a Spanglish presence.

In August of 2001, just weeks before the second annual Latin Grammy awards were scheduled to take place in Miami, they were canceled because of security concerns due to possible anti-Castro protests. In a statement made by Michael Greene, the president and CEO of the Recording Academy, the awards were moved to Los Angeles due to serious concerns for the safety and dignity of the guests, nominees, performers, and sponsors, as well as the threat of a disruption during the telecast itself. The Latin Grammy awards themselves became a flashpoint for controversy in Miami, leading to the resignation of more conservative members of the CANF, who were against bringing the awards to town in the first place. An attempt to move the CANF to a more moderate position by the late Jorge Mas Canosa's son, Jorge Mas Santos, had only resulted in tearing it apart and giving Miami another public relations black eye.

Most people think that Cuba's reintegration into the free-market world is inevitable, something that will happen soon after Fidel Castro's inevitable death. But while multinational corps and Miami Cubans are poised to storm in and repossess what they feel is rightfully theirs, the last forty-odd years of revolutionary Cuba won't just disappear into the capitalist night. Despite their "indoctrination," it is self-serving and dismissive to think that Cubans will embrace the new world order so immediately. While many Cubans may find Castro's rule constricting and not ideal, they have lived with a certain dignity unknown to most Latin Americans.

Whether there is a revolution, naked tyranny, or a slowly crumbling welfare state in Cuba right now is up to the interpreter. When I've interviewed Cuban musicians and theater people who come to New York to perform, or talked to their peers on the streets of Havana, they are careful what they say about the government. Some refuse to comment about politics at all. There is a gnawing feeling of hunger in Havana—from the literal hunger for food to the hunger for fulfillment. The block after block of empty storefronts and the weary pronouncement of revolutionary catchphrases like "the true wealth of Cuba is its people" seem to taunt the average Cuban.

But one thing is certain—the idea of Cuba's being stuck in time, made so popular by the images of crumbling Art Nouveau buildings and old '40s and '50s autos from Detroit, is only valid on the surface. Havana Cubans and Miami Cubans, no matter how far apart politically, are joined at the hip when it comes to the evolution of the Cuban soul. Despite political differences, Cuba shares an inexorable destiny with America, and the more Spanglish it gets, the more these seemingly opposite fates are inseparable.

9.

PUERTO RICO—THE FIRST SPANGLISH NATION

We are a Sovereign State of Mind, well aware of the fact
That it is almost 1898 once again and our own Embassy is
Long overdue for the most interesting minds of our great
Multicolorful generation to congregate as Heads of State
And keep our own aesthetic sancocho warm enough to escort
Our eternal tropical contemporary urban life style into
The 21st Century phase of the pursuit of liberty & justice
On the dance floor of the happiness promised our existence,
By the multi-lingo Spanglish creator of man & womankind!
        —PEDRO PIETRI, *"El Puerto Rican*
          Embassy Manifesto"

Puerto Rico is a place where my spirit comes from, the center of a circular migration that goes north, then south, then back again. Somewhere around the turn of the nineteenth century my maternal grandfather moved deep into the Luquillo Mountain range, about twenty-five miles east of San Juan, and settled on a three-acre plot of land where he grew coffee, bananas, mangoes, and kept livestock like cows, roosters, hens, and pigs. The village community of Barcelona, as it is now known, was a ramshackle gathering of *jíbaro* farmers who probed deeper and deeper into the island's untamed forests, knowing the exceptionally fertile conditions of the Luquillo range could easily support large families. My mother came from a family of nine children, and my father, who was raised on the western slope of the same range, was one of twelve.

When the Depression struck in the early '30s, conditions in Puerto Rico grew even worse than in the colonial fatherland, the continental U.S., and the *jíbaro* dream of my parents' parents began to die. Twenty years later, it seemed as if almost the whole island was leaving on cheap flights to New York, part of the industrialization plan that would save the island's economy by subtracting its untrainable agricultural labor force. At first glance, it would seem as if this migration was the pure opposite of the Cuban flight after Castro's revolution in 1959. A huge chunk, if not the vast majority, of Puerto Rico's darker-complected lower classes, under the care and vigilance of the U.S. State Department, flew north to a major American city to start a new life. But there was a huge difference between the Cuban and Puerto Rican migrations of the postwar years. Puerto Ricans, with less education and support networks, facing a more hostile climate (both in the meteorological and societal sense), and lacking an evil bogeyman dictator to prevent their return, began to go back home. Then they began to come back to the U.S. again. And then they returned to the island. Rather than a vicious cycle, this movement, which predicted the instantaneously mobile work force created by multinational capital, became a central characteristic of being Puerto Rican. We were, and are, engaged in a circular migration.

These visits were the essence of the Nuyorican rediscovery of roots, revealing a place that differed considerably from the way I had come to understand the Nuyorican world. In New York, bonding with Puerto Ricans consisted of hanging out at the Village Gate or the Palladium for salsa shows, checking out an opening at Museo del Barrio, a play at Pregones Theater in the South Bronx, or a break-dancing jam by Ghetto Originals (a mostly Nuyorican group). But up in the Luquillo Mountains, I felt the cool cosmic humidity of El Yunque, the rain forest that houses the only U.S. national park outside the fifty states, and with that moist caress came the inescapable chorus of the *coquí*—small tree frogs indigenous to the island. "Co-QUÍ? Co-QUÍ?" they ask, insistently, melodically, their small brown bellies busting out in a two-note sweet song interminably into the night. Many Taino legends surround the *coquí*, the most notable involving the tragic defeat of the mountain's resident god, Yukiyú. After a long struggle with Huracán, the storm god, Yukiyú had to leave this earth, and it fell upon the tiny *coquís* to forever chant in his memory. "Co-QUÍ?"

In Puerto Rico I felt the living reality behind the nationalism that only exists metaphorically in New York. Nuyoricans feel their nationalism as a constant presence in the heart, as an unstoppable song of an imagined freedom, a tropical paradise that is always sweet. On the island, I became drunk with the smell of the fruit-bearing trees and fertile soil and damp morning air, filled with so much humidity you can almost see it simmering. Old *jíbaros* skulk by on back roads carrying machetes, their hands withered and wrinkled by years of hard farmwork. Fiery red *flamboyan* trees are in full bloom in June, invoking a hyper-nationalist stupor tempered by souped-up Toyotas prowling around blasting dance-hall hip-hop, on their way to the mall for important shopping at Walgreen's and a movie from Blockbuster. Puerto Rico is more Americanized than some parts of America. Puerto Rico is not a sovereign country, it's the biggest Puerto Rican neighborhood in the United States. In the age when the nation has become irrelevant, Puerto Rico is the first Spanglish nation of America.

The way we became a Spanglish nation isn't a mystery—we were cajoled from the beginning, promised freedom by association with the United States, then forced to speak English as the price of admission. The coercion in the educational system for this purpose is legendary, as is the stubborn refusal of Puerto Ricans, who had been speaking Spanish for four hundred years. The practice continued in U.S. classrooms forty years later, and although it was more understandable that we be required to speak English in New York, the culture clash came to define us in important ways. Despite the writings of an array of social critics who labeled us clannish and self-contained, Puerto Ricans, like many immigrant groups before them, were learning English. But we refused to stop speaking in Spanish. Actually, we were speaking Spanglish. The new Puerto Rican nationalism, despite all the insistence of hard-core *independentistas* on the worship of an idealized national culture, started out as a hybrid. We absorbed the lessons of American democracy and found ourselves as we were liberated from Spanish colonialism. We were operating in the sphere of a fascinating contradiction: Our nationalism was intensifying as a function of our Americanization.

Inevitably hot and sticky day and night, the cobblestoned streets of Old San Juan are still incredibly inviting. As I walk up the steep incline to Calle San Sebastian, I think about how Old San Juan reminds me a little bit of New York's East Village. Fifteen years ago it had a reputation for seediness and crime and people were afraid to go there, but now it has become a cool, colorful oasis of artiness and youth, which parade up and down all night long. I peek into La Bombonera, an old-style cafeteria whose denizens harken back to a time when San Juan looked more to Havana and Madrid for spiritual sustenance than New York and Miami. As I step across the Plaza Baldiority, with its flock of pigeons and street kids swarming, I hear the song I was listening for. Inside a cluttered cafeteria, a group of middle-aged men in guayaberas and women in frilly dresses dance slowly and precisely. A mustachioed man with black tortoise shell glasses stands in the middle of the room holding the ukulele-like *cuatro* and serenades them with Puerto Rico's unofficial national anthem, "En Mi Viejo San Juan." Pedro Pietri even wrote a Nuyorican version of the poem that reflects his transnational journey through Manhattan.

I keep rambling, past beer-heavy saloons and flowery bistros, and I stop to admire, as I always do, the remarkably untouched mural painting of Pedro Albizu Campos that covers the wall of a building across the street from Hijos de Borinquen, a down-home salsa–*nueva cancion cantina* for *independentistas* and freethinkers. Even though he's been dead for over forty years, Albizu Campos is the most important symbol of Puerto Rican nationalism. The son of a Basque immigrant and an Afro-Rican mother, Albizu Campos was the first Puerto Rican to graduate from Harvard College, which he did in the early '20s. He went on to get a medical degree from a Vermont med school, but returned to Puerto Rico incensed at what he felt were the racist and patronizing attitudes he encountered up north.

In the '30s, Albizu Campos founded the Nationalist Party and began to tour the island making incendiary speeches about the need for Puerto Rico to stand up to its captor and break free. In 1936, a Nationalist Party rally held in Ponce, the island's second-biggest city, ended in tragedy when police opened fire on the crowd, killing four. It was the seminal moment for the Nationalist cause, the incident that would allow Nationalists to forever castigate America (which had taken possession of Puerto Rico at the end of the Spanish American war in an ostensibly peaceful manner) as an occupying force with blood on their hands. Following this episode, both sides became entrenched, with the U.S. government actively spying on and sabotaging the Nationalist movement, and, in a way not nearly as heinous as their interventions in countries like Guatemala and Chile, inserting their man into the mix.

The man in this particular case was Luis Muñoz Marin, a lawyer-turned-politician who had a colorful past as a man about town in New York's Greenwich Village. Connections with Franklin Roosevelt and a well-marketed political campaign that recognized the need for drastic economic reform without condemnation of the U.S. President catapulted Muñoz Marin to become the island's first native-born governor. Muñoz Marin, who campaigned on the slogan "Pan, Tierra, y Libertad," (Bread, Land, and Liberty), became permanently etched into Puerto Rican history as the Good Guy, assigning fiery Pedro Albizu Campos to the role of troublemaker. The Muñoz Marin/Albizu Campos dichotomy is a powerful one in Puerto Rican attitudes—my dad was a fan of the former; I, of course, was drawn to the Che Guevara–like militancy of the latter. Albizu Campos is another well-educated Latino who said fuck you to the U.S. government (Fidel was a lawyer, of course). But instead of succeeding in rallying the masses, Albizu was slowly poisoned and sabotaged by various levels of counter-insurgency operatives. A group of passionate disciples of Albizu, including Lolita Lebrón and Rafael Cancel Miranda, made a bizarre attempt at attracting U.S. attention to the independence cause by taking some wild potshots from the gallery of the House of Representatives in 1954.

By the end of the '50s, much of Puerto Rico's lower class had been displaced to the north, Albizu Campos was dead of illnesses that had accumulated during the counterinsurgency campaign against him (as well as a few prison terms), Lebrón and her comrades were in federal prison, and Luis Muñoz Marin's Operation Bootstrap, which was turning Puerto Rico into an industrial economy, was in full bloom. Soon after, Puerto Rican television was running shows hosted by Lucecita Benitez and Danny Rivera, two singers who would be boycotted by the CANF Cubans for you-know-what. Benitez and Rivera were playing rock and roll and were forerunners of Menudo, who prefigured both Ricky Martin and the Backstreet Boys.

In 1967, the U.S. allowed a plebiscite, or a referendum vote on the status of Puerto Rico with three choices: the status-quo commonwealth, Muñoz Marin's clever invention (in Spanish known as "free associated state"); statehood (usually backed by the most pro-Republican elements); and independence (the Marxist-oriented successors to Albizu's Nationalist Party). Independence supporters denounced the election as a farce, beginning a line of thought that purported that any election while Puerto Rico was owned by the U.S. would not be fair because it would ultimately be coerced. I tended to agree with that, with the caveat that if you believe that, then you also believe the electoral process isn't really fair in the U.S. either.

During this period, a noisy coalition of leftists, students, and workers began to rock Puerto Rico with demonstrations and bombings, angrily calling for independence, or at least a break from U.S. foreign policy and the Vietnam war. This is the Puerto Rico that the Young Lords didn't understand when they came down to announce they were taking over leadership of the independence movement. But this was also a Puerto Rico that was developing a substantial middle class with substantial disposable income; it was on its way to becoming the "Shining Star of the Caribbean," as one advertising campaign put it. Puerto Rico was becoming a kind of Hispanic version of Southern California (anticipating the actual middle-class Hispanic version of Southern California called East Los Angeles), with J. C. Penneys and Burger Kings and Fotomats and even the Gap. In 1989, at the Plaza Las Americas mall, there was even a simulacrum of El Yunque rain forest, complete with *coquís* singing on carefully choreographed backing tapes.

Puerto Rico had come full circle. Again. It's been a painstakingly slow process. Columbus first showed up in 1493, but it wasn't until Fountain of Youth searcher Ponce de León arrived in the early sixteenth century that it seemed Spain was very interested in the island. It took them about two and a half years to get out the little gold that could be mined, and the population didn't vary much from about three thousand-plus for over a hundred years. The breakdown in the beginning was about 1,300 blacks, 1,100 indigenous, and 600 white Spaniards. Many of them were criminals or debtors. The indigenous Tainos died off as real tribes but remained alive as genetic integrants to the Puerto Rican miscegenation process; they assimilated into a Spanish-speaking creole model and took on Hispanic names and were assumed to have died of disease, which some did. When the nineteenth century and the Latin American independence wars came around, Puerto Rico became a haven for Spanish loyalists, bringing an increased conservative bent to the mores of the upper classes. We became more conservative than Colombians and Venezuelans, and it wasn't until increased immigration from Europe that Puerto Rico developed an independence movement.

Not as dismissive of our Spanish component as Aztlan purists, Puerto Rican nationalism starts with a lot of nostalgia for things Spanish. When the conquerors came in the sixteenth century, they brought with them coffee, sugar, bananas, mangoes, livestock, horses, and even coconut palm trees. All those things nationalists reminisce about are Spanish. There is a small band of Taino revivalists with a site on the Internet who like to stress the interaction the Tainos had with African slaves in the early part of the colonial process, contact that yielded a hybrid cooking tradition, centered especially on viands like yuca and *ñame*. But much of what comprises the idea of Puerto Rican nationalism has to do with Spain, although whatever was Spanish was absorbed and refashioned by the African-Taino assimilators.

Now we live the American life. An act of Congress in 1917 gave Puerto Ricans automatic U.S. citizenship, and very few of us actively turn it down. (A longtime member of the Puerto Rican Socialist Party, Juan Mari Bras, refused his U.S. citizenship in 1998 and was detained at the San Juan airport for trying to reenter the island with his own Puerto Rican passport. A court ruled that he had the right to refuse his U.S. citizenship and still be allowed to travel back and forth to Puerto Rico.) Pedro Pietri and a photographer, Adal Maldonado, have staged art exhibition/poetry readings based on the theme of a fantasized Puerto Rican passport. But Puerto Ricans still live American lives.

Spanglish is everywhere in Puerto Rico. Instead of the proper Spanish verb, *estacionar*, for parking, we use *parquiar*. When driving on a highway, a motorist will moan *"dame un breaque"* (give me a break) when changing lanes. A rave club kid will sigh in amusement about something psychedelic by saying *"que tripioso!"* (how trippy). Pepsi issues the "Janga card" for teenagers to spend like plastic cash while "hanging" at the mall. And I almost fell out of my rented car one summer when a blaring ad waxed ecstatic in thickly accented Spanish about the opportunity to get "Blockbuster Rewards."

So I head for the Piñones section of the coastline just east of the highly developed tourist area Isla Verde. The last time I was there I'd brought my significant other, Adriana, and my video camera, and we filmed a scene from our Spanglish version of Jean-Luc Godard's *Pierrot le Fou*. It's the scene where Jean-Paul Belmondo and Anna Karina have run away from Paris and are discussing existentialism on a deserted beach. After being harangued by Belmondo for several minutes, Karina breaks away down the beach, moaning, "What will I do? What will I do?"

It once occurred to me that Puerto Rico's political status is a little bit like a single woman kept by a rich married man. She is supported by the man, has all the necessities of life and some luxuries, but society considers her to be immoral, and what's worse, an unfree woman. But the woman smiles and knows she is the one who is the keeper—her status as a "possession" is merely semantic. She is getting over and the married man is her captive.

Adriana is spinning around in front of the crashing waves, now, playing up to the camera, and my eyes look skyward.

High above the palm trees that line Piñones, I can make out the spectacle of two birds of vastly unequal size struggling. Both were indigenous to the island; it was the small *pitirre* wrestling with the eaglelike *guaraguao*. Legend has it that the persistent *pitirre* often wears down the hulking *guaraguao* like David usurping Goliath with sharp, short relentless attacks. They spin in the air, and I can see the *pitirre* making slow progress. It is a pure fantasy of the underdog's inevitable triumph, a New York fantasy, an immigrant fantasy. The late Nuyorican rapper Big Pun's video, filmed on urban Puerto Rican streets, has a chorus that goes: "Even though you player-hate it, we made it to the top." The Puerto Rican/Nuyorican fantasy is the ultimate triumph over America, not through brutal conquest but by subversion. It's sort of parallel to the Aztec interpreters who believe that Cortés's conquest was part of the plan, that the humiliating defeat at the hands of the blond man they mistook for God was a necessary one. But how can Puerto Ricans, who make up one of the poorest groups by average income of any in the United States, suffer in every index or measure of property ownership, education, and accumulated wealth that is known in the post-industrial economy, make it to the top?

In 1992 and 1997 there were plebiscites held in Puerto Rico that were meant to move the island out of its seemingly permanent purgatory, commonwealth status, and into either statehood or independence. Throughout the decade, there was enormous attention paid in the Puerto Rican media to what was thought to be a momentous issue that the U.S. government, along with Puerto Rico, was trying to bring to a fruitful conclusion. But the votes, which both went for the status quo commonwealth option, were difficult to take seriously because neither was binding. This is not to mention the embarrassment of the paucity of coverage by the stateside media. Outside New York, it was difficult to even know that plebiscites were taking place.

The plebiscites had the function of making the statehood party, led by the roundly criticized Pedro Rosselló, seem more and more out of step with the heart and soul of the people. It was a serious setback for the statehooders, who had worked hard to free themselves of the pro-Republican, ultraconservative image they had in the years following the Cerro Maravilla incident. The subject of several books in both languages, and *Show of Force*, a movie directed by Bruno Barreto and starring Amy Irving, the incident was named after a mountain where two college-age Puerto Rican independence party activists were killed by Puerto Rican national police. The shootings occurred on July 26, 1978, the anniversary of the Marines landing at Guánica in 1898, a day that the three political parties in Puerto Rico use as a kind of Fourth of July to hold rallies and represent their positions. Two young university activists—one who was the son of the author Pedro Juan Soto, whose book *Spiks* was influential in the evolution of Spanglish—were lured into a bombing attempt on a radio station tower by an infiltrator who was working for the Puerto Rican government. When they were "caught" in the act by the police, they were executed while they were on their knees. The police covered up the shooting, saying the killings happened in a shoot-out, but when the facts were uncovered by a determined investigative reporter, Carmen Jovet (the part Amy Irving played in the movie), the island became transfixed with a series of televised hearings in the late '70s that became Puerto Rico's Watergate.

The governor at the time, Romero Barceló, was, like his predecessor Luis Ferré, a buddy with the right elements of the Republican party, most notably Nixon and Reagan. The trial took on an embarrassing tone because evidence showed the FBI was involved in advising Barceló, whose rhetoric about making sure communism didn't threaten Puerto Rico was discredited. After Barceló, the pro-Commonwealth party took over with Rafael Hernández Colón, who was, of course, a Hispanophile, dating a Spanish woman, and blowing big sums of money for a Puerto Rico pavillion at the Barcelona Olympics. Charges of corruption began flying, Hernández Colón lost and moved to Spain with his new bride. Enter Roselló, the kinder, gentler face of statehood politics, a kind of Puerto Rican Giuliani. But a new specter of Puerto Rican nationalism began to emerge. A strike by the Puerto Rican Telephone Company rank and file, protesting Roselló's plan to privatize the company, drew huge support for the workers. Roselló, in his role as the man who would clean up accounts and make Puerto Rico presentable as a potential fifty-first state, was seen as cold and distant from the people.

In the summer of 1999, I traveled to the picturesque mountain town of Lares, where a brief but dramatic rebellion against Spanish rule occurred in 1868. Every year on July 18, El Grito de Lares (The Shout of Lares) is a boisterous gathering of the island's various leftist tribes, featuring passionate oratory, earnest folk musicians, and table upon table of Puerto Rican artisanship. Although a slew of speakers stridently denounced U.S. "aggression," resurrecting militant slogans like "Violating the law of the imperialist is following the law of the homeland," the 1999 event had an unprecedented mainstream appeal. That year's Grito was focused on ending the U.S. Navy's use of the island of Vieques, just off Puerto Rico's east coast, for large-scale maneuvers and target practice, and the crowd felt the whole world was watching.

They wanted everyone to know that despite all this façade of commonwealth and free associated state, Puerto Rico is a colony. Period. America's dirty little secret. The people of Vieques, subject to several major bombing runs a year as part of Navy training maneuvers, have no formal representation in Congress and cannot vote for President. Two-thirds of its fifty-one square miles has been occupied by the Navy since the '40s for maneuvers supposedly essential to America's "combat readiness." Vieques's 9,300 inhabitants live closest to a live firing range (nine miles) than any other U.S. citizens, and as a result, they have a 27 percent higher incidence of cancer than their fellow Puerto Ricans. Some support groups claim that the population has been exposed to an accidental barrage of uranium-tipped bombs. But what really set off Puerto Ricans was a bombing run that made a base security guard, David Sanes, Vieques's first civilian casualty.

The people gathered in Lares that day were giddy about the resurgence of nationalism in Puerto Rico. The unpleasant reminders of the centennial of the U.S. takeover the year before got mixed up with the PRTC strike and Roselló's imposition of a nonbinding plebiscite, which meant virtually nothing, just a month after most of the island was reeling from Hurricane George. But there was a new pride that was being fueled partially by events up north. Even though fear of a hegemonic U.S. culture and the encroaching use of English made Roselló's statehood gambit unpopular, the same island cognoscenti who were miffed when Madonna rubbed a Puerto Rican flag on her crotch in a mid-'90s San Juan concert were taking strong nationalist pride in the success of recording stars Ricky Martin, Jennifer Lopez, and Marc Anthony. The canonization of boxer Felix "Tito" Trinidad completed the cycle, when he entered the ring accompanied by rappers Big Pun and Fat Joe, along with the legendary sign depicting the Navy-held lands in Vieques, calling for peace now.

Now, everyone wants a piece of the nationalist action. The ruling statehood party (PNP), which has long shied away from actions that might annoy the U.S., has had no choice but to declare solidarity with Vieques. During his last year in office, former governor Roselló claimed he wouldn't stand for the resumption of naval activity there. Even ex-governor Romero Barceló finds himself in the same camp with those who would defy the "arrogance of imperialism."

It has long been said that most Puerto Ricans favor independence in their hearts, but only around 5 percent of the electorate have chosen that option in national elections or in the four status plebiscites that have been held since 1952. Puerto Rico's main political battle this century has been over national identity, but the expression of that identity can be ambivalent. For example, although "Tito" Trinidad spoke out for Vieques, he appeared in a *pava*, a *campesino* hat co-opted as a symbol of the status quo Commonwealth party (PDP), and boxing trunks with the logo of Westernbank, an institution the pro-corporate statehood party has done its best to accommodate.

When Puerto Ricans exude nationalism, they are acknowledging the fire of Pedro Albizu Campos—we are not to be messed with. But in this postcolonial age of neoliberal free trade policies, the nationalist revival can be read more as a form of self-empowerment than an explicit call for independence. It's clear that an independent Puerto Rico could not shield itself from the marauding wage-depressing agenda of multinational capital any better than Mexico or even Cuba—which, like Puerto Rico, uses the Yankee dollar as currency and is still the home of a large U.S. military base—can. It may be that George W. Bush's (and corporate America's) most profitable way out of the Puerto Rico mess is to kiss the island, and the substantial federal benefits it pays out to its pseudo-American citizens, good-bye.

On May 4, 2000, forty-six years after Lolita Lebrón and fellow Puerto Rican nationalists shot up the House of Representatives, Lebrón, along with Puerto Rican members of Congress Luis Gutiérrez and Nydia Velázquez, were arrested for resisting the Navy's attempt to clear demonstrators, including Independence Party president Rubén Berríos, from the bombing range in Vieques. "Puerto Rico has been invaded again," said New York City Councilman José Rivera as he was led away.

Clinton's position on Vieques was weak—his plan, negotiated in conjunction with Rosselló, provided for an immediate forty million dollar boost to the Vieques economy and the resumption of limited Navy training using "dummy bombs" occurred a few days after the eviction of the protesters. A referendum, scheduled by the Navy for January 2002, would allow the residents of Vieques to vote on whether the Navy should pull out entirely after three years; a vote to retain the Navy would garner the island another fifty million dollars in aid. This combined stalling tactic and overt bribe might pave the way for the Navy to resume its flouting of agreements, as it did when it ignored a 1983 accord to improve the local economy.

Rosselló's complicity with this agreement was the last straw for Puerto Ricans, now clearly influenced by the latest wave of nationalism. The day after the removal of the protesters, Rosselló activated units of the National Guard, and an angry crowd of more than a thousand demonstrators forced the cancellation of a ceremony at a renovated federal building in Old San Juan. The demonstrators smashed the windshield of pro-statehood former governor Luis Ferré's car as he tried to drive through them. Rosselló's party absorbed a blow it would not recover from in 2000's gubernatorial elections, and the Independence Party, whose leader, Rubén Berríos, was virtually canonized as the patron saint of the Vieques squatters, will score some gains. But the big winner was the status quo Commonwealth Party, which has always absorbed voters with nationalistic sentiments who are not ready for the left-leaning *independentistas*

In November 2000, Sila María Calderon of the Commonwealth party was elected governor of Puerto Rico. Through her alliance with New York politicans from José Rivera to Republican governor George Pataki, she was able to force newly elected George W. Bush to make a decision on Vieques. (Al Sharpton and several other activists were arrested and jailed for their part.) Bush agreed to having the Navy leave Vieques in May 2003 if Vieques residents opted for a binding referendum that was held in November 2001. In the wake of the World Trade Center attacks, the referendum was rescheduled for January 2002, and the Vieques issue has become complicated by the war in Afghanistan. Still, various leaders vow to continue protests.

Vieques, whose name is of Taino origin ("Biekes"), has become a flashpoint for nationalist feelings about Puerto Rico, but it's not so clear that it will be the root of Puerto Rico's final push for independence. Like most Puerto Ricans, I'm for independence in my heart, but I don't know if that's the best thing for the island. I have fallen for the romantic stories about Lebrón, Albizu Campos, and their martyred lives. I was ecstatic when Puerto Rican independence activists draped a Puerto Rican flag over the crown of the Statue of Liberty on Independence Day 1976. I even interviewed Filiberto Ojeda-Rios and Juan Segarra, two infamous Puerto Rican militants in the late '80s.

I took the bus up to Hartford in the fall of 1989 to seek out Juan Segarra, who was under house arrest for his part in a Wells Fargo robbery that occurred in 1983. It was raining so hard in Hartford that when we finally arrived at Juan Segarra's apartment it was like finding sanctuary. We were greeted at the door by his daughter, who led us into the kitchen where we could dry off. Lucy, Juan's wife, was blow-drying her hair as her daughter answered the phone and took messages. In that modest apartment in a modest section of Hartford a few minutes from downtown, it was hard to imagine that I was in what the government considered a safe house for "terrorists."

Soon Segarra came in, nattily dressed in a suit, wearing glasses that enhanced his profile—Harvard graduate, polished, intelligent. His arrival created a swirl of excitement. He kissed his wife and children, and then launched into a recounting of legalisms that had made up his day's work. But Juan was not the lawyer he had once aspired to be. He was the defendant, and he was facing over two hundred years in prison.

Juan Segarra and his wife, Lucy Berríos, are committed to the liberation of their native Puerto Rico from the U.S. They once belonged to a clandestine organization called Los Macheteros which, with the help of the still-fugitive Victor Gerena, staged a robbery of over seven million dollars from a Wells Fargo depot in West Hartford. Juan admitted taking and transporting some of that money, in addition to participating in a bizarre Three King's Day giveaway of toys to poor Puerto Rican children in Hartford and San Juan. Juan, along with several other *independentistas*, dressed up as Santa Claus and gave out the toys in a carnival atmosphere that became a legendary event. Lucy had admitted helping to plan the giveaway. For these crimes, both Juan and Lucy, as well as thirteen other defendants, were held for two and a half years without bail under the Bail Reform Act of 1984. Juan and Lucy are considered to be a threat to national security.

"I'm against terrorism," Juan said, now seated with us in his kitchen. "There's a very clear definition of what it is. It's the intentional taking of civilian lives to pursue political ends. Now, any action attributed to Los Macheteros, or claimed by Los Macheteros, from the moment that they first went public, we don't have a single civilian victim. Not one. Not even accidentally, let alone intentionally." Segarra's voice rose and fell as his passions are balanced by his analysis. At one moment he speaks with rage over what he feels is repression and intolerance; then his voice softens when he speaks of his convictions, based on youthful Catholicism, as is the case for most Puerto Ricans. Segarra claims ancestry that took part in rebellions one hundred years past, but his Ivy League academic persona peeks through when he draws parallels between his plight and that of a band of colonies that raised hell in 1776. Having come of age during the '60s, he gives off "movement" vibes, and even evokes Cheech and Chong when aping what he imagines are the reactions of the FBI agents who listened to his private conversations.

I felt a strong identification with Segarra because of his New England university training, his pseudo-hippie demeanor, and his down-home lack of pretension. I had a different kind of reaction when I met Filiberto Ojeda-Rios in the Borough of Manhattan Correctional Center later that week. Ojeda-Rios was older, bearded, a kind of Che who had grown into middle age. He was from Naguabo, yet another side of the Luquillo Mountain chain that birthed my parents. His mother's maiden name, Rios, was strangely close to my mother's, Rijos, and his skin tone, manner of speaking, and warm smile were exactly like the Rijoses. He could easily have been my uncle.

When he described the reason for his arrest, his wounding of an FBI agent who had come to arrest him, I gave him the benefit of the doubt. The island had just been through the Cerro Maravilla trials, and it was plausible that he had every right to suspect the FBI might take a shot at him. But Ojeda-Rios was clearly committed to the Cuban revolution—two of his children had been educated in Cuba, and his point of view was typically didactic. There is no denying that the U.S. presence in Puerto Rico persists in being colonial, and there is nothing Puerto Ricans can do about that within the laws of their own constitution. Every action that could be taken about Puerto Rico's political status must first be approved by Congress and signed off on by the President. Becoming a loyal Cuban revolutionary could be seen as the only dignified way out of an undignified situation.

A few years later, while in San Juan to cover a film festival, I came across a rally in support of Ojeda-Rios, who was now being housed in a prison not far from the headquarters of Banco Popular, the island's principal capitalist institution. His brother walked back and forth, handing out literature. A month or so later, I heard that Ojeda-Rios had escaped. It was oddly thrilling that a man I once interviewed, who seemed like a living portrait of my own family, had gone on the lam from the U.S. government, which had seen him as such a threat. Now Ojeda-Rios is presumed to be living in Cuba, along with William Morales, an FALN activist whose hands were blown off while he was trying to build a bomb. Morales's message of solidarity was read to the crowds at Lares at the Grito that I attended years later, his ex-wife having just been released from state prison by the Clinton administration in a much-publicized pardoning of many of the Puerto Rican *independentista* prisoners. Juan Segarra, who refused to go along with the terms of the release, is still in a maximum-security prison in Kansas.

While some of the acts that Puerto Rican independence activists have been involved with have been violent and at times cost human lives, I feel for their frustration, and history will show that the violence they have committed is a response to a violence, sometimes real and sometimes metaphoric, that has been committed on the Puerto Rican people by the U.S. But these days I wonder if independence is the noble and prudent option in this situation. In 1997, a small group of Puerto Rican academics who teach both on the island and in the U.S. proposed a different and intriguing option for the resolution of Puerto Rico's status conundrum: Radical Statehood. The argument, posed by Juan Duchesne, Chloe Georas, Ramón Grosfoguel, Agustín Lao, Frances Negrón, Pedro Angel Rivera, and Aurea María Sotomayor, calls for Puerto Ricans to reconsider how independence would affect the island.

The Radical Statehood missive, which so far has had little impact on a broad popular level, acknowledges that with the cold war over, the U.S. has little fear of Puerto Rico defecting to become a socialist country in the image of Cuba, nor does it need absolute possession over the island to continue the limited use of Puerto Rico for military strategy. In fact, the Vieques training ground may be the most important military use of the entire Puerto Rican archipelago. Economic policy over the last few years toward the island has eroded the free tax ride that U.S. corporations get when they do business there (commonly referred to as IRS Tax Code Section 936), and the Republicans in Congress would love to dispense with the large transfer payments now being sent to the island for the purposes of Welfare and Food Stamp programs. So, the proposal says, "The handwriting is on the wall: we can either press for statehood, or get ready to become an Associated Republic."

Radical Statehood would attempt to seize the statehood agenda from conservative and neoconservative types like Roselló, and project Puerto Rico as a fifty-first state that would be a major force on the left in America, as well as for the inevitable Spanglishization of the country. The idea goes basically like this: By becoming a state, Puerto Rico would not be condemned to losing its culture—Spanish and Spanglish have now been spoken widely in barrios across the country without change for the last fifty years. Most of the intolerant sectors of the U.S. oppose Puerto Rican statehood, perhaps for good reason: If Puerto Rico were to become a state, it would force

America to acknowledge a hybrid, bilingual culture as officially part of its framework. So if you really want to stick it to Uncle Sam, support Radical Statehood!

A second, crucial reason to support statehood is the increasing meaninglessness of "nationhood" in the international legal sense (not in the sociocultural sense) in the multinational economy. "In order for transnational and local businesses to compete on the world market," says the proposal, "the Republic of Puerto Rico would be forced to lower or freeze the minimum wage, neuter its environmental legislation, and eliminate important labor and civil rights which are in force under current federal laws. All the Latin American and Caribbean republics are now competing to sell themselves the cheapest to transnational capital. Puerto Rico, as a regional extension of the U.S. economy, would worsen its current position by joining that list of competitors."

If Puerto Rico were to become a state, say the proponents of Radical Statehood, two senators and possibly five U.S. representatives would have more of an influence on U.S. policy than an ambassador to the U.N. As the population of Latinos grows in the U.S., the state of Puerto Rico would be in a much better position to make alliances with them, as well as affect U.S. foreign policy toward Latin American nations.

In the last fifty years, Puerto Ricans have increased their participation on many institutional levels in the U.S., and we have benefited from our increased understanding of the democratic process, as well as the civil rights movement. As Raquel Rivera states in an essay in *Puerto Rican Jam*, a book edited by two of the Radical Statehood proponents, the lessons of race Puerto Ricans have learned in the U.S. have expanded the idea of race relations among us, and exposed the incipient racism in the Puerto Rican national culture. Being in the U.S. has enabled us to participate in the civil rights movement and the creation of hip-hop, and realize on a more popular level the Africanist ideal that Puerto Rican arts and letters have proposed in the last century.

If Puerto Rico were "set free," wouldn't it just become another servile nation on the Caribbean periphery, perhaps reverting to a colonial mentality that would reverse some of the gains made by people of color, women, and gay people? Even at Grito de Lares, one of the pro-independence speeches I heard compared Puerto Rico's lack of autonomy to a father who was unable to rule his own family. Is it possible that the independence rhetoric of '60s' Puerto Rico has ossified and lost touch with today's politics?

In some way, it repulses all Puerto Ricans who have a sense of national pride to actually become part of the U.S., after all these years we've struggled to maintain our identity apart from it. But we have become some of the most practiced and typical Americans of the current era, and much of the cultural and political energy of Puerto Rico is coming from Spanglish Nuyoricans who are embracing American institutions while at the same time not letting go of who they are.

Under the Radical Statehood logic, the U.S. is looking for a way to push us into independence. It can almost seem like the whole Vieques issue is the perfect kind of Gaza Strip conflict that could fester for years and finally make the U.S. throw up its hands and say, okay, maybe you guys should be independent! We tried! And all the Puerto Rican flags will fly madly all over the island and New York, Philadelphia, and Hartford, Connecticut, and we will all feel "free at last, Thank God almighty, we are free at last." And then the Puerto Rican economy will find itself with an inability to sustain a viable currency and wages will go down to the level of Mexico, and perhaps that of a "free" Cuba.

Of course, it's very possible that if Puerto Rico decides it wants to become a rogue state, a perpetual thorn in Congress's side, an unflinching defender of the Spanglish and working peoples' rights, America will never let us in. The Radical Statehooders say we should demand it like Martin Luther King demanded civil rights in the '60s, but somehow I don't think it will work that way.

Right now, it seems inconceivable that the Puerto Rican nationhood we carry in our hearts will reconcile itself under another flag. But as the years hold, and Spanglish forces reverse continental drift, it may be inevitable that a changed American will welcome us with open arms, and Puerto Ricans will see nothing wrong with it.

It may be that for now the Spanglish solution is to continue to attend the rites of El Spirit Republic de Puerto Rico, the performance/plastic art ceremonies kept alive by Pedro Pietri and Adal Maldonado in memory of Eddie Figueroa. To paraphrase Marx (and Marshal Berman), our nationalism, like all that is solid, will melt into air. Tropical Puerto Rico exists in New York as a virtual landscape outside of time, in memory, as a hunch, a feeling, a certainty. Not to worry that we might become irrelevant, swallowed up by big, bad nations intent on devouring difference. "Our surrealistic history has proven that we are immune to mediocrity!" proclaims Pietri.

I, who once stood on a mountaintop of Vieques with a group of squatters, trying to claim a strip of land just inside Navy territory, watching the fake bombs explode/I, who feel the exhilaration of the rich soil surrounding my grandfather's house as part of my genetic code/I, who can't stop from weeping when "Mi Viejo San Juan" or "Lamento Borincano" comes on the jukebox/I, who feel like a free bird alone in a driving rainstorm on Route 3 between San Juan and my mother's hometown, Rio Grande. . . . No matter how many Manhattan streets I prowl or L.A. freeways I patrol, I will not be separated from this magic land for however long my spirit walks on this Spanglish hemisphere.

10.

TOWARD A SPANGLISH HEMISPHERE

The authentic mestizo has conquered the exotic Creole . . .
  — JOSÉ MARTÍ, *Nuestra America*

If you are a dreamer, like me, you know that we are moving toward a Spanglish hemisphere. That is, an America that is united, a region where the inevitable mixing of north and south comes to full fruition. The end of the twentieth century witnessed a chain of events that would make this inevitable: The end of the cold war and the beginning of the information age has brought about the unfettered expansion of multinational corporations and a seemingly infinite number of new ways that the north and south can communicate. The end of the industrial age has increased the movement of private companies to the south, and cheap labor to the north. The end of East-West has focused our attention on North-South.

But besides these material exigencies (and I am a firm believer in the material basis for existence), there is a very important social reality to consider in this development. I will grant that the idea of nationalism and nations is rapidly becoming irrelevant, but it is absurd to think that because the cold war is over that we have reached the end of ideology. Still there is one ideology, a cultural ideology and not a political one, that is certain to meet death in the coming years, and that is the ideology of racial purity. Intermarriage is rising in America at spectacular rates, a fact that will further expose the myth that there are racially pure Americans. In an article by Jeffrey Lind that appeared in *The New York Times* in 1998, the author suggests that rising rates of intermarriage between whites and Asians and whites and Latinos, combined with much lesser rates of intermarriage between whites and blacks, will create a new race dynamic in American society. No longer will we be a white-black society; we will become a beige-black society. On the surface, at least, the population of North America will more closely resemble that of Latin America, which is also comprised of a significant majority of mixed-race people. In fact, one of the main complaints about racism from Latin Americans who come to America is that their mixed-race "beige" status no longer means "white."

But if America comes to resemble Latin America in terms of racial dichotomy, nothing about the "race problem" will be solved. What will change is that fewer people will be considered "other," while blacks, and perhaps pure indigenous people and Asians (whose numbers will dwindle with intermarriage) will remain discriminated against. This is why Spanglish culture can be so important to America's future. The Spanglish valorization of African and indigenous culture was in large part made possible through its incubation in North America. When we came here, we were made aware of the more overt racism of the North, and participated in the movements against racism, making a leap forward that we couldn't have in our home countries. The race ideology of Latin America, with its beige and black dichotomy, allowed for more of us to imagine we were white. When we came northward, we discovered that wasn't true.

Africa begins at the Pyrenees
— ALEXANDRE DUMAS

To understand the process that may someday become crucial in American history, we should look back at European history, specifically that of Spain. As Cuban scholar Roberto Fernández Retamar argues in his essay "The Black Legend Revisited," Spain, unlike other western European countries, always had a kind of double consciousness. Owing to its "marginalization to the development of the capitalist system," there was the duality of Spain versus the rest of Europe. Then there was an internal duality, which became doubly opposed at the very moment of the "discovery" of the New World: the Gallic-Gothic alliance of the north, which took it upon itself to expurgate the Moorish south. The five hundred-year Moorish occupation of Spain was one with perhaps the most successful multicultural society ever achieved in Europe. Through the occupation, Retamar says, "Europe gained access to the achievements of Greece, Persia, and India that the Arabs had assimilated." In southern Spain, Moors, Jews, Catholics, and Gypsies lived together for centuries, and their cultures intertwined to create the basis of what most people consider "Spanish culture": flamenco, mosque-influenced mosaic architecture, the romance of black and red. As a result of the Spanish Inquisition, which occurred simultaneously with Columbus's first voyages, a vast portion of the mixed-race, non-"Western European" people were exiled to the Americas, often to live secret lives, as the Sephardic Jews of New Mexico still do.

In other words, just as thousands of poor, unskilled Puerto Ricans were exported from the island's countryside to the slums of New York, and just as displaced agricultural workers from Mexico and Central America have been redeposited in South Central Los Angeles, the vital elements of a dynamic, mixed-race hybrid culture were the first colonists of the New World, creating the first cities of the Americas. The Spanglish essence comes from this displacement: Five hundred years ago it was pushed westward to go into hiding; one hundred years ago it was reencircled from the north and sucked upward. And now it has nowhere to go except inside. Inside the fabric of a society obsessed with increased telecommunications. Inside the language that controls the communicative force of the world. Inside the very rhythms of life in America.

As we move toward a Spanglish hemisphere, North and South are converging. The continuing importation of Latino labor into North America is crucial to the current economy, because it reduces labor costs to the point where venture capitalists are willing to throw money around at high rates of return. Economic crises in Mexico and the rest of Latin America also increase the flow of immigration.

At the same time, the increasingly sophisticated cable networks of North America continue to penetrate the South. MTV, HBO, Showtime, CNN, Discovery, TBS, Fox, and ESPN all have Spanish-language affiliates, spreading a Spanish version of American culture into the hinterlands of Latin America. The constant exposure to North American lifestyles through television has created enormous societal changes in Latin America. In general, the effect has been a hybrid, inclusive one: American attitudes, like tolerance for women's rights, gay lifestyles, and punk rock are added to, rather than replacing, traditional totems like the church, the traditional music, and the language.

Border Crossers

We are a Nation of one and many millions of eternal Ricans
Who need to visit each other more often to keep up with
The latest bochinches in the artistic and political circles
—Pedro Pietri, "El Spirit Republic de
Puerto Rico Manifesto"

— While so much is happening as a result of migration, emigration, and immigration, and communities are congealing right now in so many variations of Spanglish style in Brooklyn, Boston, Detroit, Orlando, Atlanta, Milwaukee, El Paso, Denver, Tulsa, ad infinitum, the movement back and forth, the circular migration, is key to the sophistication of Spanglish. North and South Americans must become border crossers, which is a process of simultaneous creation and destruction. Increased awareness of "bordered" cultures, which exist in the overlap, helps deny the existence of the border.

The trauma of the Spanglish soul revisiting the homeland is one of the key elements that reinforce our need to be Spanglish, that is, hybrid border crossers who can't be at home in the U.S. nor in Latin America, as both places are presently constituted. It's always puzzled me how alienated many Chicanos feel when they travel to Mexico City. I feel uncomfortable reading Richard Rodriguez's essay "India," in which he seems separated from his Mexican hosts by his affiliation with a credit card company junket. Or when he goes to Tijuana, confronts his fear of the water, and does not drink. The punchline: You might as well face it, you're addicted to America.

Understandable, in some ways. The Mexican is so clearly defined, so "far from God, so close to America," that Americans must be regarded with suspicion. Chicanos, unfortunately, fall under the definition of "American," especially for Mexicans. But these sentiments are also expressed vehemently, famously by Nuyoricans. The origins of Nuyorican are attributed at least partially to a trip poet Miguel Algarín took to the island where he felt snubbed by intolerant islanders. Algarín's case has added power because part of that snubbing was racist, since he is darker skinned. And of course my story is no better than the rest. When I first started returning to the island in the '80s, my Spanish in no way resembled that spoken in Puerto Rico. First, it was wholly inept. Then, after some practice, it became too mannered, as if I approached a New Yorker speaking in a British accent.

What happens when you speak Spanish like an outsider in Puerto Rico is that they answer you in English. Cleverly bilingual of them. Oh, how Spanglish. I finally learned that the only way to convince a native Puerto Rican that I was legit was to speak as unintelligibly as possible, and it worked. I dropped syllables, always the letter *s* at the end of words, pronounced *r*'s like *l*'s, aspirated consonants. One day, at the fresh coconut kiosk at Luquillo beach, I ordered two coconuts and a bottled water—*"Po'l favo'l, dame doh cocoh y una botella de awa,"* and the guy answered me in Spanish. I knew it was the beginning of something special.

Not good enough to be Americans, not good enough to be Puerto Ricans (or Mexicans). Caught in between. "I felt like a stranger." Neither, nor (coincidentally the name of an East Village club where Nuyorican poet Miguel Piñero hung out just before his death). True, some of this reaction is based on island Puerto Ricans' feeling of classism or racism toward darker and poorer Nuyoricans, the losers that had to take the cheap plane ride and screw up everyone's reputation in *West Side Story*. But it's not good enough for me to merely write this off as the inevitable sadness of being Spanglish. It's not good enough for Spanglish citizens to become another version of Hollywood's Tragic Mulatto, the mixed-race daughter in *Imitation of Life* who throws it all away for a no-good beatnik.

I have become fascinated with every last Latino culture. Using my limited funds, and the occasional privilege that being a member of the press accords me, I have made the pilgrimage to five different Latin American countries besides the first Spanglish nation, Puerto Rico. Each time I find epiphanies in their slightly different variations of Latin-ness, as if I'd found lost tribes of a treasured order. And each time I find evidence of the new Spanglish order.

About two hundred miles east of Caracas, at the end of a long, winding road with speed bumps in seemingly every town on the way, which stretch a journey in a beat-up '75 LTD to almost nine hours, lies Carupano, one of the heartlands of Spanglish America. Situated on the northern coast of Venezuela, in the middle of the semi-arid peninsular state of Sucre, Carupano is a quintessential model of postmodern Third World contradiction. It's a place where people cruise in sports utility vehicles searching for the old woman who makes black bean empanadas from scratch on a street corner. It's a place where people use cell phones to make arrangements with friends and neighbors to go see the elaborate nativity scene at the local 350-year-old church. It's a place where people rumba on the beach to the beat of children drumming on milk cartons, and party at night in clubs where Eurodisco hits like "Barbie Girl" are all the rage.

I had come to Venezuela partly out of the urgings of Los Amigos Invisibles, an ultrahip acid-jazz dance band who told me stories about mobile DJ parties and a club scene that rivaled Miami's. The Amigos dressed like space-age bachelors of the early '60s, looking like extras from an obscure Peter Sellers movie that had been dubbed into Spanish for Mexican television. They understood the silly hyperbole that lurked just under the surface of Latin America's hard-core machismo and somehow transformed it into an infectious groove that made it all the way to New York and Los Angeles. They seemed to be the voice of Latin America's youth, parodying the vacant MTV manner of their counterparts to the north, while adding the irrepressible soul of the south.

But what I didn't understand about the sardonic cast of Los Amigos was not limited to their jaded Caracas background, nor just the major cities of Latin America like Bogotá, Buenos Aires, or Mexico City. The alternative universe of postindustrial consumer culture had taken deep root in obscure outposts like Carupano. As I flitted from house to house in this Christmas season, bearing witness to increasingly complex, kitsch-laden nativity scenes (called *pesebres* in the local dialect), I found myself in a world that didn't quite resemble the corrugated-tin-shack stereotype of Latin America. I was taking in a typical outer periphery town that was busily playing out the suburban dramas that have shaped North America's postwar life.

One night, on a club crawl through Carupano, I found myself in Shooters, a cheesy dancehall not unlike what you'd find in Miami, Dallas, or Milwaukee, chatting up single mothers and thirty something men. The women were lamenting their increased responsibilities while enjoying new creative freedoms, while the men talked about cars, and the annoyance of having to leave Carupano to find work in the new, finance-driven tourist companies in towns to the distant south. MTV Latino played on the video screens overhead, flashing videos of Argentine groups like Soda Stereo and Illya Kuryaki and the Valderramas. At one point, as I leaned across a pool table to make myself heard, my eyes froze on a wacky postmodern juxtaposition. Under the disco ball that marked the dancing area, a swarm of couples were shuffling the folksy and erotic *cumbia* while the English hard-techno group, Prodigy, performed in all their pierced and tattooed glory to a horde of headbangers in Moscow on the monitors behind the dancers.

During the cold war era, Mexico City was filled with Soviet spies, who coordinated communist contact with sympathizers throughout Latin America. Mexico City became a home base of sorts for leftists from Central and South America, even Brazil. In Mexico City, I am a secret agent for such cross-cultural experiments, investigating the alternative arts scene, as well as finding the rebirth of rock and roll in the mystical underground of that city's music world. Mexico City is a modern leviathan in the middle of the Valley of Mexico, a labyrinth of neighborhoods clashing starkly in tone, fractured by an '80s earthquake yet still incredibly sure of itself. Not only are Chicanos making pilgrimages here, but New York Latinos like writers Junot Díaz (Dominican) and Francisco Goldman (Guatemalan/ Jewish), filmmaker Alex Rivera (Peruvian/Anglo), and photographer Joe Rodriguez (Nuyorican). When I first traveled to Mexico City in 1993, the rate of exchange was three pesos to a dollar. A lunch for two at the Zona Rosa restaurant, Fonda El Refugio, set me back about fifty dollars. As I returned several times over the next few years, I felt fearless flagging cabs, going anywhere at night, to places like El Habito, operated by feminist performance artist Jesusa Rodriguez, where I could just as likely see sarcastic *ranchera* singer Astrid Hadad, who sang songs about being beaten by men, as an impromptu reunion of the avant-rock band Tuxedo Moon, having just moved to Mexico after years in exile in Europe. But after NAFTA began to sink in, the party was over, and there was an acute crisis in the Mexican peso—by '96 the rate of exchange was over nine pesos to a dollar. Fonda El Refugio became ridiculously inexpensive and the green and white VW Beetle taxis I was fond of became notoriously crime-ridden. The circus jugglers that bummed change at the magnificent Parisian traffic circles became whole families, led by a beleaguered mother. I was warned not to take the subway.

In the historic centro district of Mexico City, the famous Café Tacuba, a kind of tourist trap for seekers of the "old" city, suffered major damage from a fire. Almost simultaneously, the rock group Café Tacuba introduced their new album, *Reves*, which reinvigorated one of their old themes: Europeans have conquered the world in various ways, but the point is, however, to reverse the cycle. After all, in the climactic lyric of an earlier song, "El Ciclón," Tacuba had proclaimed that "Life always returns to its circular form."

In a music conference in Miami, Tacuba screened the video inspired by the music on *Reves*, which was directed by an old school chum, Adolfo Davila. "We wanted to work on the assumption that music could generate images, not the reverse," said bassist Quique Rangel. The video began with a staccato swirl of images reflected through a hubcap—again, the circular narrative ploy—moving through life in Mexico City from the point of view of a petty street criminal and a working woman. Shantytowns are juxtaposed with PCs, tabloid TV violates an ancient pyramid, the visuals pulsing to the rhythmic imperatives of Tacuba's composition. "This is a rhythm that's played in reverse," Tacuba chant, as a boxer comes back up from the canvas, and one of the famous Acapulco divers zips back up the cliff. The turning of the wheel had begun.

It seemed no coincidence that Mexican rock began to sound angrier, more inflected with North American overtones. Rock-rap became the rage in Mexico, with bands like Molotov, Control Machete, and Resorte, all of whom worked with California-based

Anglo producers, supplanting the earnest idealism of early '90s Mexican rock. Cypress Hill went to Mexico to record the Spanish-language version of their English hit, "How I Could Just Kill a Man," and Rage Against the Machine filmed an MTV special in a warehouse-club in town. Rage itself is a proto-Spanglish band, featuring half-Mexican, half-Anglo Zack de la Rocha and half-African, half-white Tom Morello. Morello, born out of an idealistic marriage between an American political activist and a revolutionary leader from Kenya, Africa, grew up half-black in a white suburb of Chicago. Like de la Rocha, another product of a mixed marriage, he grew up listening to trashy '70s and '80s rock while feeling somewhat alienated from a middle American environment insensitive to his otherness. "I used to listen to Alice Cooper, Black Sabbath, Kiss," said Morello. "Even as a sixteen-year-old, I had twin ambitions. One was to be in a rock band and the other was to find my convictions as a rebel and as an activist."

The Mexico City show coincided with a months-long takeover of the Autonomous National University of Mexico campus protesting the privatization of the university. De la Rocha and Morello have long been associated with supporters of Subcomandante Marcos of the Zapatistas. While it is undoubtedly a contradiction that Rage makes millions from a corporate system they are dedicated to defeat, it doesn't seem to bother Morello, who points to the massive audience the band has created for their radical message.

> The phrase "political correctness" evokes not only the neo-conservative caricature of socialist, feminist, gay, lesbian, and multiculturalist politics but also a real tendency within the left . . . but if political correctness evokes a preachy, humorless austerity, the phrase "popular culture" evokes a sense of pleasure. . . . How do we critique the dominant Eurocentric media while harnessing its undeniable pleasures? Assume imperfection and contradiction."
>
> —ROBERT STAMM/ELLA SHOHAT,
> Unthinking Eurocentrism

Messy contradictions aside, the most interesting thing about Rage is the way they represent the demographic change that is sweeping the U.S., and affecting who is playing and listening to rock music. As people of mixed race, de la Rocha and Morello were willing to mix their musical influences and pioneer the rap-rock sound years before acts like Limp Bizkit and Sugar Ray. It's not only de la Rocha's partial Mexican ancestry that makes Rage very much like a rock en Español band. "While I'm not as familiar with the roots and genesis of the rock en Español movement, I think that clearly in the '90s there's been a breaking down of musical barriers in rock," said Morello. "Where there was formerly a much greater segregation between hiphop and rock communities, now it's really difficult to find a band that at least in some measure doesn't combine some of those different elements. I think another important development has been that not just the musical segregation but also the ethnic segregation in rock music has become less of a force."

Both Cypress Hill and Rage Against the Machine have established a significant presence in Latin America, although they are still not directly communicating; their appearances there feel staged, almost intrusive, despite the seeming loyalty of the fans who no doubt think highly of them. They still haven't achieved the kind of connection that salsa singer Willie Colón has when he does a show there, and recently, starred in a local soap opera. But the dialogue is just beginning. Latin alternative kids are way ahead of the North American bands they worship; they have fully appropriated the style and content of North America while most of us are still total strangers to the Latin American way of life.

One of the more alarming manifestations of hemispheric convergence is the exportation of Salvadoran youth gangs from Los Angeles to their ancestral country. Many of these gang members, who belong to groups like *Mara Salvadurena* and *Calle 108*, came north as a result of the U.S.-sponsored war against Marxist rebels in the '80s. The classic profile is of a young man who lost his father to that violence, moves to a city like Los Angeles or Washington, D.C., and learns the gang/prison culture around him. Salvadoran gangs have carved out most of the territory of cities and towns in El Salvador, and their agenda is completely beholden to their leaders in Los Angeles. They speak Spanglish and are involved in a similar form of extortion as Colombian rebels—they kidnap children of middle- to upper-class families and demand a ransom.

The entire violent process that the U.S. exported to El Salvador in the '80s has been renewed in the new century; the same strongholds that the FMLN rebels used to employ are now being held by roving gangs of extortionists and drug dealers. The legacy of military-style violence, propped up by weapons that have made the transition from being toted by revolutionary soldiers to being brandished by a SoCal-style gang, persists. The violent subtext of the New World Economy, which necessarily implies a large-scale decimation of the lower classes both inside and outside the U.S.'s borders, is one of the worst things about hemispheric convergence. The unequal distribution of wealth, and the inadequacy of democratic systems in addressing that since the collapse of industrialism, is the biggest issue underlying the recent "recovery." Spanglish can play a large part in forcing a change; most of the citizens of Latin America and their counterparts in the U.S. are on the losing side of the equation. Movements like that of the Zapatistas, ensconced in rural areas of Chiapas, using the Internet as a tool for dissemination of information, could be duplicated. The remnants of liberation theology, combined with a new kind of radical democratic thinking, are ripe for development in Latin America and Latino barrios in America. Leaders like Richie Perez, a key figure from New York's Young Lords Party, have created the groundwork for a new activism, especially around the issues of police brutality and prisoners' rights. And the left is not the only arena for Spanglish politics—the new politics has already established itself as a hybrid force—Democratic social liberalism plus Republican economic conservatism.

Spanglish style can add to new coalitions of race plus class politics; maybe we can also solve the riddle that the Yippie fringe of
'60s activism could not. Maybe we can dance and have fun while
we change the world. As much as I have been attracted to the punk
aesthetic, its rejection of "flower power" was subliminally also a
rejection of the Latin influence on the counterculture in California.
("We were dressed in black leather, they dressed in wild colors"—
Mary Woronov recalled about the encounter between the Warhol
crowd and the San Francisco Summer of Love.) The punk aesthetic's self-destructive nature was testament to the impossibility of
the White Negro. Maybe it was no coincidence that the late rock
critic Lester Bangs, who deserved credit for at least confronting the
issue of racism in the punk scene, wore a T-shirt that said THE LAST
OF THE WHITE NIGGERS.

The idea that Spanglish culture is America's new bohemia has
been expressed before by Juan Flores. The emphasis that I place
on the history of Spanglish bohemia in the U.S. is no coincidence.
Rather than tell the success stories of Hispanic businessmen and
politicians, who operate with their share of cross-cultural contradictions and can be just as Spanglish as Miguel Piñero or Luis
Valdez, I focus on the bohemian vanguard because they took the
most chances to protect their Latino identities. But as Spanglishness makes itself better understood, or the very rhythm of language and communication reflects the collapse of categories and
the end of race purity, North becomes South and South becomes
North.

The Media is the Mensaje

North America is in a cultural crisis, wringing its hands over the coming of the electric world, the media world, where literacy deteriorates, and electric images dominate. Critics fret that either there is no story line or meaning in everything from the novel to polite conversation, or that the most powerful pop figures today are sitcom stars and rap MCs. The intelligentsia throws up its hands in dismay when white rapper Eminem grafts his Detroit suburban ethos on the imperatives of gangsta—hit first and hit hard, fuck women and gays, get over. The oral tradition, so highly prized by anti-Eurocentrists, serves the ambitions of a postliterate white boy. Eminem is the ultimate media presence, so convincing a hiphop figure that he is backed by Dr. Dre, his producer and a significant Los Angeles rap pioneer, and his music has been canonized as authentic hiphop.

Right now, there exists very little understanding in North America that the everyday salsa or merengue star is actively engaged in a project of multiracial artistry. He/she is completely fluent in the language that celebrates a union of and contradiction between European romanticism and African call and response. (Of course, according to works like Martin Bernal's *Black Athena*, the Hellenophilic tendencies of romantics might actually be an unacknowledged passion for Egypt or Phoenicia, whose contributions to Greek culture were written out of textbooks by pro-Aryan racial purists.) And, because the bi- and tricultural syncretism is so seamless, many Latinos are unaware of it, and simply think of salsa/merengue as "Latin" music.

—We are multicultural. Not in the vastly misunderstood, overused, and overly condemned sense of the word. We are not a society of people who came to live with each other because we were "politically correct" and found a way to send our children to the same schools and went to theater only with nontraditional casting and frequented clubs and restaurants with a "mixed crowd." We are multicultural because we slept with each other. For five hundred years. It's in our genetic code.

To paraphrase McLuhan again, for Latinos, the "medium," that is, the multicultural framework through which we perceive the world, is at this time more important than the actual messages being spread by the information age. Biculturalism, or bilingualism, can be a great advantage during a time when a philosophical leap of faith is necessary. During a conversation I once had with Willie Colón, we realized we shared the same belief about how literate we became, despite our humble origins in the Bronx. The mere circumstance of being bilingual in two related languages gave us added perceptivity. Certain words that were routine, almost street words in Spanish, like "charlatan" and "equivocate," were higher-level vocabulary words in English.

What may be more important in the long run, however, is the perspective of bilingual, biculturalism. Just being bilingual sheds light on *language* itself, the fact that it has structure. When one grows up monolinguistic, one may never really understand language's abstract structure. The same goes for culture. The same goes for race.

At the same time, this "electric" existence, of highly energetic and contrasting sights, sounds, and concepts, resists linear explanation. The definition of Latino or Spanglish can easily be lost in the process of shedding light on it. We live in a never-ending echo chamber of overlapping. The echoing sound might be a writing teacher, shouting, "What's the story?" or "Show, don't tell."

Let's imagine, then, that we are Narcissus. And that Echo, the monocultural North American claiming to be our teacher, is running toward us, arms outstretched, saying, "I want to love you, just tell me, objectively who you are." But, like Rodriguez putting the glass of water to his lips, and never drinking, you can't answer. You can't accept Echo's love. Instead we are staring into a pool that holds our image. Not because we're vain, not because we can't love anyone but ourselves, but because we're the only ones who can see it, and we have to stay alive. Narcissism is transformed from a character flaw into an act of survival.

With all of this in mind, it's easy to see why Latinos and Spanglish culture have been all but invisible in the media. While African Americans suffered from invisibility for a long time, this was mostly because of the white majority's desire to ignore the problem it had created. Once the civil rights movement came, and whites were forced to look into the face of black rage and accomplishment, some changes, if still inadequate, were made. Through the appropriations of White Negroes and the inevitable lust of the networks, certain aspects of black culture, because it was an "other" culture, were made intelligible and visible.

But Latinos, in addition to being a third wheel, are difficult to present in a linear fashion. Our multicultural reality is confusing; our ability to identify with widely divergent social contexts will never make our families "average." Still, as we continue to live our Spanglish realities and develop discrete communities, the possibilities of representation grow. New story lines are fleshed out. In recent years, Latinos have come to dominate the boxing world. In quick succession, the movie industry has trotted out two films, *The Price of Glory* and *Girlfight*, which focus on Latino/Latinas who are boxers. A new television series, *Resurrection Boulevard*, is a kind of intelligent soap opera about a family with boxers in it, but the female characters, who aren't boxers, are given important roles that amplify Spanglish contradiction and ambivalence. *Resurrection Boulevard* is also a strong show because it is situated in East Los Angeles, which has been a Chicano stronghold for so long that it has a particular feel with recognizable totems and traditions.

— Another strength of *Resurrection Boulevard* is the fact that the cast, writers, and producers are almost entirely Latino (though a diverse crew at that—Chicanos, Puerto Ricans, Colombians, and Cuban Americans are all involved). At the risk of engaging in what some might see as didacticism, I believe the problem of lack of representation of Latinos in the media is directly related to the lack of

Latinos working as media professionals. In 1996, I wrote a cover story for the *Village Voice* called "Brownout," which detailed the sad statistical tale of Spanglish invisibility in newsrooms, behind the camera, and on film sets.

Here are some numbers (keep in mind Latinos make up about 12 to 13 percent of the population right now): The percentage of Latino employees at major newspapers in the U.S. stands at 3.66 percent, down slightly from the previous year. In broadcast media, the figures are slightly higher, from 5 to 11 percent. Only 2 percent of the continuing characters on network television shows are Latino.

My own involvement in journalism was nontraditional and fraught with contradiction. I followed the path of least resistance, and inspired by the great African-American alternative journalist Greg Tate, I tried to become a gonzo Latino specialist. Many people in the business told me that I shouldn't pigeonhole myself, but should pick an area of expertise and establish myself as a mainstream writer. But as conversant as I was in mainstream culture, I wasn't trusted to interpret it very often. So I stuck to my people, my beat. Doing so freed me from being a film critic and spending my life in dark screening rooms, or being a street reporter, forever digging through court records and pestering local politicians, or being a music critic, trapped in a living room with thousands of CDs, finding myself graying and middle-aged at a rave in San Francisco with a swarm of nineteen-year-olds.

Since so few people were covering Latinos as a beat, I became a general expert in the subject, "discovering" movements like Latin alternative music, a new activism in the Dominican neighborhood of Washington Heights, reinventing myself as a poet-journalist at the Nuyorican Poets Café, writing about police brutality against minority communities six years before the Abner Louima episode. It wasn't easy; editors had told me at various times that police brutality against Latinos was a fabrication, that a drug-dealing background of one victim justified his death at the hands of the police. One editor, who actually served as my advocate at one point, had written this about Puerto Ricans in the '70s: "Spics. Specks. The name fit. They were barnacles . . . And if they got too close—well, the smell of beans and beer, whole families and chicken, gnawing down to the bone, pink walls and cockamammie music, endless bongos in the night—well, there would be this greaser with hair like an oily palm tree, and he'd be sitting next to you in the subway in his Desi Arnaz shoes and his silver sharkskin pants and his jukebox-boleros shirt, and you just knew he had a razor up his sleeve." In my entire mainstream journalism career, a period spanning fifteen years, I have only dealt with one Latino editor, and she was let go after only six months.

While there have been Spanglish media success stories like *Latina* magazine, which is partly the product of a partnership with African American–oriented *Essence* magazine, there has been no explosion of traditional media in Spanglish. *Latina*, which pioneered the bilingual presentation of stories, is still constricted by its beauty-and-health-tips format, although its hewing to a specific identity strategy is a major accomplishment. The hot process for dissemination of Spanglish right now is in .com start-ups, many of which actively use Spanglish as a way of defining their base.

The different Web sites that have hit the Internet at the turn of the century reflect different Spanglish sensibilities. The aptly named Yupi.com appeals to a middlebrow Latino professional type, as well as other Miami-based sites like El Sitio, Terra.com, and Quepasa.com. Web sites following the *Urban Latino* magazine perspective, that is, a black cultural assimilative model (with some hybrid inclusion of Latino signifiers), like latinflava.com and loquesea.com, combine hiphop English with Spanglish. Loquesea.com (meaning "whatever") is one of the few sites in English, Spanish, and Spanglish—words like "La Clicka" and "Checkalo" fuel the growth of Spanglish through cyberspacisms. In fact, the Internet has accelerated the expansion of Spanglish because of its specialized terms that are untranslatable into Spanish.

Although there is a huge struggle going on right now to define how Latinos prefer to receive their information, that is, either in English or Spanish, the role of the Spanish-language media is important. In fact the Spanish language media is becoming more sophisticated, especially with the advent of CNN en Español and CBS Telenoticias, two organizations owned by U.S. networks. The existing giants, Telemundo and Univision, at times score extremely high ratings in cities like Los Angeles and Houston. While there is something dreadfully backward about much of the prime-time programming on Spanish-language television (shows like the extremely popular *Sabado Gigante*, a game show with similarities to *Ted Mack's Original Amateur Hour*, infantilize the viewer and serve as an extension of the colonial past that immigrants could gain from to escape), there have been some attempts to create viable new programming. Telemundo began a series of semi-bilingual shows that copy some American formats (most notably a *Charlie's Angels* imitation with an Afro-Latina cast member to combat the persistent racism in Latin American television), and the news departments keep up a steady stream of Latino-issues coverage that makes North American news seem myopic. But there are still sizable complaints from Latinos about the heavy-handed, conservative nature of Cuban American hegemony over much of the programming.

Perhaps the most dynamic Spanglish media happening today is in radio, the one area where Spanish and Spanglish-speaking radio stations actually become the top-rated carriers in large markets like New York and Los Angeles. The late '90s were a significant period for the ascension of Spanish language radio, because advertisers and radio programmers began to realize that Latinos have many different nationality identifications and varying degrees of assimilation. The number of Latinos in the New York area, with a huge community of recently arrived immigrants, who prefer their information in English has risen to almost 50 percent of the market. WSKQ-FM, otherwise known as La Mega, took that revelation and a concept that recognized that New York listeners were far more interested in salsa and merengue than Latin "lite" ballads, and became the number-one radio station in New York. They also anchored their rise to the top around a Spanglish announcer. Nuyorican Manuel Navarro, also known as Paco. Paco was perhaps more influential to the explosion of the disco era as any Latino was in the origin of hiphop. During his tenure at the legendary WKTU, Paco virtually invented the disco format, and was a major celebrity at Studio 54. Now he's hawking Cadillacs for Potamkin Brothers car dealership and subscriptions to *The New York Times* on a radio station playing those songs about hot, horny men and their *mulatas*.

While I was researching a piece about Spanish-language radio I found some disconcerting revelations about racism in the advertising industry when it came to selling time on Latino-themed radio stations. Amcast, a division of Katz Radio Group, which sold advertising time to stations, warned companies in an internal memo against buying too many ads on black and Latino radio stations, because "advertisers should want prospects, not suspects." Others in the field claimed that many businesses, such as Ikea, have what he calls a "no-Hispanic dictate." While figures like New York–based minority-issues advocate Al Sharpton have been active in trying to correct this, racism of this kind might be only the tip of the iceberg. Still, by its nature, advertising is so manipulative and culture-flattening that I can't insist on its being crucial to bringing about a Spanglish hemisphere. The official national identity of Puerto Rico is now manufactured by a consortium of advertisers that include the island's biggest bank, Banco Popular. But Puerto Ricans sussed their role out in the midst of the telephone strike in 1998, and the institution came under heavy criticism.

Advertisers are still trying to figure out how to avoid making mistakes translating things from English. A story in *The McKinsey Quarterly*, a trade magazine, told the story of how Chevrolet, when marketing the Nova to Latinos, overlooked the fact that *"no va"* in Spanish means "doesn't go." Advertisers may have come a long way since Teddy Roosevelt, once the governor of Puerto Rico, introduced a general to an island audience as a "tapeworm" (*solitaria*), when he meant "bachelor" (*soltero*). But the advertising world is merely a reflection of a reality; Spanglish is still struggling to find ways to make itself more intelligible.

SOUTH AMERICAN WAY

Outside of the massive immigration of Mexicans and Central Americans into the Southwest and the major cities, and their further dispersion into unlikely areas of the South and the Midwest, the most dynamic new influence on the future of Spanglish right now comes from South America. Long aware of their status as "sub" Americans, lower- and middle-class immigrants from countries like Colombia, Peru, and even southern Coners from Bolivia, Uruguay, and Argentina are part of a new chapter in Spanglish history. They are adding new kinds of experience to Latino life in the U.S., ones that aren't as determined by U.S. influence as previous immigrants from the Caribbean. Colombia and Peru in particular offer the perspective of countries with large indigenous and African populations, more like the U.S., and the southern Cone countries are almost shockingly American in their aspirations and racial mix.

In 1996, a pair of writers from Chile and Bolivia put out an anthology of short stories called *McOndo*, a title designed to satirize their connection to North American fast-food culture and their disaffection for Gabriel García Márquez's seat of magical realism, the fictional town of Macondo. Alberto Fuguet and Edmundo Paz Soldán variously allude to several levels of trash culture, rock, comic books, and the ever-expanding lexicon of info-tech terminology. They have been roundly criticized by the traditional Latin American literary establishment. Although some of this criticism is deserved—they can be excessively steeped in merely referring to the transformative nature of the new South American cities—what they are accomplishing is a necessary moment in the convergence of our hemisphere. The internalization of English words into the South American language has a bit of a democratizing effect, and the movement away from the flowery and the sappy, left over from the Spanish colonial legacy, is necessary to free Latin America from the last vestiges of its patriarchal racism.

The cool versus hot paradigm is very much a part of considering the North-South interchange—it even refers to the punk-hippie conflict, the city mouse–country mouse divide. The Brazilian singer Caetano Veloso once told me that '70s rock star Raul Seixas despised Veloso and his fellow Tropicalistas because their synthesis of bossa nova and rock was not "real" rock. The fact that Brazil had this debate fifteen to twenty years before the development of Latin alternative rock and hiphop is evidence of how far ahead Brazil is from the rest of Latin America.

In the '30s, *The Masters and the Slaves*, a now-controversial book by Gilberto Freyre, was a kind of anthropological manifesto that urged Brazilians to identify with blackness as essential to their identity. His attitudes about the days of slavery are naïve to racist at worst, but his writing helped to popularize the samba as central to Brazilian identity in the '30s, much as Dominican dictator Trujillo posited the African-influenced merengue as that country's national dance (although he denied its African origin).

Veloso went on to tell me about *Minha Formacão* (My Formation) by Joaquim Nabuco, who was writing at about the same time that Martí, Vasconcelos, and Rodó were. At the same time Spanish-speaking Latin America was debating over whether or not they should identify with North America or Europe. Nabuco was concerned with one central idea: "Slavery will remain for a long time to come, the defining national characteristic of Brazil." He felt that the process and structure of slave relations were so imbedded in Brazilian society that, as Veloso reiterated, even the Brazilian with the whitest skin considered himself nonwhite.

It's this very attitude that I consider the saving grace of Latin American and Spanglish culture. But Veloso explained that in some ways this can be a very bad thing. The illusion of nonwhiteness that white Brazilians have can allow them to believe that racism doesn't exist in Brazil. So, in Brazil, we have a culture that exults in African-derived carnival celebrations, the African-derived *candomble* religion, the African-derived samba, the legends of escaped slave heroes like Zumbi. Brazil has confronted its reality as an Afro-European society in ways North Americans couldn't dream of (except maybe in New Orleans, and I mean maybe). But the syrupy status quo surrounding this notion can be infuriating for black people in Brazil. This is evidenced by the predilection for Brazilian rappers to name themselves with North American–sounding, English-derived names.

The corny, peace-love idea of race utopia in Latin America is a big lie—it doesn't work. But the head-in-the-sand denial of racial disharmony in the U.S. is obviously not a success either. That's why the process of the Spanglification of the hemisphere, which includes Portuguese-speaking Brazil, is necessary for us to get somewhere on the race question. We need to get to a place where race ceases to exist, where there are no longer hyper-segregated communities of black, white, and brown *razas*, not because we ignore it, but because we acknowledge it.

Resurrecting La Malinche

> *Our lord, you are weary. The journey has tired you, but now you have arrived on the earth. You have come to your city, Mexico . . . This was foretold by the kings who governed your city, and now it has taken place. You have come back to us; you have come down from the sky. Rest now and take possession of your royal houses. Welcome to your land, my lords!*
> —Moctuzema, upon meeting Cortés for the first time

The story is so familiar it's almost forgotten. When Cortés came to Mexico, he had been preceded by a number of bad omens and an Aztec mythology that predicted the return of Quetzalcoatl, the feathered serpent, as a bearded white man. Just as Andalusia had been invaded by the north from Castille, Tenochtitlán was being taken by a Spanish mercenary. Four hundred years later, Cuba and Puerto Rico were seized with a large assist from a mustachioed man who was once the police commissioner of New York City, Theodore Roosevelt. First they raped us, then they talked down to us. They thought we were children.

There was a woman who was along for the ride with Cortés, an indigenous woman from the Gulf Coast of Mexico, whom the Spanish called Doña Marina and the Aztecs dubbed La Malinche. She was a translator for Cortés, and in Mexican history she has taken all the blame for any corruption on Mexican culture visited by Europeans. She was said to have had a son with Cortés who was almost immediately whisked away to Spain to be married to Castillian royalty in return for his forever giving up any claim to the lands in Mexico because of his birthright. He was bought off.

The resurrection of La Malinche, orchestrated by a loose affiliation of Chicana academics in the '80s, was a centerpiece to the feminist twist that spun West Coast Spanglish on a new course. Gloria Anzaldua turned macho *carnalismo* on its head constructing this pentathon neither/nor: "you are neither *hispana india negra española ni gabacha, eres mestiza, multata*, half-breed caught in the crossfire between camps while carrying all five races on your back." She is the voice I hear when I realize La Malinche got a bad rap. It's not surprising that a woman got blamed for a failure of a culture to defend itself against a brutal attack. Why did we let it happen? It was that damned woman who betrayed us and ruined us before we could get it together. La Malinche may have been an opportunist, like the insipid Rosie Perez character in the Dreamworks film *The Road to El Dorado* (2000), a cartoon fantasy about a benign European conquest. But maybe she was the first Spanglish person.

La Malinche was not so much selling out as she was embarking on the cultural fusion that would play a crucial role in the future of the Americas. She was a translator, just as any writer is a translator, whether it's for the other side or one's own people. The Spanish cognate of translate, *trasladar* means less to interpret than to move, to transfer. I would like to push that envelope a little further and claim the role of translator as *transformer*.—

Can Spanglish style transform society? In part, perhaps, but only in conjunction with similar-thinking groups, willing to abandon the particularity of Eurocentrism for the universality of hybridity. The contradictory flow of postcolonial "others" from Asia, Africa, the Caribbean, Oceania, and all the internal colonies of North America and Europe are feeling the same impulse. The spirit of Spanglish flows through everyone from Salman Rushdie to New Zealand's Maori.

The Spanglish future is more stories like New York–born ex-Dominican president Leonel Fernandez, the first transnational head of state. It's the clicking sounds of keyboards across Latin America, *chateando* about *rocanrol*. It's updated versions of liberation theology grafted onto post-Marxist prison gangs, like the Latin Kings, who hold meetings that are like a cross between a Catholic mass, a twelve-step meeting, and a slam poetry reading. We surge toward a Spanglish hemisphere, where the information techno-imperative of the North has an on-line affair with the tragicomic humanity of the South. The border, like Marx's postrevolutionary state, will wither away, and everywhere will be on the border and nowhere will be on the border. There will just be America, the New Old World.

The netherworld of in-between is netherworld no longer, it is a cool world, a place I thrive in. In the Yoruban pantheon, I feel closest to Elegua, the trickster, the gatekeeper of all roads; I cast darkness on the most promising situations and shed light on the most negative ones. My astrological sign is Gemini, and my twin sides are a harmony of opposition, both sides of the human story.

Let me speak *hablar* Spanglish here *aqui* and fullfill *mi* role *como* the in-between *traslador* who can help you see *el futuro*. *Mi* inner Woody Allen says, *yo quiero ser* Zelig. Chaotic cross-*identificación* happens *automaticamente*, almost genetically, telekinetically. It's not that I'm *mas o menos* comfortable with any particular *identidades*, it's just easy for me to be *todos*. I have no suitable explanation.

'Splain, Lucy, 'Splain.

When I grew up, Ricky Ricardo sounded strange to me. I was like Lucy, making fun of how my parents spoke. I was intolerant of their bilingual beauty. *Yo quería ser perfecto*, a perfect little Puerto Rican/American robot *que lo sabía todo*, the Acts of Contrition, the Constitution, Hail Mary, full of grace, blessed is the fruit of thy womb, Vietnam. The priests turned the altar around to face me, stopped speaking Latin, and said the war was justified.

Pero somehow I still *quería ser Boricua. Aunque tu no me creas*, you won't believe it, I couldn't escape the feeling that something was stuck inside me that won't let me go. Something stuck inside me something *algo* something *algo*. A little bird told me, a *pajaro*. A *pitirre* flying upside a *guaraguao. Algo* is some algae in my *alma*, soul. It amalgamates me. It's *algo*, a *ritmo*, a rhythm makes my words go. It's *algo-ritmo*, an attitudinal algorithm, a syncopated beat that's impossible to know. Perhaps europeo, perhaps africano, perhaps indio. Most likely some *arabe* from a funky cold medina in Morocco. A mathematical solution to Caribbean culture's chaotic flow. You could say I'm a series of syllabic fragments analogous to archipelago. Baby we're dancing some serious mambo.
I'm not your idea
Of silly Puerto Ricans
Just dancing all day
Incapable of thinking
I'm not the *other*. I am you.

INDEX

Magical Urbanism (Davis), 3
Mailer, Norman, 59, 65
Maldita Vecindad, 195
Maldonado, Adal, 91, 130, 258, 271
Mambo Kings Play Songs of Love, The
  (Hijuelos), 44, 51, 160
  film, 133
Mambo Mouth (revue), 137, 138
"Mambo No. 5" (song), 152
Marcantonio, Vito, 84
Mari Bras, Juan, 258
María Calderone, Sila, 265
Marin, Cheech, 63, 179
Mariposa, 112, 115
Martí, José, 17, 19, 35, 226, 238, 273
Matador (film), 130
Martin, Darnell, 134
Martin, Ricky, 23, 25, 135, 142, 150, 263
Martinez, Ruben, 118
Marzán, Julio, 99
Masucci, Jerry, 158
McLuhan, Marshall, 5
McOndo (Fuguet & Paz Soldán), 293
McWilliams, Carey, 34, 46
Media
  information in Spanish or English, 291
  lack of Latinos in, 289–90
  Latin magazines, 290–91
  radio, Spanish language, 291
  Web sites, 290
  See also Television
Megalopolis (Olalquiaga), 167, 285
Melendez, Micky, 85
Memories of Underdevelopment
  (Gutiérrez Alea), 233
Mendiola, Jim, 38, 220
Menudo (group), 256
Mexican, The (film), 130–31, 147
Mexicans in U.S., 27, 53–56, 203–23
  film depiction of, 38–40
  food, 152
  Los Hijos de America, 43
  mestizo, 54–55, 84
  music (mambo), 152
  music (rock), 155–56, 172–75, 195
  new immigration versus indigenous
    population, 43–44, 207
  pachuco, 44, 45–46, 54–55, 156
  percent of Latino population, 206
  Peter Hernandez v. Texas, 207

pocho (word used by), 193
urbanization of, 43
radical politics, 1960s–70s, 76–82
Selena and, 173–75
Texas vs. California, 212–16
Texas and, 219–22
zoot suit and riots, 44–46, 53–54, 73
  See also California; Chicano; Los
    Angeles; Texas
Mexico
  African component, 15
  bands and music, 162–67, 168–69,
    173–74, 205, 213–14, 280–83
  Chilangos, 212
  conquest of, by Cortés, 32, 295–97
  education, 166
  el nahual, 46
  identity, 13
  Mexican War, 33–34
  Mexican Revolution, 12, 163, 220
  Mexico City, 280–83
  Muralist school, 13, 166
  National University, motto of, 14
  nationalism, 10, 219
  Nortec, 173–74
  politics and foreign policy, 206–7,
    208–9
  rasquache, 191, 191n.
  slamming, 166
  Teotihuacán pyramids, 163–64
  Treaty of Guadalupe Hidalgo, 33–34,
    76, 77, 78
  Virgen de Guadalupe, La, 82, 191,
    213–14
Miami, 27, 217–18, 228, 229–30, 239
  music industry, 242–45, 248–49
  González, Elián, and, 227, 244, 247–48
  Miami Sound Machine (MSM [band]),
    244
Mi Familia (film), 209
Milanes, Pablo, 218, 225
Minha Formacão (My Formation
  [Nabuco]), 294
Miranda, Carmen, 40
Mohr, Nicolasa, 123
Molina, Alfred, 132
Monsiváis, Carlos, 45
Montalban, Ricardo, 136
Montañez, Andy, 245
Montoya, José, 89, 92, 190, 196

Puerto Ricans (*continued*)
  Nuyorican radical politics, 83–89, 284
  West Side Story and depiction of,
    57–59, 61
Puerto Ricans Out of Focus
  (photography), 130
Puerto Rico, 251–72
  advertisers and, 292
  ceding to U.S., 34
  Cerro Maravilla incident, 260–61, 267
  Cubans and, 218, 225–26, 245
  flag, 41
  Grito de Lares, 262–63, 271
  history, 252, 253–58
  jíbaro, 50–51, 72, 252
  labor movement, 42
  language of, 277–78
  Morales family, 251–52
  nationalism and FALN, 88–89, 92, 208,
    219, 228, 253, 255–58, 260–72
  Nuyorican Journey (circular
    migration), 70–77, 252
  Operation Bootstrap, 71, 252, 256
  politicians and politics, 208, 255–59,
    260–72
  San Juan, 254–55
  skin color and, 214–15
  Spanglish used in, 254, 258–59
  Spirit Republic de Puerto Rico, 271, 276
  Vieques, 208, 264–65, 271, 272
  as U.S. commonwealth, 41, 256–57,
    260, 262–72

Q & A (film), 133–34
Quasimodo (film), 131
Quinn, Anthony, 25, 136
Quintanilla, Abraham, 56

Race
  biracialism, 16–17
  class and, 19–21
  color line or border, 3–4
  conflict, 67
  cosmic (*La raza cósmica*), 12–15, 163,
    166, 214
  end to, call for, 14, 274, 295
  intermarriage, 34, 203, 221–22, 274
  Latino and Hispanic vs. Spanglish, 1–5
  mejorar la raza, 4–5, 221–22
  Mi raza is tu raza, 14, 21

miscegenation, 5, 13, 15–18, 31–32, 46,
    61, 82, 189
mulatto (*mulata*), 4, 51, 115, 150, 215
multiracialism, 8–9, 70, 168, 283
negritude movement, 50
normalizing the idea of race-mixing,
    15–18
"one drop" rule, 15, 49
racism in Latino society, 107, 115,
    214–15
raza, 15
skin color and, 4–5, 15, 49–51, 66, 115,
    214–15, 274, 294–95
West Side Story and, 5
White Negro and, 59–63, 154
Rage Against the Machine (band), 196,
    239, 282
Rangel, Quique, 281
Re (album), 167, 191
"Rebirth of New Rican" (Morales),
    100–101
Refried Elvis (Zolov), 163, 206
Religion
  escapulario (saint emblem), 171
  espiritista, 66, 91
  Roman Catholicism, 10, 203
  Santería, 19, 165, 215, 229, 232,
    234–38
  voodoo, 19
Resurrection Boulevard (TV series), 198,
    288–89
Reves (album), 281
Revolt of the Cockroach People (Acosta),
    181, 182
Reyes, Senen, 187
Reyes, Silvestre, 207
Ringolevio (Grogan), 64
Rivas, Bimbo, 101
Rivera, Alex, 280
Rivera, Danny, 245, 256
Road to El Dorado, The (film), 296
Roberts, John Storm, 43
Rodó, José Enrique, 35
Rodríguez, Abraham, 56, 121–22
Rodriguez, Clara E., 208
Rodriguez, Jesusa, 280
Rodriguez, Joe, 280
Rodriguez, Luis, 23, 122, 218
Rodriguez, Richard, 11, 19, 277
Rodriguez, Robert, 130–31, 147